PHILOSOPHY AND SCIENCE

The Age of Enlightenment, which has been edited by the renowned teacher, lecturer, and writer, Sir Isaiah Berlin, presents the basic writings of the major eighteenth-century philosophers and provides a brilliant commentary on their thoughts, times, and impact on philosophy.

The philosophers of the eighteenth century tried to prove that everything—or almost everything—in the world moved according to unchangeable and predictable physical laws. Sir Isaiah's extensive selections from the major works of Locke, Berkeley, and Hume, as well as La Mettrie, Reid, Condillac, and their German critics, shed light upon this period when it seemed that philosophy might almost have been converted into a natural science. His penetrating introduction and interpretation of the key ideas of these influential philosophers explain their significance in the eighteenth century and today.

SIR ISAIAH BERLIN is considered England's greatest living political thinker. He has taught at Harvard University and Bryn Mawr College, was Chichele Professor of Social and Political Theory, Oxford University and President of Wolfson College in Oxford. Professor Berlin is the author of numerous collections of essays, including FOUR ESSAYS ON LIBERTY, CONCEPTS AND CATEGORIES, RUSSIAN THINKERS, and PERSONAL IMPRESSIONS.

THE AGE OF ENLIGHTENMENT

The 18th Century Philosophers

SELECTED, WITH INTRODUCTION AND INTERPRETIVE COMMENTARY

by

ISAIAH BERLIN

A MERIDIAN BOOK

MERIDIAN
Published by the Penguin Group
Penguin Books USA Inc., 375 Hudson Street,
New York, New York 10014, U.S.A.
Penguin Books Ltd, 27 Wrights Lane,
London W8 5TZ, England
Penguin Books Australia Ltd, Ringwood,
Victoria, Australia
Penguin Books Canada Ltd, 10 Alcorn Avenue,
Toronto, Ontario, Canada M4V 3B2
Penguin Books (N.Z.) Ltd, 182–190 Wairau Road,
Auckland 10, New Zealand

Penguin Books Ltd, Registered Offices:
Harmondsworth, Middlesex, England

Published by Meridian, an imprint of New American Library, a division of Penguin Books USA Inc.

First Meridian Printing, 1984
15 14 13

Contents

Acknowledgments

My thanks are due in the first place to Mr. Marcus Dick, Fellow of Balliol College, Oxford, for his most valuable assistance to me in preparing this volume. I should also like to thank Mr. Stuart Hampshire for his help in selecting texts.

In addition, I have to thank the University of North Carolina, Chapel Hill, for permission to quote from *Unity and Language, A Study in the Philosophy of Johann Georg Hamann,* by James C. O'Flaherty.

THE AGE OF
ENLIGHTENMENT

Introduction

PHILOSOPHICAL PROBLEMS ARISE WHEN MEN ASK QUES-
tions of themselves or of others which, though very diverse,
have certain characteristics in common. These questions
tend to be very general, to involve issues of principle, and
to have little or no concern with practical utility. But what
is even more characteristic of them is that there seem to
be no obvious and generally accepted procedures for answering them, nor any class of specialists to whom we
automatically turn for the solutions. Indeed there is something peculiar about the questions themselves; those who
ask them do not seem any too certain about what kind of
answers they require, or indeed how to set about finding
them. To give an illustration: if we ask "Have any ravens
been seen in Iceland in 1955?" we know how to set about
answering such a question—the correct answer must obviously be based on observation, and the naturalist is the
expert to whom we can appeal. But when men ask questions like "Are there any material objects in the universe
(or does it, perhaps, consist rather of minds and their
states)?" what steps do we take to settle this? Yet outwardly there is a similarity between the two sentences. Or
again, supposing I ask "Did the battle of Waterloo take
place in the seventeenth century?" we know how to look
for the relevant evidence, but what are we to do when
asked "Did the universe have a beginning in time?" We
know how to answer "Are you quite certain that he knows
you?" But if someone wonders "Can I ever be quite certain about what goes on in the mind of another?" how do
we satisfy him? It is easier to reply to "Why is Einstein's
theory superior to Newton's?" than to "Why are the pre-
dictions of scientists more reliable than those of witch doc-
tors (or vice versa)?", or to "How many positive roots are
there of the equation $x^2 = 2$?" than to "Are there irrational

numbers?", or to "What is the exact meaning of the word 'obscurantist'?" than to "What is the exact meaning of the word 'if'?". "How should I mend this broken typewriter?" seems different in kind from "How should I (or men in general) live?"

In each case the attempt to answer the second question of the pair somehow seems to encounter an obstacle. There is not, as there is for the first member of the pair, a well-attested, generally accepted, method of discovering the solution. And yet questions of this kind seem definite enough, and have proved, to some men, very puzzling and indeed tormenting. Why, then, is there such difficulty in arriving at answers which settle the matter once and for all, so that the problems do not crop up afresh in each generation? This failure to provide definite solutions creates the impression that there is no progress in philosophy, merely subjective differences of opinion, with no objective criteria for the discovery of the truth.

The history of such questions, and of the means employed to provide the answers, is, in effect, the history of philosophy. The frame of ideas within which, and the methods by which, various thinkers at various times try to arrive at the truth about such issues—the very ways in which the questions themselves are construed—change under the influence of many forces, among them answers given by philosophers of an earlier age, the prevailing moral, religious and social beliefs of the period, the state of scientific knowledge, and, not least important, the methods used by the scientists of the time, especially if they have achieved spectacular successes, and have, therefore, bound their spell upon the imagination of their own and later generations.

One of the principal characteristics of such questions— and this seems to have become clearer only in our own day —is that, whatever else they may be, they are neither empirical nor formal. That is to say, philosophical questions cannot be answered by adducing the results of observation or experience, as empirical questions, whether of science or of common sense, are answered. Such questions as: "What is the supreme good?" Or "How can I be sure that your sensations are similar to mine? Or that I ever genuinely understand what you are saying, and do not merely seem to myself to do so?" cannot be, on the face of it, answered by either of the two great instruments of human knowledge: empirical investigation on the one hand, and deductive reasoning as it is used in the formal disciplines on the other—the kind of argument which occurs, for example, in mathematics or logic or grammar.

Indeed it might almost be said that the history of philosophy in its relation to the sciences, consists, in part, in the disentangling of those questions which are either empirical (and inductive), or formal (and deductive), from the mass of problems which fill the minds of men, and the sorting out of these under the heads of the empirical or formal sciences concerned with them. It is in this way that, for instance, astronomy, mathematics, psychology, biology, etc., became divorced from the general corpus of philosophy (of which they once formed a part), and embarked upon fruitful careers of their own as independent disciplines. They remained within the province of philosophy only so long as the kinds of way in which their problems were to be settled remained unclear, and so were liable to be confused with other problems with which they had relatively little in common, and from which their differences had not been sufficiently discerned. The advance both of the sciences and of philosophy seems bound up with this progressive allocation of the empirical and formal elements, each to its own proper sphere; always, however, leaving behind a nucleus of unresolved (and largely unanalyzed) questions, whose generality, obscurity, and, above all, apparent (or real) insolubility by empirical or formal methods, gives them a status of their own which we tend to call philosophical.

Realization of this truth (if it be one) was a long time in arriving. The natural tendency was to regard philosophical questions as being on a level with other questions, and answerable by similar means; especially by means which had been successful in answering these other questions, which in fact did turn out to be either empirical or *a priori*, even though the distinction between the two was not always consciously drawn. When some branch of human inquiry, say physics or biology, won notable successes by employing this or that new and fertile technique, an attempt was invariably made to apply analogous techniques to philosophical problems also, with results, fortunate and unfortunate, which are a permanent element in the history of human thought. Thus the unprecedented successes of the mathematical method in the seventeenth century left a mark on philosophy, not merely because mathematics had not clearly been discriminated from philosophy at this time, but because mathematical techniques—deduction from "self-evident" axioms according to fixed rules, tests of internal consistency, a priori methods, standards of clarity and rigor proper to mathematics—were applied to philosophy also; with the result that this particular model dominates the philosophy as well as the natural science of the period. This led to notable successes and equally notable failures, as the over-enthusiastic and fanatical application of techniques rich in results in one field, when mechanically applied to another, not necessarily similar to the first, commonly does. If the model that dominated the seventeenth century was mathematical, it is the mechanical model, more particularly that of the Newtonian system, that is everywhere imitated in the century that followed. Philosophical questions are in fact *sui generis,* and resemble questions of mechanics no more closely than those of mathematics (or of biology or psychology or history); nevertheless the effect upon philosophy of one model is very different from that of another; and it is this that forms a common characteristic of all the very different philosophers whose views are assembled in this volume.

The eighteenth century is perhaps the last period in the history of Western Europe when human omniscience was thought to be an attainable goal. The unparalleled progress of physics and mathematics in the previous century transformed the generally held view of the nature of the material world, and, still more, of the nature of true knowledge, to such a degree, that this epoch still stands like a barrier between us and the ages which preceded it, and makes the philosophical ideas of the Middle Ages, and even the

Renaissance, seem remote, fanciful and, at times, almost unintelligible. The application of mathematical techniques —and language—to the measurable properties of what the senses revealed, became the sole true method of discovery and of exposition. Descartes and Spinoza, Leibniz and Hobbes, all seek to give their reasoning a structure of a mathematical kind. What can be said must be statable in quasi-mathematical terms, for language less precise may turn out to conceal the fallacies and obscurities, the confused mass of superstitions and prejudices, which characterized the discredited theological or other forms of dogmatic doctrine about the universe, which the new science had come to sweep away and supersede. This mood persists into the eighteenth century, with Newton's influence as the strongest single factor. Newton had performed the unprecedented task of explaining the material world, that is, of making it possible, by means of relatively few fundamental laws of immense scope and power, to determine, at least in principle, the properties and behavior of every particle of every material body in the universe, and that with a degree of precision and simplicity undreamt of before. Order and clarity now reigned in the realm of physical science:

> Nature and Nature's Laws lay hid in Night:
> God said, Let Newton be! and all was Light!

Yet the ancient disciplines of metaphysics, logic, ethics, and all that related to the social life of men, still lay in chaos, governed by the confusions of thought and language of an earlier and unregenerate age. It was natural, and indeed almost inevitable, that those who had been liberated by the new sciences should seek to apply their methods and principles to a subject which was clearly in even more desperate need of order than the facts of the external world. Indeed this task was of crucial importance: for without a true and clear picture of the principal "faculties" and operations of the human mind, one could not be certain how much credence to give to various types of thought or reasoning, nor how to determine the sources and limits of human knowledge, nor the relationships between its varieties. But unless this was known the claims of ignoramuses and charlatans could not be properly exposed; nor the new picture of the material world adequately related to other matters of interest to men—moral conduct, aesthetic principles, laws of history and of social and political life, the "inner" workings of the passions and the imagination, and all the other issues of central interest to human beings. A science of nature had been created; a science of mind had yet to be made. The goal in both cases must remain the same: the formulation of general laws on the basis of observation ("inner" and "outer"), and, when necessary, experiment; and the deduction from such laws, when established, of specific conclusions. To every genuine question there were many false answers, and only one true one; once discovered it was final—it remained for ever true; all that was needed was a reliable method of discovery. A method which answered to this description had been employed by "the incomparable Mr. Newton"; his emulators in the realm of the human mind would reap a harvest no less rich if they followed similar precepts. If the laws were correct, the observations upon which they were based authentic, and the inferences sound, true and impregnable conclusions would provide knowledge of hitherto unexplored realms, and transform the present welter of ignorance and idle conjecture into a clear and coherent system of logically interrelated elements—the theoretical copy or analogue of the divine harmony of nature, concealed from the view by human ignorance or idleness or perversity. To comprehend it, is, for a rational creature, tantamount to conforming to it in all one's beliefs and actions; for this alone can make men happy and rational and free.

It was essential to guarantee the efficacy of the instruments of investigation before its results could be trusted. This epistemological bias characterized European philosophy from Descartes's formulation of his method of doubt until well into the nineteenth century, and is still a strong tendency in it. The direct application of the results of this investigation of the varieties and scope of human knowledge to such traditional disciplines as politics, ethics, metaphysics, theology, and so on, with a view to ending their perplexities once and for all, is the program which philosophers of the eighteenth century attempted to carry through. The principles which they attempted to apply were the new scientific canons of the seventeenth century; there was to be no *a priori* deduction from "natural" principles, hallowed in the Middle Ages, without experimental evidence, such as that all bodies come to rest when no longer under the influence of any force, or that the "natural" path sought after by heavenly bodies, in the quest for self-fulfillment, is necessarily circular. The laws of Kepler or Galileo contradicted these "natural" principles, on the basis of observation (the vast mass of data, for instance, accumulated by the Danish astronomer Tycho Brahe), and experiment (of the kind conducted by Galileo himself). This use of observation and experiment entailed the application of exact methods of measurement, and resulted in the linking together of many diverse phenomena under laws of great precision, generally formulated in mathematical terms. Consequently only the measurable aspects of reality were to be treated as real—those susceptible to equations connecting the variations in one aspect of a phenomenon with measurable variations in other phenomena. The whole notion of nature as compounded of irreducibly different qualities and unbridgeable "natural" kinds, was to be finally discarded. The Aristotelian category of final cause—the explanation of phenomena in terms of the "natural" tendency of every object to fulfill its own inner end or purpose—which was also to be the answer to the question of why it existed, and what function it was attempting to fulfill—notions for which no experimental or observational evidence can in principle be discovered—was abandoned as unscientific, and, indeed, in the case of inanimate entities without wills or purposes, as literally unintelligible. Laws formulating regular concomitances of phenomena—the observed order and conjunctions of things and events—were sufficient, without introducing impalpable entities and forces, to describe all that is describable, and predict all that is predictable, in the universe. Space, time, mass, force, momentum, rest—the terms of mechanics—are to take the place of final causes, substantial forms, divine purpose, and other metaphysical notions. Indeed the apparatus of mediaeval ontology and theology were to be altogether abandoned in favor of a symbolism referring to those aspects of the universe which are given to the senses, or can be measured or inferred in some other way.

This attitude is exceedingly clear in the works not only of Locke and Hume, who had a profound respect for natural science, but also in those of Berkeley, who was deeply concerned to deny its metaphysical presuppositions. To all of them the model was that of contemporary physics and mechanics. The world of matter for Newton, and indeed for those pre-Newtonian physicists with whose works Locke was probably acquainted rather better, was to be described in terms of uniform particles, and the laws of its behavior were the laws of the interaction of these particles. The British empiricist philosophers, whose work gradually came to dominate European thought, applied this conception to the mind. The mind was treated as if it were a box containing mental equivalents of the Newtonian particles. These were called "ideas." These "ideas" are distinct and separate entities, "simple," i.e., possessing no parts into which they can be split, that is, literally atomic, having their origin somewhere in the external world, dropping into the mind like so many grains of sand inside an hourglass; there, in some way, they either continue in isolation, or are compounded to form complexes, in the way in which material objects in the outer world are compounded out of complexes of molecules or atoms. Locke attempts something like the history of the genesis of ideas in our minds and an account of their movement within it, their association and dissociation from each other, like a contemporary chemist analyzing the ingredients and physical behavior of a compound substance. Thought, at least reflective thought, is for Locke a kind of inner eye, corresponding to the outer physical eye which takes in the external world. When Locke defines knowledge as "the perception of the connection and agreement or disagreement and repugnancy of any of our ideas," this "perception" is conceived by him as something which inspects two ideas as if they were discriminable particles; the inner eye is then able to see whether they agree or not, and so whether the proposition asserting their connection is or is not true, much as the outer eye can inspect two colored objects and see whether the colors match each other or not. When Berkeley criticizes Locke's theory of abstract general ideas, what he is principally attacking is the notion that there can be an idea which is not an absolutely determinate image, since ideas are entities; and "abstract ideas," as invoked by Locke in order to explain how general terms mean, seem to Berkeley a contradiction in terms, because if they are ideas, they must be concrete entities, and cannot also be abstract, that is, not determinate, not having any particular properties given to the senses or the imagination. Whether his attack upon Locke is fair or not, what is characteristic is the assumption common to both (and to Hume and many other contemporary empiricists, particularly in France) that the mind is a container within which ideas like counters circulate and form patterns as they would in a complicated slot machine; three-dimensional Newtonian space has its counterpart in the inner "space" of the mind over which the inner eye—the faculty of reflection—presides.

Philosophy, therefore, is to be converted into a natural science. The facts with which it is to deal are to be discovered by introspection. Like every other genuine human investigation it must begin with empirical observation. Hume echoes this: "As the science of man is the only solid foundation for the other science, so the only solid foundation we can give to this science itself must be laid on experience and observation." Philosophy is in reality a kind of scientific psychology; among the extreme followers of this doctrine, particularly in France, it becomes a kind of physiology—an early version of behaviorism or "physicalism." The French disciples of Locke and Hume, Condillac, Helvétius, La Mettrie, push this to extreme limits. Condillac undertakes to reconstruct every human experience—the most complex and sophisticated thoughts or "movements of the soul," the most elaborate play of the imagination, the most subtle scientific speculation—out of "simple" ideas, that is, sensations classifiable as being given to one or the other of our normal senses, each of which can, as it were, be pin-pointed and assigned to its rightful place in the stream of sensations. The great popularizers of the age, whose writings reached educated readers in many lands beyond the borders of their native France, headed by Voltaire, Diderot, Holbach, Condorcet, and their followers, whatever their other differences, were agreed upon the crucial importance of this sensationalist approach. There are "organic"—anti-atomic—notions in the writings of Diderot as well as those of Maupertuis or Bordeu, and some of these may have influenced Kant; but the dominant trend is in favor of analyzing everything into ultimate, irreducible atomic constituents, whether physical or psychological. Hume, who believes "that the sciences of mathematics and natural philosophy (i.e., natural science) and natural religion have such a dependence on the knowledge of man," believes this because the task of philosophy is to deal with the ultimate ingredients of all that there is. His theory of the mind is mechanistic, and conceived by analogy with Newton's theory of gravitational attraction, the association of ideas being called upon to perform the same function in the mind as gravitation does in the material world. This association of ideas is described by him as "a kind of attraction, which in the mental world will be found to have as extraordinary effects as in the natural, and to show itself in as many and as various forms." La Mettrie conceives the true philosopher as a kind of engineer who can take to pieces the apparatus that is the human mind; Voltaire describes him as an excellent anatomist, who (he is speaking in praise of Locke) can explain human reason as he can explain the springs of the human body. Scientific images abound in the philosophical treatises of the French *philosophes* and their disciples in other countries; Nature, which was conceived as an organism by Butler in the beginning of the century, was compared to a watch by Dean Paley half a century later. "Natural morality" and "natural religion" (common to all men, but more evident in the least corrupt—rural or primitive—societies) can be studied scientifically like the life of plants or animals. Diderot compares social life to a great workshop factory.

Berkeley, so far from finding this empiricism unpalatable because he is a Christian and a bishop, on the contrary finds it alone compatible with the spiritualism which impregnates all his beliefs. For him Locke is, if anything, not empiricist enough. And, in a sense, Berkeley is right; the science of the seventeenth century which Locke admires and which he seeks to apply to mental phenomena, was anything but strictly empiricist. On the contrary, the world of the senses is regarded by Galileo and Descartes as vague, deceptive and blurred, full of phenomena only describable in qualitative terms, that is, not admissible in a properly quantitative, scientific world picture. The "primary" qualities with which the sciences deal are not themselves directly given to the senses. There are two domains: the quantitative, precisely measurable, domain of objects in space, possessing such properties as motion and rest, determinate shape, solidity, specific temperatures which are the motions of particles, and so forth; this is contrasted with the domain of colors, smells and tastes, degree of warmth and cold, loud and soft sounds, etc., which are subjective, and therefore unreliable. Locke, who starts from the principle that we have no knowledge except that which comes from the senses, finds it difficult to explain why the "primary" qualities, which for him, must, if he is to be consistent, depend as much on the evidence of the senses as the "secondary" ones, should nevertheless be accorded the kind of primacy and authority which physical science seemed to give them. And so he alternates between inconsistency and half-hearted attempts to represent the secondary qualities as in some way generated by the primary ones, which are not so much themselves sensible, as somehow causally responsible for the data of the senses. And he finds himself in similar difficulties with regard to material substance, which for the physicists was certainly something not directly given to the senses, nor anything that could be so given, and must therefore be unacceptable to strict empiricism. Berkeley quite consistently rejects attempts at "appeasement" of physics, and rejects all efforts at compromise with its alleged demands. Indeed he looks at such dualism as incompatible with the out-and-out empiricism which he advocates. The contrast between subjective sensations and objective properties of matter is specious. The senses are the sole source of knowledge. The world consists of thoughts, feelings, sensations—"ideas" in the minds of agents, of God, and his creatures, men. Beyond that there is nothing, at least so far as the material world is concerned. He combines a consistent empiricism with regard to the material world with belief in the reality of spiritual substances—eternal souls or spirits—active beings, whose existence does not depend, as that of passive entities must, on being sensed, or being otherwise the content of someone's experience—substances of which we possess not "ideas" but (as his predecessors in the seventeenth century had called this non-sensible awareness) "notions," which may also embrace relations since these are, apparently, not sensible either. His position in this regard—a peculiar union of Platonism and sensationalism —is not as inconsistent as it has too often been taken to be by his critics from Hume onwards.

For Berkeley the notion of external substances so cut off from possible sensible experience that no idea of them can in principle be formed is unintelligible. He is at once a complete spiritualist and a consistent sensationalist. And his whole argument rests upon the view that, if we do not allow ourselves to be befuddled by scientific terminology which suggests the existence of imperceptible matter, while at the same time basing all our knowledge upon the evidence of what can be perceived and it alone, we shall arrive at an orthodox Christian position that the universe is spiritual in character. And whereas for Locke and Hume mathematics represents the most perfect form of knowledge—indeed the ideal of lucidity and impregnable certainty, in comparison with which all other claims to knowledge are defective—for Berkeley mathematics suggests the existence of mythological entities which have no existence in the world. Geometrical figures for Berkeley are not ideal entities, free from the need that all real entities have to justify themselves by empirical observation, but are the contents of sensation no less than anything else. A line consists of a certain, in principle countable, number of *minima sensibilia*—and if it consists of an odd number of these, cannot be precisely bisected whatever geometers may say. This eccentric view is interesting if only as evidence of what extremes empiricism and nominalism can reach.

Both Locke and Hume hold a more plausible view of mathematics, and although their accounts of mathematical reasoning are not altogether convincing, they realize no less clearly than Leibniz the difference between it and statements of empirical fact. Hume, in particular, is clear about the difference between statements of formal entailment, i.e., those of logic and arithmetic or algebra (he is confused and hesitant about geometry) and those of a factual kind, i.e., those asserting existence. Indeed, his major achievement rests precisely on the recognition that since such notions as necessity and identity, strictly interpreted, belong to the world of formal disciplines—what the Rationalists had called "truths of reason," known to be such because their contradictories are self-contradictory, (as opposed to "truths of fact," which cannot be tested by any purely formal process)—they have no place in the realm of statements about the world, the assumption that they have, being largely responsible for the very existence of the false science of metaphysics.

Necessity and identity are relations not to be discovered by either observation of the external world, or introspection, nor by any combinations of the data of these "faculties." They are, therefore, not real relations uniting real entities, or discoverable in the real world. Knowledge must therefore be of two types: either it claims to be "necessary," in which case it rests on formal criteria and can give no information about the world. Or it does claim to give information about the world, in which case it can be no more than probable, and is never infallible; it cannot have certainty, if what we mean by this is the kind of certainty only achieved by logic or by mathematics. This distinction between the two types of assertion, closely related to the distinction between "synthetic" and "analytic," "a posteri-

ori" and "a priori," is the beginning of the great controversy which awakened Kant from his dogmatic slumber
and transformed the history of modern philosophy.

The heroic attempt to make philosophy a natural science
was brought to an end by the great break with the traditions
both of rationalism and of empiricism as they had developed hitherto, inaugurated by Kant, whose philosophical
views are the source of much of the thought of the nineteenth century, and are not included in the compass of this
volume. It was he who first grasped firmly the truth that
the task of philosophy is—and has always been—not to
seek answers to empirical questions of fact, which are answered by the special sciences, or at another level by
ordinary common sense. Nor can it be a purely deductive
discipline as used by the formal sciences such as logic or
mathematics. He was the first great philosopher to realize
that the principal questions of philosophy are neither those
for which there is a clear method of solution by empirical
investigation (e.g., the question of the genesis of our ideas
—the attempt to find out where they "come from," which
is a question for psychologists, physiologists, anthropolo-
gists, and the like) nor those to be answered by deduction
from self-evident or a priori axioms, as had been held by
the schoolmen and rationalists; for what is self-evident—
or a matter of faith and direct revelation—to one person
may not be so to another. Kant rightly held that mere
deduction cannot add to our knowledge either of things or
of persons: and does not answer those questions, or solve
those puzzles, which seem characteristically philosophical.
The questions which he asked, and the methods which he
employed (whether valid or not), were concerned rather
with analyzing our most general and pervasive concepts
and categories. He distinguished the types of statements we
make in the light of the kinds of evidence they require,
and the relations to each other of the concepts which they
presuppose.

Kant is particularly clear on an issue, confusion about
which lies at the heart of the major fallacies of eighteenth-
century philosophy, namely that questions concerning types
of judgments and kinds of categories involved in normal

experience are far from identical with questions about the "sources" of our data or beliefs or attitudes. It is obvious that there must be differences of logical principle (and not merely of origin) between such propositions as "every event has a cause" or "this sheet of paper cannot be both blue and brown in the same place at the same time" on the one hand, and such propositions as "there are no snakes in Ireland" or "I had a headache yesterday," on the other. If someone doubts whether every event has a cause, or whether Pythagoras's theorem is true, or whether this piece of paper is both brown and blue at the same time, it is useless to accumulate for his benefit more and more instances of, say, events in this or that relation to one another; or more and more right-angle triangles together with instruments for measuring the areas of the squares on the sides; or further sheets of paper, some entirely brown, others entirely blue, but none simultaneously and wholly both. These methods of confuting the doubter are useless, because the way to convince someone of the truth of such propositions is clearly quite different from the way in which we demonstrate the truth of factual propositions about the world, that is, by the production of empirical evidence of some kind. The question here is "What is the correct sort of evidence or guarantee which one should produce for the truth of such and such a proposition?", and this is altogether different from such a question as "How do I, or you (or men in general) come to learn the truth of such and such a proposition?" The answer to this last question is one of genetic psychology, and depends on many empirical accidents and vicissitudes of a man's life. It is characteristic of the great classical empiricists (even of Hume who was so keenly aware of differences of logical type, and so triumphantly, and with such devastating results, proved that precisely because inductive argument could never be rendered deductive, therefore there was a sense in which certainty was impossible about matters of fact) that they confused these two questions, and supposed that a certain kind of answer to the latter question—the question of the genesis of knowledge or of the ways of learning—automatically entailed a certain sort of answer to the first, namely the question of what was the correct proceeding for establishing the truth of, and what concepts were involved in, a given proposition.

This confusion emerges in the way in which these philosophers tend to conflate these two distinct questions into one unclear inquiry: "How can we know proposition X?", which is neither "What is the right evidence for, or proof of, propositions like X?" nor yet "Whence do we acquire the knowledge (or impression) of X?" One of the best examples of this muddle is to be found in the first book of Locke's *Essay,* where he tells us that children, for example, are not born with the knowledge of the law of non-contradiction, and seems to think that this proves something about the logical status of such propositions. The question of the sources of knowledge is one of fact, and the empiricists who, following Hobbes or Locke, argued that it was neither "innate," that is, "imprinted" on the mind before birth by God or nature, nor derived by "intuition," i.e., some channel other than and superior to the senses, were in effect saying that the answer to this question could be provided only by psychology, correctly conceived as an empirical science. It was the attempt to show that philosophy consisted in this empirical procedure (for if it is not to be based on observation, what value can it have?) that led to some of the most illuminating insights of eighteenth-century thought, as well as the major fallacy which vitiates it—the identification of philosophy with science.

Kant himself is by no means free from this kind of error; nevertheless, he did shift the center of philosophical emphasis from the two questions "What is deducible from what?" and "What entities are there in the world, whether outside, or in, the mind?" to an examination of the most general concepts and categories in terms of which we think and reason—frames of reference or systems of relations— like space, time, number, causality, material thinghood, of which we seem unable to divest ourselves, save very partially, even in imagination, and which are not dealt with in the textbooks devoted to special sciences, because they are too universal and too pervasive, and, *prima facie* at any rate, do not fit into any classification, either empirical or formal. The history of philosophy has largely consisted in dealing with such questions, whose subject matter is difficult to classify; in seeking to solve, or at least to elucidate, puzzles which haunt many men's minds in a way quite different from perplexities within the field of some special science, where the method of finding the answer, however difficult, is not itself a puzzle. These philosophical problems change from one age to another, representing no straight line of progress (or retrogression), as human thought and language change under the impact of the factors which determine the forms and the concepts in which men think, feel, communicate—factors which seem to pursue no regular pattern of a discernible kind.

These considerations were relatively remote from the minds of the great empirical philosophers of the eighteenth century, selections of whose writings are to be found in this volume. To them everything seemed far clearer than it can ever have done to any but a very few of their successors. What science had achieved in the sphere of the material world, it could surely achieve also in the sphere of the mind; and further, in the realm of social and political relations. The rational scheme on which Newton had so conclusively demonstrated the physical world to be constructed, and with which Locke and Hume and their French disciples seemed well on the way to explaining the inner worlds of thought and emotion, could be applied to the social sphere as well. Men were objects in nature no less than trees and stones; their interaction could be studied as that of atoms or plants. Once the laws governing human behavior were discovered and incorporated in a science of rational sociology, analogous to physics or zoology, men's real wishes could be investigated and brought to light, and satisfied by the most efficient means compatible with the nature of the physical and mental facts. Nature was a cosmos: in it there could be no disharmonies; and since such questions as what to do, how to live, what would make men just or rational or happy, were all factual questions, the true answers to any one of them could not be incompatible with true answers to any of the others. The

ideal of creating a wholly just, wholly virtuous, wholly satisfied society, was therefore no longer utopian.

Nor is this view confined to the natural scientists and
their allies and spokesmen. It was held no less confidently
by the rationalist followers of Leibniz and his disciple
Wolff. They held that rational thought was a means of ob-
taining truth about the universe vastly superior to empirical methods. But they also believed, if anything even
more strongly than their empiricist adversaries, that the
truth was one single, harmonious body of knowledge;
that all previous systems—religions, cosmologies, mythol-
ogies—were but so many different roads, some longer or
wider, some more twisted and darker, to the same rational goal; that all the sciences and all the faiths, the most
fanatical superstitions and the most savage customs, when
"cleansed" of their irrational elements by the advance of
civilization, can be harmonized in the final true philosophy
which could solve all theoretical and practical problems
for all men everywhere for all time. This noble faith ani-
mated Lessing who believed in reason and Turgot who
believed in the sciences, Moses Mendelssohn who believed
in God, and Condorcet who did not. Despite great differences of temperament and outlook and belief this was
the common ground. Theists and atheists, believers in auto-
matic progress and skeptical pessimists, hard-boiled French
materialists and sentimental German poets and thinkers,
seemed united in the conviction that all problems were sol-
uble by the discovery of objective answers, which, once
found—and why should they not be?—would be clear for
all to see and valid eternally. It is true that dissident voices,
first in Germany, then in England, were beginning to be
raised in the middle of the century, maintaining that neither men nor their societies were analogous to inanimate
objects or even to the zoological kingdom; and that the
attempt to deal with them as if they were would necessarily
lead to disaster. Johnson and Burke, Hamann and Herder
(and to some degree even Montesquieu and Hume) began
the revolt which was destined to grow in strength. But
these remained isolated doubts.

A very great deal of good, undoubtedly, was done, suffering mitigated, injustice avoided or prevented, ignorance exposed, by the conscientious attempt to apply scientific methods to the regulation of human affairs. Dogmas were refuted, prejudices and superstitions were pilloried successfully. The growing conviction that appeals to mystery and darkness and authority to justify arbitrary behavior were, all too often, so many unworthy *alibis* concealing self-interest or intellectual indolence or stupidity, was often triumphantly vindicated. But the central dream, the demonstration that everything in the world moved by mechanical means, that all evils could be cured by appropriate technological steps, that there could exist engineers both of human souls and of human bodies, proved delusive. Nevertheless, it proved less misleading in the end than the attacks upon it in the nineteenth century by means of arguments equally fallacious, but with implications that were, both intellectually and politically, more sinister and oppressive. The intellectual power, honesty, lucidity, courage, and disinterested love of the truth of the most gifted thinkers of the eighteenth century remain to this day without parallel. Their age is one of the best and most hopeful episodes in the life of mankind.

CHAPTER I

John Locke

JOHN LOCKE, WHOSE PHILOSOPHY EXERCISED UNDISPUTED sway over the ideas of the entire eighteenth century, was born in 1632, and at the age of twenty-six took his Master's degree at Oxford, where he lived and taught on and off, until, in 1683, four years before the Glorious Revolution which his ideas had done much to mold, he was expelled on suspicion of complicity in the machinations of the Whigs, and in particular of his patron, Lord Shaftesbury, whom he served as political adviser and physician. He fled to Holland and returned only after the accession of William of Orange. It was during the last fifteen years of his life, spent peacefully in the country, that he published the great treatises on philosophy and politics which transformed human thought.

He was a man of gentle, shy and amiable disposition, widely liked and esteemed, without enemies, and endowed with an astonishing capacity for absorbing and interpreting in simple language some of the original and revolutionary ideas in which his time was singularly rich. He was in harmony with his age, and all that he touched prospered. He is the father of the central philosophical and political tradition of the Western world, especially in America; nor were his practical gifts negligible, for he left the imprint of his good sense on the machinery of modern British administration particularly in matters dealing with trade.

If Descartes broke the spell of scholasticism by attempting to apply the methods, standards, and some of the concepts of the mathematical and natural sciences (which he had himself done so much to advance) Locke, whose scientific attainments were exceedingly modest,

emancipated philosophy from even this degree of speciali-
zation. And for the eighteenth century, at least, he rendered it no longer an esoteric study, but a discipline based
on normal powers of empirical observation and common-
sense judgment. Descartes only recognizes as worthy of
attention arguments which proceed by rigorous deduction
from premises which are self-evident or known to be true
a priori; Locke appeals to observation of the natural world,
seeks to examine present beliefs and states of mind by
tracing them to their psychological origins and giving an
account of their "natural" growth therefrom. Above all,
like Hobbes, he looks on man as an object in nature, not
fundamentally different from other natural objects, and to
be described and explained by the genetic methods of the
natural science of psychology—although he did not call it
that. His own theories are often fanciful enough; he is
guilty of many inconsistencies and obscurities and lapses
into modes of thought which he is supposing himself to
combat. Nevertheless, his ideas, or at least the effects of
his skill in presenting them (the literary taste of the latter
part of the seventeenth and the whole of the eighteenth century is clearly different from our own) were genuinely revolutionary. His view that many cardinal errors are due to
the mistaking of words for things; that minds—or their
thoughts—are capable of having their natural histories
written no less than plants or animals, with equally startling and fruitful results; that the findings of philosophers
must not depart too widely from the beliefs of balanced
common sense (Locke may almost be said to have invented
the notion of common sense); that philosophical problems
are as often as not due to confusion in the mind of the
philosopher rather than the difficulties inherent in the
subject—all this transformed the ideas of men. Voltaire's
unbounded admiration alone is sufficient testimony to the
impact of Locke's works. He supposed himself to be prac-
ticing the method of Newton; but in fact he far more resembles the physician (that he was) who seeks to cure the
diseases (in this case delusions about the external world
and the mental faculties of men), and as part of this process traces them to their origins and examines their symp-

toms, and so finds himself compiling something which is partly a textbook of anatomy, partly a manual on methods of healing. It is written in plain and lucid language which does a good deal to conceal the vagueness and obscurity of much of the thought itself. The opening Epistle is of a characteristic intellectual modesty and charm, and predisposes the contemporary reader in its favor by telling him that he need not, to obtain true knowledge, soar in the clouds with theologians, descend dark wells with metaphysicians, but only study his own nature, which, if done conscientiously, will sweep away the "sanctuary of vanity and ignorance"—the clouds of meaningless words—and so clear a path for a solid, empirical science of man.

All the selections from Locke that follow are from *An Essay Concerning Human Understanding*.

{ THE EPISTLE TO THE READER

Were it fit to trouble thee with the history of this essay, I should tell thee that five or six friends meeting at my chamber, and discoursing on a subject very remote from this, found themselves quickly at a stand by the difficulties that rose on every side. After we had awhile puzzled ourselves, without coming any nearer a resolution of those doubts which perplexed us, it came into my thoughts that we took a wrong course, and that before we set ourselves upon inquiries of that nature, it was necessary to examine our own abilities, and see what objects our understandings were, or were not, fitted to deal with. This I proposed to the company, who all readily assented; and therefore it was agreed that this should be our first inquiry. Some hasty and undigested thoughts on a subject I had never before considered, which I set down against our next meeting, gave the first entrance into this discourse; which having been thus begun by chance, was continued by entreaty; written by incoherent parcels; and after long intervals of neglect, resumed again, as my humour or occasions permitted; and at last, in a retirement, where an attendance on my health gave me leisure, it was brought into that order thou now seest it. . . .

. . . The commonwealth of learning is not at this time without master-builders, whose mighty designs in advancing the sciences will leave lasting monuments to the admiration of posterity; but every one must not hope to be a Boyle[1] or a Sydenham[2]: and in an age that produces such masters as the great Huygenius[3] and the incomparable Mr. Newton, with some others of that strain, it is ambition enough to be employed as an under-labourer in clearing the ground a little, and removing some of the rubbish that lies in the way to knowledge; which certainly had been very much more advanced in the world, if the endeavours of ingenious and industrious men had not been much cumbered with the learned but frivolous use of uncouth, affected, or unintelligible terms, introduced into the sciences, and there made an art of, to that degree that philosophy, which is nothing but the true knowledge of things, was thought unfit or incapable to be brought into well-bred company and polite conversation. Vague and insignificant forms of speech, and abuse of language, have so long passed for mysteries of science, and hard or misapplied words, with little or no meaning, have, by prescription, such a right to be mistaken for deep learning and height of speculation, that it will not be easy to persuade either those who speak or those who hear them that they are but the covers of ignorance, and hindrance of true knowledge. To break in upon the sanctuary of vanity and ignorance will be, I suppose, some service to human understanding; though so few are apt to think they deceive or are deceived in the use of words, or that the language of the sect they are of has any faults in it which ought to be examined or corrected, that I hope I shall be pardoned if I have in the third book dwelt long on this subject, and endeavoured to make it so plain, that neither the inveterateness of the mischief nor the prevalence of the fashion shall be any excuse for those who will not take care about the meaning of their

[1] The Hon. Robert Boyle (1627-91). British physicist and chemist, one of the founders of the Royal Society.
[2] Thomas Sydenham (1624-89). English physician.
[3] Christian Huyghens (1629-95). Dutch mathematician, physicist and astronomer.

own words, and will not suffer the significancy of their expressions to be inquired into.]

HAVING SPECIFIED HIS GENERAL APPROACH, LOCKE GIVES a more detailed account of what he proposes to do and how, and gives an outline of the painful but necessary task of turning oneself into one's own object—of "thought trying to catch its own tail"—which has ever since formed the core of modern philosophy, superseding the clear and naïve vision, untroubled by neurotic self-consciousness, which characterized the bulk of classical and mediaeval thought.

The following is from Book I, "Of Innate Notions."

[CHAPTER I. *Introduction*

1. *An Inquiry into the Understanding, pleasant and useful.*—Since it is the understanding that sets man above the rest of sensible beings, and gives him all the advantage and dominion which he has over them, it is certainly a subject, even for its nobleness, worth our labour to inquire into. The understanding, like the eye, whilst it makes us see and perceive all other things, takes no notice of itself; and it requires art and pains to set it at a distance, and make it its own object. But whatever be the difficulties that lie in the way of this inquiry, whatever it be that keeps us so much in the dark to ourselves, sure I am that all the light we can let in upon our own minds, all the acquaintance we can make with our own understandings, will not only be very pleasant, but bring us great advantage in directing our thoughts in the search of other things.

2. *Design.*—This, therefore, being my purpose, to inquire into the original, certainty, and extent of human knowledge, together with the grounds and degrees of belief, opinion, and assent, I shall not at present meddle with the physical consideration of the mind, or trouble myself to examine wherein its essence consists, or by what motions of our spirits or alterations of our bodies we come to have any sensation by our organs, or any ideas in our understandings; and whether those ideas do, in their for-

mation, any or all of them, depend on matter or not. These are speculations which, however curious and entertaining, I shall decline, as lying out of my way in the design I am now upon. . . .

3. *Method.*—It is therefore worth while to search out the bounds between opinion and knowledge, and examine by what measures, in things whereof we have no certain knowledge, we ought to regulate our assent and moderate our persuasions. In order whereunto I shall pursue this following method.

First, I shall inquire into the original of those ideas, notions, or whatever else you please to call them, which a man observes and is conscious to himself he has in his mind; and the ways whereby the understanding comes to be furnished with them.

Secondly, I shall endeavour to show what knowledge the understanding hath by those ideas, and the certainty, evidence, and extent of it.

Thirdly, I shall make some inquiry into the nature and grounds of faith, or opinion; whereby I mean that assent which we give to any proposition as true, of whose truth yet we have no certain knowledge: and here we shall have occasion to examine the reasons and degrees of assent.

7. *Occasion of this Essay.*—This was that which gave the first rise to this essay concerning the understanding. For I thought that the first step towards satisfying several inquiries the mind of man was very apt to run into, was to take a survey of our own understandings, examine our own powers, and see to what things they were adapted. Till that was done, I suspected we began at the wrong end, and in vain sought for satisfaction in a quiet and sure possession of truths that most concerned us, whilst we let loose our thoughts into the vast ocean of being; as if all that boundless extent were the natural and undoubted possession of our understandings, wherein there was nothing exempt from its decisions, or that escaped its comprehension.]

THIS SUMS UP LOCKE'S "EPISTEMOLOGICAL" APPROACH TO philosophy, and his conception of the task of the philosopher as clarification ("to be employed as an under-labourer in clearing the ground a little, and removing some of the rubbish that lies in the way to knowledge") whose work is to be ancillary to the work of the scientist in discovering objective facts.

He goes on to introduce the term which is central to his exposition, and which was destined to play a crucial role in later philosophy—the "idea."

[8. *What Idea stands for.*—Thus much I thought necessary to say concerning the occasion of this inquiry into human understanding. But, before I proceed on to what I have thought on this subject, I must here in the entrance beg pardon of my reader for the frequent use of the word "idea," which he will find in the following treatise. It being that term which, I think, serves best to stand for whatsoever is the object of the understanding when a man thinks, I have used it to express whatever is meant by phantasm, notion, species, or whatever it is which the mind can be employed about in thinking; and I could not avoid frequently using it.

I presume it will be easily granted me that there are such *ideas* in men's minds. Every one is conscious of them in himself, and men's words and actions will satisfy him that they are in others.

Our first inquiry, then, shall be, how they come into the mind.]

THIS USE OF THE WORD "IDEA"—WHICH IS FAR WIDER than, but had obvious affinities with, such later notions as "impressions," "phenomena," "appearances," "percepts," "sensibilia," "sense data," "the given," etc.—is part and parcel of this semimechanical conception of the mind, and the view that the philosopher is, as it were, engaged upon the natural history (the description of the origin, growth, behaviour) of certain entities called "ideas" in the mind.

[CHAPTER II. *No Innate Principles in the Mind*

1. *The way shown how we come by any knowledge, sufficient to prove it not innate.*—It is an established opinion among some men, that there are in the under-

standing certain innate principles; some primary notions, κοιναί 'έννοιαί, characters, as it were, stamped upon the mind of man, which the soul receives in its very first being, and brings into the world with it. It would be sufficient to convince unprejudiced readers of the falseness of this supposition, if I should only show (as I hope I shall in the following parts of this discourse) how men, barely by the use of their natural faculties, may attain to all the knowledge they have, without the help of any innate impressions, and may arrive at certainty, without any such original notions or principles. . . .

2. *General Assent the great Argument.*—There is nothing more commonly taken for granted, than that there are certain principles, both speculative and practical (for they speak of both), universally agreed upon by all mankind, which therefore, they argue, must needs be constant impressions which the souls of men receive in their first beings, and which they bring into the world with them, as necessarily and really as they do any of their inherent faculties.

3. *Universal Consent proves nothing innate.*—This argument, drawn from universal consent, has this misfortune in it, that if it were true in matter of fact that there were certain truths wherein all mankind agreed, it would not prove them innate, if there can be any other way shown how men may come to that universal agreement in the things they do consent in, which I presume may be done.

4. *"What is, is," and "it is impossible for the same Thing to be and not to be," not universally assented to.*— But, which is worse, this argument of universal consent, which is made use of to prove innate principles, seems to me a demonstration that there are none such; because there are none to which all mankind give an universal assent. I shall begin with the speculative, and instance in those magnified principles of demonstration, "Whatsoever is, is," and "It is impossible for the same thing to be, and not to be"; which, of all others, I think, have the most allowed title to innate. These have so settled a reputation of maxims universally received that it will no doubt be thought strange if anyone should seem to question it. But yet I take liberty to say that these propositions are so far

from having an universal assent that there are a great part of mankind to whom they are not so much as known.

5. *Not on the Mind naturally imprinted, because not known to Children, Idiots, &.*—For, first, it is evident that all children and idiots have not the least apprehension or thought of them; and the want of that is enough to destroy that universal assent which must needs be the necessary concomitant of all innate truths: it seeming to me near a contradiction to say that there are truths imprinted on the soul which it perceives or understands not; imprinting, if it signify anything, being nothing else but the making certain truths to be perceived. For to imprint anything on the mind without the mind's perceiving it, seems to me hardly intelligible. If therefore children and idiots have souls, have minds, with those impressions upon them, they must unavoidably perceive them, and necessarily know and assent to these truths; which since they do not, it is evident that there are no such impressions. For if they are not notions naturally imprinted, how can they be innate? And if they are notions imprinted, how can they be unknown? To say a notion is imprinted on the mind, and yet at the same time to say that the mind is ignorant of it, and never yet took notice of it, is to make this impression nothing. No proposition can be said to be in the mind which it never yet knew, which it was never yet conscious of.]

BEFORE ADVANCING HIS OWN THEORY OF KNOWLEDGE IN Book IV, Locke seeks to demolish what he regards as a rival epistemological theory, namely that at least some knowledge is innate.

The argument is a dilemma. Either in saying that a proposition (e.g. "Whatever is, is" or "It is impossible for the same thing to be and not to be," the so-called Law of Identity and Law of Non-Contradiction of Classical Logic) is innate, we mean literally that a knowledge of its truth is already explicitly present in the consciousness of each man as soon as he is born, or we mean something less radical, for example, that all men are born with a capacity or faculty for knowing its truth, a capacity which is exercised only when we "come to the use of reason." But the first claim, which rests on the evidence of actual experience, is false, as he demonstrates in the passage above; for it is a necessary (though not, as Locke points out above, a sufficient) condition of the truth of this claim that all men must agree to the "innate" proposition. And this is obviously not so—Locke cites the case of children and idiots. Whereas, if we take the second horn of the dilemma, then (1) the use of the term "innate" is "a very improper way of speaking," but, (2) worse still, the theory now fails to distinguish between the small, privileged class of supposedly innate propositions, and any other propositions (say those of mathematics) whose truth men can come gradually to know.

What has puzzled (and still puzzles) students of Locke, is the precise identity of his opponents. Few of his contemporaries can have held a theory that knowledge was literally innate (though some attributed such a theory to Plato); and many took pains explicitly to deny it. The possible targets of the attack are three. (a) Descartes and some of his followers who did make a confused use of the term "innate idea,"[4] (b) Certain contemporary English philosophers, the Cambridge Platonists, and especially Henry More, who also held a kind of weakened theory of innate knowledge. And (c) many surviving followers of Scholasticism who maintained that all knowledge was *ex praecognitis et praeconcessis,* i.e., was obtained by deduction from previously known self-evident truths. Perhaps it is at the third group that Locke's polemic was principally directed. And in the attacks both here and in the Fourth Book Locke is not only fulfilling the narrower philosophical purpose of destroying a rival theory of knowledge, but also, on a much wider front, making a claim of central theological and political importance, for the primacy of individual judgment against authority and dogma: since "This [i.e. the theory of innate knowledge] being once

[4]Leibniz, who attacked Locke in his *New Essays,* held a form of the "weaker" theory about innate faculties, common to all men, for recognizing absolute "truths of reason"—potentialities rather than actual truths permanently present to the mind—like veins in the marble which the sculptor must take into account, and which form its character whether he does so or not.

received, it eased the lazy from the pains of search, and stopped the inquiry of the doubtful concerning all that was once styled innate. And it was of no small advantage to those who affected to be masters and teachers to make this the principle of principles, 'that principles must not be questioned.' "

The attack on innate ideas is, historically, if not the first, the greatest blow struck for empiricism and against the vast metaphysical constructions which rested on axioms for which no evidence could be discovered. All these rival systems claimed their origins and their validity in the exercise of pure reason: and Locke—like Hobbes before him—although with hesitations and inconsistencies, questioned the existence of any such instrument for discovering facts about the world. Upon its existence the very possibility of metaphysics directly depends. In the passages which follow (from Book II, "Of Ideas") Locke provides his own positive accounts of the matter.

[CHAPTER I. *Of Ideas in General, and their Original*

1. *Idea is the Object of Thinking.*—Every man being conscious to himself that he thinks, and that which his mind is applied about whilst thinking being the ideas that are there, it is past doubt that men have in their mind several ideas, such as are those expressed by the words "whiteness," "hardness," "sweetness," "thinking," "motion," "man," "elephant," "army," "drunkenness," and others. It is in the first place then to be inquired, how he comes by them. I know it is a received doctrine that men have native ideas and original characters stamped upon their minds in their very first being. This opinion I have at large examined already; and I suppose what I have said in the foregoing book will be much more easily admitted, when I have shown whence the understanding may get all the ideas it has, and by what ways and degrees they may come into the mind; for which I shall appeal to every one's own observation and experience.

2. *All Ideas come from Sensation or Reflection.*—Let us then, suppose the mind to be, as we say, white paper,

void of all characters, without any ideas; how comes it to
be furnished? Whence comes it by that vast store which
the busy and boundless fancy of man has painted on it
with an almost endless variety? Whence has it all the materials of reason and knowledge? To this I answer, in one
word, from experience; in that all our knowledge is
founded, and from that it ultimately derives itself. Our
observation, employed either about external sensible objects, or about the internal operations of our minds, perceived and reflected on by ourselves, is that which supplies
our understandings with all the materials of thinking. These
two are the fountains of knowledge, from whence all the
ideas we have, or can naturally have, do spring.

3. *The Objects of Sensation one Source of Ideas.*—
First, our senses, conversant about particular sensible objects, do convey into the mind several distinct perceptions
of things, according to those various ways wherein those
objects do affect them; and thus we come by those ideas
we have, of yellow, white, heat, cold, soft, hard, bitter,
sweet, and all those which we call sensible qualities; which
when I say the senses convey into the mind, I mean they
from external objects convey into the mind what produces
there those perceptions. This great source of most of the
ideas we have, depending wholly upon our senses, and
derived by them to the understanding, I call "sensation."

4. *The Operations of our Minds, the other Source of
them.*—Secondly, the other fountain, from which experience furnisheth the understanding with ideas, is the perception of the operations of our own mind within us, as
it is employed about the ideas it has got; which operations,
when the soul comes to reflect on and consider, do furnish
the understanding with another set of ideas, which could
not be had from things without; and such are perception,
thinking, doubting, believing, reasoning, knowing, willing,
and all the different actings of our own minds; which we
being conscious of, and observing in ourselves, do from
these receive into our understandings as distinct ideas, as
we do from bodies affecting our senses. This source of ideas
every man has wholly in himself; and though it be not
sense, as having nothing to do with external objects, yet

it is very like it, and might properly enough be called "internal sense." But as I call the other "sensation" so I call this "reflection," the ideas it affords being such only as the mind gets by reflecting on its own operations within itself. By reflection, then, in the following part of this discourse, I would be understood to mean that notice which the mind takes of its own operations, and the manner of them; by reason whereof there come to be ideas of these operations in the understanding. These two, I say, viz., external material things, as the objects of sensation, and the operations of our own minds within, as the objects of reflection, are to me the only originals from whence all our ideas take their beginnings. The term "operations" here I use in a large sense, as comprehending not barely the actions of the mind about its ideas, but some sort of passions arising sometimes from them, such as is the satisfaction or uneasiness arising from any thought.

5. *All our Ideas are of the one or the other of these.* —The understanding seems to me not to have the least glimmering of any ideas which it doth not receive from one of these two. External objects furnish the mind with the ideas of sensible qualities, which are all those different perceptions they produce in us; and the mind furnishes the understanding with ideas of its own operations.

These, when we have taken a full survey of them, and their several modes, combinations, and relations, we shall find to contain all our whole stock of ideas; and that we have nothing in our minds which did not come in one of these two ways. Let any one examine his own thoughts, and thoroughly search into his understanding; and then let him tell me, whether all the original ideas he has there, are any other than of the objects of his senses, or of the operations of his mind, considered as objects of his reflection: and how great a mass of knowledge soever he imagines to be lodged there, he will, upon taking a strict view, see that he has not any idea in his mind but what one of these two hath imprinted; though, perhaps, with infinite variety compounded and enlarged by the understanding, as we shall see hereafter.

24. *The original of all our Knowledge.*—In time the

mind comes to reflect on its own operations about the ideas got by sensation, and thereby stores itself with a new set of ideas, which I call "ideas of reflection." These are the impressions that are made on our senses by outward objects that are extrinsical to the mind, and its own operations, proceeding from powers intrinsical and proper to itself. . . .

25. *In the Reception of simple Ideas, the Understanding is for the most part passive.*—In this part the understanding is merely passive; and whether or not it will have these beginnings, and, as it were, materials of knowledge, is not in its own power: for the objects of our senses do, many of them, obtrude their particular ideas upon our minds, whether we will or not; and the operations of our minds will not let us be without at least some obscure notions of them. No man can be wholly ignorant of what he does when he thinks. These simple ideas, when offered to the mind, the understanding can no more refuse to have, nor alter when they are imprinted, nor blot them out and make new ones itself, than a mirror can refuse, alter, or obliterate the images or ideas which the objects set before it do therein produce. As the bodies that surround us do diversely affect our organs, the mind is forced to receive the impressions, and cannot avoid the perception of those ideas that are annexed to them.}

NO OTHER TEXT GIVES A CLEARER PICTURE OF THE CEN-tral notions underlying the new theory of knowledge developed in Britain in the eighteenth century, especially the first two paragraphs:

(1) *Ideas as entities.* In the mind of man, conceived as a sort of hollow vessel or container, there are to be found a number ("a vast store") of perfectly distinct and separable entities called *ideas.* This is taken to be self-evident.

(2) *The philosopher as a natural scientist.* The starting point of the philosopher is to function as a descriptive psychologist—to draw up an inventory of these entities, sorting them into kinds, describing their activities, transformations, and so forth.

(3) *The genetic approach.* These entities must come

from somewhere—they cannot originate in nothing; it is next the business of the philosopher to answer the question "Where do these ideas come from?" "What is their source?"

(4) *The Empirical Method*. These tasks are to be carried out by a sort of simple quasi-botanical inspection.

In this passage Locke advances the classical empiricist thesis of eighteenth-century epistemology: "All our ideas come from experience." It later transpires that only "simple" ideas come directly from experience; "complex" ideas are built up from simple ideas by "the operations of the mind"; hence they too have their final source in experience. "Experience" itself Locke distinguishes into sensation directed upon (and stimulated by) external objects, and reflection (we should now call it "introspection"), directed within upon the workings of the mind itself.

We can here discern already the origins of many of the difficulties which Locke will encounter. How, one may ask, can he distinguish ideas of sensation solely by the fact that they come from external objects, if he has *ex hypothesi* only the ideas themselves, and no external objects, to inspect? They cannot in these conditions be distinguished unless there exists some criterion internal to the ideas themselves. This is connected with Locke's misconception of the logical relations between epistemology on the one hand and physics and the physiology of the sense organs on the other. In the following paragraphs he offers a kind of taxonomy—a classified catalogue of the ultimate constituents of experience—the "ideas."

[CHAPTER II. *Of Simple Ideas*

1. *Uncompounded Appearances.*—The better to understand the nature, manner, and extent of our knowledge, one thing is carefully to be observed concerning the ideas we have; and that is, that some of them are simple, and some complex.

Though the qualities that affect our senses are, in the things themselves, so united and blended that there is no separation, no distance between them; yet it is plain the

ideas they produce in the mind enter by the senses simple
and unmixed. For though the sight and touch often take
in from the same object, at the same time, different ideas—
as a man sees at once motion and colour, the hand feels
softness and warmth in the same piece of wax; yet the
simple ideas thus united in the same subject are as perfectly distinct as those that come in by different senses:
the coldness and hardness which a man feels in a piece
of ice being as distinct ideas in the mind as the smell and
whiteness of a lily, or as the taste of sugar and the smell
of a rose. And there is nothing can be plainer to a man
than the clear and distinct perception he has of those
simple ideas; which, being each in itself uncompounded,
contains in it nothing but one uniform appearance or conception in the mind, and is not distinguishable into different ideas.

2. *The Mind can neither make nor destroy them.*—
These simple ideas, the materials of all our knowledge, are
suggested and furnished to the mind only by those two
ways above mentioned, viz., sensation and reflection.
When the understanding is once stored with these simple
ideas it has the power to repeat, compare, and unite them,
even to an almost infinite variety, and so can make at
pleasure new complex ideas. But it is not in the power of
the most exalted wit, or enlarged understanding, by any
quickness or variety of thoughts, to invent or frame one
new simple idea in the mind, not taken in by the ways
before mentioned; nor can any force of the understanding
destroy those that are there. The same inability will everyone find in himself, who shall go about to fashion in his
understanding one simple idea not received in by his
senses from external objects, or by reflection from the
operations of his own mind about them.

3. This is the reason why, though we cannot believe it
impossible to God to make a creature with other organs
and more ways to convey into the understanding the notice
of corporeal things than those five, as they are usually
counted, which he has given to man; yet I think it is not
possible for anyone to imagine any other qualities in bodies, howsoever constituted, whereby they can be taken

notice of, besides sounds, tastes, smells, visible and tangible qualities. And had mankind been made but with four senses, the qualities then which are the objects of the fifth sense had been as far from our notice, imagination, and conception, as now any belonging to a sixth, seventh, or eighth sense, can possibly be. . . . I have here followed the common opinion of man's having but five senses, though perhaps there may be justly counted more; but either supposition serves equally to my present purpose.]

LOCKE HERE DRAWS THE DISTINCTION, CARDINAL TO HIS psychological atomism (the conception of ideas as irreducible ultimate elements) between simple and complex ideas. He maintains that when we see, hear, smell, etc., a material object, although this object itself has many qualities, the mind receives the "ideas" of each of these qualities as a quite separate simple idea, which itself cannot be further analyzed.

Complex ideas are built up from simple ideas by various "operations of the mind" which Locke will presently describe. But the simple ideas themselves all come from experience. Since they are the basic stuff of which all thoughts, feelings, etc., consist, the imagination cannot generate a simple idea not previously sensed directly, only reproduce and shuffle them in new combinations. It is worth comparing this with Hume's treatment of the problem of imagining a color one has never seen (see below p. 171).

Having classified types of ideas, Locke considers their relationship to material reality with which they are our sole link, sometimes by mirroring it faithfully, sometimes less directly. The whole discussion represents an effort to reconcile the data of ordinary sense perception with the findings of physicists; Locke's failure to achieve this is among the earliest attempts to solve a crucial problem which divides philosophers to this day. Among modern thinkers whose theories of perception derive from his are to be found such diverse personalities as Bertrand Russell, Santayana and Lenin, although it is fair to add that Lenin's philosophical views perhaps scarcely deserve to be taken seriously.

The doctrine of primary and secondary qualities originates with the Greek Atomists. Traces of it occur in the writings of such early Renaissance thinkers as Campanella, but its modern version and enormous influence is due in the first place to Galileo. Natural science had made astonishing progress in the seventeenth century, and this advance was due, more than to any other single factor, to the abandonment of the mediaeval practice of describing objects in terms of irreducible qualitative differences, in favor of concentration upon their quantitatively measurable properties. Precise laws of great predictive power could at last be formulated in purely mathematical terms, connecting the variations in these properties. In Galileo's case, moreover, it is only certain among the measurable properties that enter into his laws, namely mechanical properties. As has so often happened since, the methodological precept "only the mechanical measurable properties of matter are of value in formulating scientific laws" became converted into the metaphysical statement "only the mechanical measurable properties of matter are *real.*" And Galileo argued for the reality of these properties and the unreality of all others (colors, tastes, smells, etc.) by saying that he could not conceive of a body which had not got a shape, a size and a position, and was not either at rest or moving in some determinate manner, whilst he could readily conceive of one which was lacking in taste, smell or color. These latter properties he concluded were subjective illusions; only the former were objective, real, "in the body" itself.

This doctrine gained wide currency in the seventeenth century, and by Locke's time had become closely connected with two further theories: (1) That local motion and impact are the only causal agencies in the material world, so that all explanations must, in the end, be in terms of these.

(2) The Cartesian notion of man, according to which the mind was something totally different in kind from the

body which contained it like a box, in the part of itself called the brain.

These two theories combined to produce the following picture: particles emanating from material objects strike the human sense organs setting up a chain of effects in the nervous system, which somehow finally produce an entity wholly different in kind from themselves—an idea in the mind. This dualism—between "real" entities colliding in the external world endowed with mathematically transcribable "primary" qualities, and "ideas" in minds, a mere subjective counterpart or by-product—leads directly to the representative theory of perception of which Locke's version is as follows:

[CHAPTER VIII. *Some Further Considerations Concerning Our Simple Ideas*

7. *Ideas in the Mind, Qualities in Bodies.*—To discover the nature of our ideas the better, and to discourse of them, intelligibly, it will be convenient to distinguish them as they are ideas or perceptions in our minds, and as they are modifications of matter in the bodies that cause such perceptions in us, that so we may not think (as perhaps usually is done) that they are exactly the images and resemblances of something inherent in the subject; most of those of sensation being in the mind no more the likeness of something existing without us, than the names that stand for them are the likeness of our ideas, which yet upon hearing they are apt to excite in us.

8. Whatsoever the mind perceives in itself, or is the immediate object of perception, thought, or understanding, that I call "idea"; and the power to produce any idea in our mind, I call "quality" of the subject wherein that power is. Thus a snowball having the power to produce in us the ideas of white, cold, and round, the power to produce those ideas in us as they are in the snowball, I call "qualities"; and as they are sensations or perceptions in our understandings, I call them "ideas"; which ideas, if I speak of sometimes as in the things themselves, I would

be understood to mean those qualities in the objects which produce them in us.

9. *Primary Qualities.*—Qualities thus considered in bodies are, first, such as are utterly inseparable from the body, in what state soever it be; such as, in all the alterations and changes it suffers, all the force can be used upon it, it constantly keeps; and such as sense constantly finds in every particle of matter which has bulk enough to be perceived, and the mind finds inseparable from every particle of matter, though less than to make itself singly be perceived by our senses; v.g., take a grain of wheat, divide it into two parts, each part has still solidity, extension, figure, and mobility; divide it again, and it retains still the same qualities; and so divide it on till the parts become insensible, they must retain still each of them all those qualities. For, division (which is all that a mill or pestle or any other body does upon another, in reducing it to insensible parts) can never take away either solidity, extension, figure, or mobility from any body, but only makes two or more distinct separate masses of matter of that which was but one before; all which distinct masses, reckoned as so many distinct bodies, after division, make a certain number. These I call "original" or "primary" qualities of body, which I think we may observe to produce simple ideas in us, viz., solidity, extension, figure, motion or rest, and number.

10. *Secondary Qualities.*—Secondly, such qualities, which in truth are nothing in the objects themselves but powers to produce various sensations in us by their primary qualities, i.e., by the bulk, figure, texture, and motion of their insensible parts, as colours, sounds, tastes, etc., these I call "secondary" qualities. To these might be added a third sort, which are allowed to be barely powers, though they are as much real qualities in the subject as those which I, to comply with the common way of speaking, call qualities, but, for distinction, "secondary" qualities. For the power in fire to produce a new colour or consistency in wax or clay by its primary qualities is as much a quality in fire as the power it has to produce in me a new idea or sensation of warmth or burning, which I felt not

before, by the same primary qualities, viz., the bulk, texture, and motion of its insensible parts.

11. *How primary Qualities produce their Ideas.*—The next thing to be considered is, how bodies produce ideas in us; and that is manifestly by impulse, the only way which we can conceive bodies to operate in.

12. If, then, external objects be not united to our minds when they produce ideas therein, and yet we perceive these original qualities in such of them as singly fall under our senses, it is evident that some motion must be thence continued by our nerves or animal spirits, by some parts of our bodies, to the brain or the seat of sensation, there to produce in our minds the particular ideas we have of them. And since the extension, figure, number, and motion of bodies of an observable bigness may be perceived at a distance by the sight, it is evident some singly imperceptible bodies must come from them to the eyes, and thereby convey to the brain some motion which produces these ideas which we have of them in us.

13. *How secondary.*—After the same manner that the ideas of these original qualities are produced in us, we may conceive that the ideas of secondary qualities are also produced, viz., by the operation of insensible particles on our senses. For it being manifest that there are bodies, and good store of bodies, each whereof are so small that we cannot by any of our senses discover either their bulk, figure, or motion, as is evident in the particles of the air and water, and others extremely smaller than those, perhaps as much smaller than the particles of air and water as the particles of air and water are smaller than peas or hail-stones: let us suppose at present that the different motions and figures, bulk and number, of such particles, affecting the several organs of our senses, produce in us those different sensations which we have from the colours and smells of bodies, v.g., that a violet, by the impulse of such insensible particles of matter of peculiar figures and bulks, and in different degrees and modifications of their motions, causes the ideas of the blue colour and sweet scent of that flower to be produced in our minds; it being no more impossible to conceive that God should annex such

ideas to such motions, with which they have no similitude, than that he should annex the idea of pain to the motion of a piece of steel dividing our flesh, with which that idea hath no resemblance.

14. What I have said concerning colours and smells may be understood also of tastes and sounds, and other the like sensible qualities; which, whatever reality we by mistake attribute to them, are in truth nothing in the objects themselves but powers to produce various sensations in us, and depend on those primary qualities, viz., bulk, figure, texture, and motion of parts, as I have said.

15. *Ideas of primary Qualities are Resemblances; of secondary, not.*—From whence I think it easy to draw this observation, that the ideas of primary qualities of bodies are resemblances of them, and their patterns do really exist in the bodies themselves; but the ideas produced in us by these secondary qualities have no resemblance of them at all. There is nothing like our ideas existing in the bodies themselves. They are, in the bodies we denominate from them, only a power to produce those sensations in us; and what is sweet, blue, or warm in idea, is but the certain bulk, figure, and motion of the insensible parts in the bodies themselves, which we call so.

16. Flame is denominated "hot' and "light," snow, "white" and "cold," and manna, "white" and "sweet," from the ideas they produce in us, which qualities are commonly thought to be the same in those bodies that those ideas are in us, the one the perfect resemblance of the other, as they are in a mirror, and it would by most men be judged very extravagant if one should say otherwise. And yet he that will consider that the same fire that at one distance produces in us the sensation of warmth, does at a nearer approach produce in us the far different sensation of pain, ought to bethink himself what reason he has to say that his idea of warmth, which was produced in him by the fire, is actually in the fire, and his idea of pain, which the same fire produced in him the same way, is not in the fire. Why are whiteness and coldness in snow and pain not, when it produces the one and the other idea in us,

and can do neither but by the bulk, figure, number, and motion of its solid parts?

17. The particular bulk, number, figure, and motion of the parts of fire or snow are really in them, whether anyone's senses perceive them or not; and therefore they may be called real qualities, because they really exist in those bodies. But light, heat, whiteness, or coldness, are no more really in them than sickness or pain is in manna. Take away the sensation of them, let not the eyes see light or colours, nor the ears hear sounds; let the palate not taste, nor the nose smell; and all colours, tastes, odours and sounds, as they are such particular ideas, vanish and cease, and are reduced to their causes, i.e., bulk, figure, and motion of parts.

18. A piece of manna of a sensible bulk is able to produce in us the idea of a round or square figure; and, by being removed from one place to another, the idea of motion. This idea of motion represents it as it really is in the manna moving: a circle or square are the same, whether in idea or existence, in the mind or in the manna; and this both motion and figure are really in the manna, whether we take notice of them or no: this everybody is ready to agree to. Besides, manna, by the bulk, figure, texture, and motion of its parts, has a power to produce the sensations of sickness, and sometimes of acute pains or gripings, in us. That these ideas of sickness and pain are not in the manna, but effects of its operations on us, and are nowhere when we feel them not, this also everyone agrees to. And yet men are hardly to be brought to think that sweetness and whiteness are not really in manna, which are but the effects of the operations of manna by the motion, size and figure of its particles on the eyes and palate; as the pain and sickness caused by manna are confessedly nothing but the effects of the operations on the stomach and guts by the size, motion, and figure of its insensible parts (for by nothing else can a body operate, as has been proved). . . .}

AS CAN EASILY BE SEEN, LOCKE'S EXPOSITION OF THE doctrine is seriously confused:

(a) There is the false identification of epistemology as

a form of natural science. The above account (omitting the questionable "idea in the mind") may not be absurd as physiology, but physiology is not relevant in discussing the prior question (taken as already settled in their favor by physiologists) as to what we know of the external world.

(b) How can Locke know that our ideas of the primary qualities do resemble those qualities as they exist "in the body," since he can know only the ideas and cannot compare them with what they supposedly resemble?

(c) What is meant by saying that a quality is or is not "really in the body"? True, there is a distinction between sentences describing the measurable properties of bodies, and sentences describing our own sensations, namely that in the former case there are much clearer publicly accepted tests of "objective" truth made as independent as possible of "subjective" experience. But this carries no metaphysical implications about difference of "ontological status."

(d) Does Locke only mean that each material body must possess *some* determinate size, shape, and motion (or rest) as is suggested in Paragraph 9? This would seem to be a truism. For without fulfillment of these conditions we should not use the expression "material body." Or does he mean (as he seems to suggest in the passage quoted) that our perceptions of the sizes, shapes, etc., are *never* mistaken in the way in which our perceptions of colors, tastes, etc., admittedly are. But in this case he is mistaken, as, indeed, Berkeley pointed out (see p. 135, p. 147 ff.). And if we are sometimes just as mistaken with regard to size, shape or motion as with color, smell, etc., what reason have we for supposing that there exist any primary qualities at all? Because scientists assure us about them? But what means of discovering have they which ordinary mortals have not? Are they really in touch with a firm world with stable proportions, while the rest of mankind are sunk in a welter of blurred sensations, too indeterminate to be capable of exact description—and if so how have they achieved this? With what special organs of perception or intuition are they endowed? Descartes or Leibniz may have supposed that the real properties of material bodies are discoverable not by the senses but by "reason"—a parallel and superior source of information. But Locke denied this; hence his attempt at once to take over the distinction between primary (objective) qualities and secondary (subjective) ones—because Galileo and Newton built their phenomenally successful explanations on this principle—and yet preserve his own "sensationalist" premises which seem incompatible with this dualism, is not successful. But its very failure revealed the nature of this problem, which runs through his discussion of "complex" ideas, and grows still more acute when he begins to analyze the notion of substance—that which has the primary qualities—the material object the reality of which physicists and biologists took for granted. His account of how single ideas are combined into complicated wholes solves nothing.

[CHAPTER XI. *Of Discerning, and Other Operations of the Mind*

6. *Compounding.*—The next operation we may observe in the mind about its ideas is composition, whereby it puts together several of those simple ones it has received from sensation and reflection, and combines them into complex ones. Under this of composition may be reckoned also that of enlarging; wherein though the composition does not so much appear as in more complex ones, yet it is nevertheless a putting several ideas together, though of the same kind. Thus, by adding several units together we make the idea of a dozen; and putting together the repeated ideas of several perches we frame that of a furlong.

8. *Naming.*—When children have by repeated sensations got ideas fixed in their memories, they begin by degrees to learn the use of signs; and when they have got the skill to apply the organs of speech to the framing of articulate sounds, they begin to make use of words to signify their ideas to others. These verbal signs they sometimes borrow from others, and sometimes make themselves, as one may observe among the new and unusual names children often give to things in the first use of language.

9. *Abstraction.*—The use of words, then, being to stand

as outward marks of our internal ideas, and those ideas being taken from particular things, if every particular idea that we take in should have a distinct name, names must be endless. To prevent this, the mind makes the particular ideas received from particular objects to become general; which is done by considering them as they are in the mind, such appearances separate from all other existences, and the circumstances of real existence, as time, place, or any other concomitant ideas. This is called "abstraction," whereby ideas taken from particular beings become general representatives of all of the same kind, and their names, general names, applicable to whatever exists conformable to such abstract ideas. Such precise, naked appearances in the mind, without considering how, whence, or with what others they came there, the understanding lays up (with names commonly annexed to them) as the standard to rank real existences into sorts, as they agree with these patterns, and to denominate them accordingly. Thus, the same colour being observed today in chalk or snow, which the mind yesterday received from milk, it considers that appearance alone, makes it a representative of all of that kind; and, having given it the name "whiteness," it by that sound signifies the same quality wheresoever to be imagined or met with, and thus universals, whether ideas or terms, are made.

CHAPTER XII. *Of Complex Ideas*

1. *Made by the Mind out of simple Ones.*—We have hitherto considered those ideas in the reception whereof the mind is only passive, which are those simple ones received from sensation and reflection before mentioned, whereof the mind cannot make one to itself, nor have any idea which does not wholly consist of them. But as the mind is wholly passive in the reception of all its simple ideas, so it exerts several acts of its own, whereby out of its simple ideas, as the materials and foundations of the rest, the others are framed. . . . As simple ideas are observed to exist in several combinations united together, so the mind has a power to consider several of them united

together as one idea; and that not only as they are united in external objects, but as itself has joined them together. Ideas thus made up of several simple ones put together I call "complex"; such as are beauty, gratitude, a man, an army, the universe, which, though complicated of various simple ideas or complex ideas made up of simple ones, yet are, when the mind pleases, considered each by itself as one entire thing, and signified by one name.

2. *Made voluntarily.*—In this faculty of repeating and joining together its ideas, the mind has great power in varying and multiplying the objects of its thoughts infinitely beyond what sensation or reflection furnished it with; but all this still confined to those simple ideas which it received from those two sources, and which are the ultimate materials of all its compositions: for, simple ideas are all from things themselves, and of these the mind can have no more nor other than what are suggested to it. It can have no other ideas of sensible qualities than what come from without by the senses, nor any ideas of other kind of operations of a thinking substance than what it finds in itself; but when it has once got these simple ideas, it is not confined barely to observation, and what offers itself from without; it can, by its own power, put together those ideas it has, and make new complex ones which it never received so united.

8. *The abstrusest Ideas from the two Sources.*—If we trace the progress of our minds, and with attention observe how it repeats, adds together, and unites its simple ideas received from sensation or reflection, it will lead us further than at first perhaps we should have imagined. And I believe we shall find, if we warily observe the originals of our notions, that even the most abstruse ideas, how remote soever they may seem from sense, or from any operations of our own minds, are yet only such as the understanding frames to itself, by repeating and joining together ideas that it had either from objects of sense, or from its own operations about them; so that those even large and abstract ideas are derived from sensation or reflection, being no other than what the mind, by the ordinary use of its own faculties, employed about ideas received from objects

of sense, or from the operations it observes in itself about them, may and does attain unto.]

NO BETTER ILLUSTRATION IS WANTED OF THE QUASI-mechanical model of the mind with which Locke operates. Ideas exist as objects in the mind. Simple ideas of sensation and reflection pour in upon the mind, which is a passive receptacle. But the mind has, of itself, certain "active powers" by means of which it can combine several ideas to form a single new compound idea.

Compounding is the most obviously mechanical of these activities. By this ideas are put together to make a new idea, much as bricks might be put together to make a house: and can be taken apart again. The empiricist thesis is stressed again and again. However complex and remote from direct experience some of our ideas may be, yet the original materials (simple ideas) from which they are built up all come from sensation or reflection.

The philosophical doctrine of substance is ancient, complex and not readily intelligible. The most important feature of a "substance" was said to be that it is (as opposed to its "modes" or qualities) self-subsistent. The doctrine as held by Locke's Scholastic contemporaries amounted (very roughly) to this: The world consists of a plurality of independent substances, each of which is either God or a physical object or a mind, together with the modifications or qualities of these substances. Nothing else exists. Substances are distinguished from modes in that the former are self-subsistent, i.e., capable of existing by themselves, while the latter require a substance in which to "inhere." Substances, as self-subsistent, possess a higher degree of reality than the cluster of "modes" which each substance, as it were, owns.

From this (by now) scarcely intelligible ontology Locke never shook himself free. He confuses it with Galileo's or Newton's notions of material objects, and is, in consequence, involved in many embarrassments including his perplexity in the passage which follows about the "idea" of "substance in general," and his difficulty in accounting for our ideas of relations, since relations which seem to connect two or more substances, and do not uniquely belong to any given one, cannot be allowed to be real in this ontological scheme.

Locke talks principally of two sorts of ideas of substance.

(1) Our idea of substance in general. This he confesses to be very obscure, since it is *ex hypothesi* quite featureless. It is arrived at by stripping off from our idea of any particular object (whether a physical object or a mind) *all* its qualities; what is left—the self-subsistent owner of the qualities—is then an unknown substratum, an "I-know-not-what," for all that can be said of it is that "it," whatever it may be, "supports" the qualities. As a description, this seems—like Augustinian negative theology which regards God as transcendent and unknowable—incapable of explaining the physical world.

(2) Our idea of a given particular entity, e.g., the sun, or a particular lump of gold, is called our idea of *a* substance. The idea of a particular substance is a complex idea consisting of the ideas of a number of qualities which have been constantly found together with "the confused idea of something to which they belong and in which they subsist."

Both these notions, and a good many others, of what substance is jostle each other in the following passages.

[CHAPTER XXIII *Of Our Complex Ideas of Substances*

1. *Ideas of Substances, how made.*—The mind being, as I have declared, furnished with a great number of the simple ideas conveyed in by the senses, as they are found in exterior things, or by reflection on its own operations, takes notice, also, that a certain number of these simple ideas go constantly together; which being presumed to belong to one thing, and words being suited to common apprehensions, and made use of for quick dispatch, are called, so united in one subject, by one name; which, by inadvertency, we are apt afterward to talk of and consider as one simple idea, which indeed is a complication of many ideas together: because, as I have said, not imagin-

ing how these simple ideas can subsist by themselves, we accustom ourselves to suppose some substratum wherein they do subsist, and from which they do result; which therefore we call "substance."

2. *Our Idea of Substance in general.*—So that if anyone will examine himself concerning his notion of pure substance in general, he will find he has no other idea of it at all, but only a supposition of he knows not what support of such qualities which are capable of producing simple ideas in us; which qualities are commonly called "accidents." If anyone should be asked, "What is the subject wherein colour or weight inheres?" he would have nothing to say but, "The solid extended parts." And if he were demanded "What is it that solidity and extension inhere in?" he would not be in a much better case than the Indian before mentioned, who, saying that the world was supported by a great elephant, was asked what the elephant rested on? to which his answer was, "A great tortoise"; but being again pressed to know what gave support to the broad-backed tortoise, replied—something, he knew not what. And thus here, as in all other cases where we use words without having clear and distinct ideas, we talk like children, who, being questioned what such a thing is which they know not, readily give this satisfactory answer, that it is something, which in truth signifies no more, when so used, either by children or men, but that they know not what; and that the thing they pretend to know and talk of is what they have no distinct idea of at all, and so are perfectly ignorant of it, and in the dark. The idea, then, we have, to which we give the general name "substance" being nothing but the supposed, but unknown, support of those qualities we find existing, which we imagine cannot subsist *sine re substante,* "without something to support them," we call that support *substantia;* which, according to the true import of the word, is, in plain English, "standing under," or "upholding."

3. *Of the Sorts of Substances.*—An obscure and relative idea of substance in general being thus made, we come to have the ideas of particular sorts of substances, by collecting such combinations of simple ideas as are by experi-

ence and observation of men's senses taken notice of to
exist together, and are therefore supposed to flow from
the particular internal constitution or unknown essence of
that substance. Thus we come to have the ideas of a man,
horse, gold, water, &c., of which substances, whether anyone has any other clear idea, further than of certain simple ideas coexisting together, I appeal to everyone's own
experience. It is the ordinary qualities observable in iron
or a diamond, put together, that make the true complex
idea of those substances, which a smith or a jeweller commonly knows better than a philosopher; who, whatever
substantial forms he may talk of, has no other idea of those
substances than what is framed by a collection of those
simple ideas which are to be found in them; only we must
take notice that our complex ideas of substances, besides
all those simple ideas they are made up of, have always
the confused idea of something to which they belong and
in which they subsist. And therefore, when we speak of any
sort of substance we say it is a thing having such or such
qualities; as, body is a thing that is extended, figured, and
capable of motion; spirit, a thing capable of thinking; and
so hardness, friability, and power to draw iron, we say,
are qualities to be found in a loadstone. These and the like
fashions of speaking, intimate that the substance is supposed always something, besides the extension, figure,
solidity, motion, thinking or other observable ideas, though
we know not what it is.

4. *No clear Idea of Substance in general.*—Hence, when
we talk or think of any particular sort of corporeal substances, as horse, stone, &c., though the idea we have of
either of them be but the complication or collection of
those several simple ideas of sensible qualities which we
used to find united in the thing called "horse" or "stone";
yet because we cannot conceive how they should subsist
alone, nor one in another, we suppose them existing in,
and supported by, some common subject; which support
we denote by the name "substance," though it be certain
we have no clear or distinct idea of that thing we suppose
a support.

5. *As clear an Idea of Spirit as Body.*—The same thing

happens concerning the operations of the mind; viz., thinking, reasoning, fearing, &c., which we concluding not to subsist of themselves nor apprehending how they can belong to body, or be produced by it, we are apt to think these the actions of some other substance, which we call "spirit"; whereby yet it is evident that, having no other idea or notion of matter, but something wherein those many sensible qualities which affect our senses do subsist; by supposing a substance wherein thinking, knowing, doubting, and a power of moving, &c., do subsist, we have as clear a notion of the substance of spirit as we have of body: the one being supposed to be (without knowing what it is) the substratum to those simple ideas we have from without; and the other supposed (with a like ignorance of what it is) to be the substratum to those operations we experience in ourselves within. It is plain, then, that the idea of corporeal substance in matter is as remote from our conceptions and apprehensions as that of spiritual substance, or spirit; and therefore, from our not having any notion of the substance of spirit, we can no more conclude its non-existence than we can, for the same reason, deny the existence of body: it being as rational to affirm there is no body, because we have no clear and distinct idea of the substance of matter, as to say there is no spirit, because we have no clear and distinct idea of the substance of a spirit.

6. *Of the Sorts of Substances.*—Whatever therefore be the secret abstract nature of substance in general, all the ideas we have of particular, distinct sorts of substances, are nothing but several combinations of simple ideas coexisting in such, though unknown, cause of their union, as make the whole subsist of itself. It is by such combinations of simple ideas, and nothing else, that we represent particular sorts of substances to ourselves; such are the ideas we have of their several species in our minds; and such only do we, by their specific names, signify to others, v.g., man, horse, sun, water, iron: upon hearing which words everyone who understands the language frames in his mind a combination of those several simple ideas which he has usually observed or fancied to exist together under that

denomination; all which he supposes to rest in, and be, as it were, adherent to, that unknown common subject, which inheres not in anything else. Though in the meantime it be manifest, and everyone upon inquiry into his own thoughts will find that he has no other idea of any substance, v.g., let it be gold, horse, iron, man, vitriol, bread, but what he has barely of those sensible qualities which he supposes to inhere, with a supposition of such a substratum as gives, as it were, a support to those qualities, or simple ideas, which he has observed to exist united together. Thus, the idea of the sun—what is it but an aggregate of those several simple ideas, bright, hot, roundish, having a constant regular motion, at a certain distance from us, and perhaps some other? as he who thinks and discourses of the sun has been more or less accurate in observing those sensible qualities, ideas, or properties which are in that thing which he calls the "sun."

7. *Power, a great Part of our complex Ideas of Substances.*—For he has the perfectest idea of any of the particular sorts of substances who has gathered and put together most of those simple ideas which do exist in it, among which are to be reckoned its active powers and passive capacities; which, though not simple ideas, yet in this respect, for brevity's sake, may conveniently enough be reckoned amongst them. Thus, the power of drawing iron is one of the ideas of the complex one of that substance we call a "lodestone," and a power to be so drawn is a part of the complex one we call "iron": which powers pass for inherent qualities in those subjects. Because every substance being as apt, by the powers we observe in it, to change some sensible qualities in other subjects as it is to produce in us those simple ideas which we receive immediately from it, does, by those new sensible qualities introduced into other subjects, discover to us those powers which do thereby mediately affect our senses as regularly as its sensible qualities do it immediately, v.g., we immediately by our senses perceive in fire its heat and colour; which are, if rightly considered, nothing but powers in it to produce those ideas in us: we also by our senses perceive the colour and brittleness of charcoal, whereby

we come by the knowledge of another power in fire, which it has to change the colour and consistency of wood. By the former, fire immediately, by the latter it mediately, discovers to us these several qualities, which therefore we look upon to be a part of the qualities of fire, and so make them a part of the complex idea of it. . . . For the powers that are severally in them are necessary to be considered, if we will have true distinct notions of the several sorts of substances.

8. *And why*.—Nor are we to wonder that powers make a great part of our complex ideas of substances, since their secondary qualities are those which, in most of them, serve principally to distinguish substances one from another, and commonly make a considerable part of the complex idea of the several sorts of them. For, our senses failing us in the discovery of the bulk, texture, and figure of the minute parts of bodies, on which their real constitutions and differences depend, we are fain to make use of their secondary qualities, as the characteristical notes and marks whereby to frame ideas of them in our minds, and distinguish them one from another: all which secondary qualities, as has been shown, are nothing but bare powers. For the colour and taste of opium are, as well as its soporific or anodyne virtues, mere powers depending on its primary qualities, whereby it is fitted to produce different operations on different parts of our bodies.

9. *Three Sorts of Ideas make our complex ones of Substances*.—The ideas that make our complex ones of corporeal substances are of these three sorts. First, the ideas of the primary qualities of things which are discovered by our senses, and are in them even when we perceive them not; such are the bulk, figure, number, situation, and motion of the parts of bodies, which are really in them, whether we take notice of them or no. Secondly, the sensible secondary qualities which, depending on these, are nothing but the powers those substances have to produce several ideas in us by our senses; which ideas are not in the things themselves otherwise than as anything is in its cause. Thirdly, the aptness we consider in any substance to give or receive such alterations of primary qualities as that the substance

so altered should produce in us different ideas from what it did before; these are called "active and passive powers": all which powers, as far as we have any notice or notion of them, terminate only in sensible simple ideas. For, whatever alteration a loadstone has the power to make in the minute particles of iron, we should have no notion of any power it had at all to operate on iron, did not its sensible motion discover it: and I doubt not but there are a thousand changes that bodies we daily handle have a power to cause in one another, which we never suspect, because they never appear in sensible effects.

10. *Powers make a great Part of our complex Ideas of Substances.*—Powers therefore justly make a great part of our complex ideas of substances. He that will examine his complex idea of gold will find several of its ideas that make it up to be only powers: as the power of being melted, but of not spending itself in the fire, of being dissolved in aqua regia; are ideas as necessary to make up our complex idea of gold, as its colour and weight; which, if duly considered, are also nothing but different powers. For, to speak truly, yellowness is not actually in gold; but it is a power in gold to produce that idea in us by our eyes, when placed in a due light: and the heat which we cannot leave out of our idea of the sun is no more really in the sun than the white colour it introduces into wax. These are both equally powers in the sun, operating, by the motion and figure of its insensible parts, so on a man as to make him have the idea of heat; and so on wax as to make it capable to produce in a man the idea of white.

11. *The now secondary Qualities of Bodies would disappear, if we could discover the primary ones of their minute Parts.*—Had we senses acute enough to discern the minute particles of bodies, and the real constitution on which their sensible qualities depend, I doubt not but they would produce quite different ideas in us: and that which is now the yellow colour of gold would then disappear and instead of it we should see an admirable texture of parts of a certain size and figure. This microscopes plainly discover to us; for, what to our naked eyes produces a certain colour is, by thus augmenting the acuteness of our senses, discovered to

be quite a different thing; and the thus altering, as it were, the proportion of the bulk of the minute parts of a coloured object to our usual sight, produces different ideas from what it did before. Thus sand or pounded glass, which is opaque and white to the naked eye, is pellucid in a microscope; and a hair seen this way loses its former colour, and is in a great measure pellucid, with a mixture of some bright sparkling colours, such as appear from the refraction of diamonds and other pellucid bodies. Blood to the naked eye appears all red, but by a good microscope, wherein its lesser parts appear, shows only some few globules of red, swimming in a pellucid liquor; and how these red globules would appear, if glasses could be found that yet could magnify them a thousand or ten thousand times more, is uncertain.

14. *Complex Ideas of Substances.*— . . . The ideas we have of substances, and the ways we come by them; I say, our specific ideas of substances are nothing else but a collection of a certain number of simple ideas, considered as united in one thing. These ideas of substances, though they are commonly simple apprehensions, and the names of them simple terms, yet, in effect, are complex and compounded. Thus the idea which an Englishman signifies by the name "swan," is white colour, long neck, red beak, black legs, and whole feet, and all these of a certain size, with a power of swimming in the water, and making a certain kind of noise; and perhaps to a man who has long observed this kind of birds, some other properties, which all terminate in sensible simple ideas, all united in one common subject.

37. *Recapitulation.*—And thus we have seen what kind of ideas we have of substances of all kinds, wherein they consist, and how we came by them. From whence, I think, it is very evident:

First, That all our ideas of the several sorts of substances are nothing but collections of simple ideas, with a supposition of something to which they belong, and in which they subsist; though of this supposed something we have no clear distinct idea at all.

Secondly, That all the simple ideas that, thus united in

one common substratum, make up our complex ideas of several sorts or substances, are no other but such as we have received from sensation or reflection. So that even in those which we think we are most intimately acquainted with, and that come nearest the comprehension of our most enlarged conceptions, we cannot go beyond those simple ideas. And even in those which seem most remote from all we have to do with, and do infinitely surpass anything we can perceive in ourselves by reflection, or discover by sensation in other things, we can attain to nothing but those simple ideas which we originally received from sensation or reflection, as is evident in the complex ideas we have of angels, and particularly of God himself.

Thirdly, That most of the simple ideas that make up our complex ideas of substances, when truly considered, are only powers, however we are apt to take them for positive qualities; v.g., the greatest part of the ideas that make our complex idea of gold are yellowness, great weight, ductility, fusibility, and solubility in aqua regia, &c., all united together in an unknown substratum: all which ideas are nothing else but so many relations to other substances, and are not really in the gold considered barely in itself, though they depend on those real and primary qualities of its internal constitution, whereby it has a fitness differently to operate and be operated on by several other substances.]

IN ADDITION TO THE TWO MAIN SENSES DISTINGUISHED above, the word "substance" is sometimes also used by Locke, somewhat as chemists use it, to denote a natural kind, or sort, i.e., a whole class of substances in the second sense given above. In this sense, for example, our idea of gold (and not of a lump of gold) would itself be an idea of a substance. Substances in this third sense seem to be whole classes of entities, and ideas of substances are abstract and general, since they apply to types and not to individuals.

The doctrine of primary and secondary qualities reappears once again: "Powers make a great part of our complex ideas of substances," namely both those powers which cause in us ideas of secondary qualities and also the powers to interact in characteristic ways with other substances. And the theory (which will bulk so large in Book IV) that the "powers" which cause ideas of "secondary qualities" themselves depend upon the primary qualities of the minute particles of the body, is now stated more boldly.

Locke's notion of the substratum of a mind is no clearer than that of the substratum of a physical object. It is upon the substrata of material objects that Berkeley's attacks are directed; he never questions the assumption that each mind is a simple substance (in which ideas inhere), whatever additional properties it may possess—e.g., that of creation and action, and awareness of relations of other minds (and of God) by means other than ideas.

This completes Locke's investigation of the furniture of our minds. His next task is to make good his promise to clear the ground a little by examining the use of language and the ways in which it has misled philosophers and retarded the advance of knowledge. In Book III of the *Essay* he begins to do so, although with little of the genius and devastating insight of Berkeley. The most valuable portion of his long and meandering discussion (though there is much else) is that dealing with abstract ideas and his distinction between "real essences" and "nominal essences." The passages which follow give the heart of his doctrine. They can be understood only if one bears in mind that it was commonly held by the "schoolmen" of Locke's time—and by the rationalists who had not broken completely with them—that all substances belonged to one or other of a fixed number of natural kinds (or species) whose boundaries were precisely delimited by God or Nature; and further that to belong to a given natural kind was to "possess" the so-called "real essence" of that species. If we could attain to a knowledge of the real essence, then from this knowledge we could deduce with absolute certainty all the properties of every member of that species. Locke argued against this (a) that the occurrence of "monsters and changelings" is incompatible with the doctrine of a fixed number of "natural" and unalterable species or molds, and (b) that since the "real essences" of these supposed species are admitted to be impenetrable to human minds, the doctrine is of no value from the point of view of the advancement of human knowledge.

Locke does, however, find a use for the expression "real essence," giving it a scientific rather than a metaphysical interpretation. He uses it to stand for the "real and internal constitution" of a thing, i.e. (cf. above p. 63), the structure of the primary qualities of its minute particles, on which all its other properties depend. The existence of such real essences bulks large in Locke's treatment of scientific knowledge in Book IV. Locke admits that we do not at present know even these real essences, and volunteers nothing about our prospects of ever discovering their character. How then, do our general terms, which denote classes of things, function? For they are certainly indispensable to all human communication; without them we could not describe at all, or classify, or speak of the same object in different places at different times, or of differences and similarities between any two entities. Since they evidently do not denote unknowable real essences, they must be defined in terms of groups of qualities which have been consistently found together, whether this coexistence has its basis in a common atomic structure or not. The complex ideas of these groups of qualities he calls the "nominal essences" of species, and they are "abstract general ideas."

In the course of his discussion Locke makes a characteristically valuable point about words and definitions. G. E. Moore[5] maintained that words standing for certain ideas are not definable on the grounds that these ideas are simple and unanalyzable, and have no parts, for, he held, all definition consists in an analysis of a whole into its parts. This is not the point that Locke is making. Locke is emphasizing, correctly, that there are certain words whose meaning cannot be adequately taught by means of verbal definitions, for they depend for their use on that

[5] In *Principia Ethica* (London, 1903).

direct inspection without a minimum of which no symbolism or language can describe the world at all. The use of such words can only be learnt "ostensively"—in the presence of the objects which they describe, with which their connection is conveyed by pointing, or some other effective method. An example of this is the impossibility of adequately teaching the meanings of color words to a blind man. It is obvious that verbal definitions—the substitution of one set of words for another—will not convey the meaning of "red" to those who cannot see.

The following is from Book III, "Of Words."

[CHAPTER III. *Of General Terms*

1. *The greatest Part of Words general.*—All things that exist being particulars, it may perhaps be thought reasonable that words, which ought to be conformed to things, should be so too, I mean in their signification: but yet we find quite the contrary. The far greatest part of words that make all languages are general terms; which has not been the effect of neglect or chance, but of reason and necessity.

2. *For every particular Thing to have a Name is impossible.*—First, It is impossible that every particular thing should have a distinct peculiar name. For the signification and use of words depending on that connexion which the mind makes between its ideas and the sounds it uses as signs of them, it is necessary, in the application of names to things, that the mind should have distinct ideas of the things, and retain also the particular name that belongs to every one, with its peculiar appropriation to that idea. But it is beyond the power of human capacity to frame and retain distinct ideas of all the particular things we meet with: every bird and beast men saw, every tree and plant that affected the senses, could not find a place in the most capacious understanding. . . .

3. *And useless.*—Secondly, If it were possible, it would yet be useless, because it would not serve to the chief end of language. Men would in vain heap up names of particular things that would not serve them to communicate

their thoughts. Men learn names, and use them in talk with others, only that they may be understood: which is then only done when, by use or consent, the sound I make by the organs of speech excites, in another man's mind who hears it, the idea I apply it to in mine when I speak it. This cannot be done by names applied to particular things, whereof I alone having the ideas in my mind, the names of them could not be significant or intelligible to another who was not acquainted with all those very particular things which had fallen under my notice.

4. Thirdly, But yet, granting this also feasible (which I think is not), yet a distinct name for every particular thing would not be of any great use for the improvement of knowledge: which, though founded in particular things, enlarges itself by general views, to which things reduced into sorts under general names are properly subservient. . . .

6. *How general Words are made.*—The next thing to be considered is, how general words come to be made. For, since all things that exist are only particulars, how come we by general terms, or where find we those general natures they are supposed to stand for? Words become general by being made the signs of general ideas; and ideas become general by separating from them the circumstances of time, and place, and any other ideas that may determine them to this or that particular existence. By this way of abstraction they are made capable of representing more individuals than one; each of which, having in it a conformity to that abstract idea, is (as we call it) of that sort.

7. But to deduce this a little more distinctly, it will not perhaps be amiss to trace our notions and names from their beginning, and observe by what degrees we proceed, and by what steps we enlarge our ideas from our first infancy. There is nothing more evident than that the ideas of the persons children converse with (to instance in them alone) are, like the persons themselves, only particular. The ideas of the nurse and the mother are well framed in their minds; and, like pictures of them there, represent only those individuals. The names they first gave to them are confined to these individuals; and the names of "nurse"

and "mamma" the child uses, determine themselves to those persons. Afterwards, when time and a larger acquaintance have made them observe that there are a great many other things in the world that, in some common agreements of shape and several other qualities, resemble their father and mother, and those persons they have been used to, they frame an idea which they find those many particulars do partake in; and to that they give, with others, the name "man," for example. And thus they come to have a general name, and a general idea; wherein they make nothing new, but only leave out of the complex idea they had of Peter and James, Mary and Jane, that which is peculiar to each, and retain only what is common to them all.

9. *General Natures are nothing but abstract Ideas.*— That this is the way whereby men first formed general ideas and general names to them, I think is . . . evident . . . and he that thinks general natures or notions are anything else but such abstract and partial ideas of more complex ones, taken at first from particular existences, will, I fear, be at a loss where to find them. For, let anyone reflect, and then tell me wherein does his idea of "man" differ from that of "Peter" and "Paul," or his idea of "horse" from that of "Bucephalus," but in the leaving out something that is peculiar to each individual, and retaining so much of those particular complex ideas of several particular existences as they are found to agree in? Of the complex ideas signified by the names "man" and "horse," leaving out but those particulars wherein they differ, and retaining only those wherein they agree, and of those making a new distinct complex idea, and giving the name "animal" to it, one has a more general term that comprehends, with man, several other creatures. Leave out of the idea of "animal" sense and spontaneous motion, and the remaining complex idea, made up of the remaining simple ones of "body," "life," and "nourishment," becomes a more general one under the more comprehensive term, *vivens.* . . . To conclude: this whole mystery of genera and species, which makes such a noise in the schools . . . is nothing

else but abstract ideas, more or less comprehensive, with names annexed to them. . . .

11. *General and Universal are Creatures of the Understanding.*—. . . It is plain, by what has been said, that general and universal belong not to the real existence of things; but are the inventions and creatures of the understanding, made by it for its own use, and concern only signs, whether words or ideas. Words are general, as has been said, when used for signs of general ideas, and so are applicable indifferently to many particular things; and ideas are general when they are set up as the representatives of many particular things; but universality belongs not to things themselves, which are all of them particular in their existence, even those words and ideas which in their signification are general. When, therefore, we quit particulars, the generals that rest are only creatures of our own making, their general nature being nothing but the capacity they are put into by the understanding of signifying or representing many particulars; for the signification they have is nothing but a relation that by the mind of man is added to them.

12. *Abstract Ideas are the Essences of the Genera and Species.*—The next thing therefore to be considered is, what kind of signification it is that general words have. For as it is evident that they do not signify barely one particular thing—for then they would not be general terms, but proper names—so on the other side it is as evident they do not signify a plurality; for "man" and "men" would then signify the same, and the distinction of "numbers" (as grammarians call them) would be superfluous and useless. That, then, which general words signify, is a sort of things; and each of them does that by being a sign of an abstract idea in the mind; to which idea as things existing are found to agree, so they come to be ranked under that name; or, which is all one, be of that sort. Whereby it is evident, that the essences of the sorts, or if the Latin word pleases better, *species,* of things, are nothing else but these abstract ideas. For the having the essence of any species, being that which makes any thing to be of that species, and the conformity to the idea to which

the name is annexed being that which gives a right to that name, the having the essence, and the having that conformity, must needs be the same thing; since to be of any species, and to have a right to the name of that species, is all one. As, for example, to be a man or of the species man, and to have right to the name "man" is the same thing. Again, to be a man, or of the species man, and have the essence of a man, is the same thing. Now since nothing can be a man, or have a right to the name "man," but what has a conformity to the abstract idea the name "man" stands for; nor any thing be a man, or have a right to the species man, but what has the essence of that species; it follows that the abstract idea for which the name stands and the essence of the species is one and the same. From whence it is easy to observe that the essences of the sorts of things, and consequently the sorting of this, is the workmanship of the understanding that abstracts and makes these general ideas.

13. *They are the Workmanship of the Understanding, but have their Foundation in the Similitude of Things.*— I would not here be thought to forget, much less to deny, that Nature, in the production of things, makes several of them alike: there is nothing more obvious, especially in the races of animals, and all things propagated by seed. But yet, I think, we may say the sorting of them under names is the workmanship of the understanding, taking occasion, from the similitude it observes amongst them, to make abstract general ideas, and set them up in the mind with names annexed to them, as patterns or forms (for in that sense the word "form" has a very proper signification), to which as particular things existing are found to agree, so they come to be of that species, have that denomination, or are put into that *classis*. . . . And when general names have any connexion with particular beings, these abstract ideas are the medium that unites them; so that the essences of species, as distinguished and denominated by us, neither are nor can be anything but those precise abstract ideas we have in our minds. And therefore the supposed real essences of substances, if different from our abstract ideas, cannot be the essences of the species

we rank things into. For two species may be one as rationally as two different essences be the essence of one species; and I demand, what are the alterations may or may not be in a horse or lead, without making either of them to be of another species? In determining the species of things by our abstract ideas, this is easy to resolve: but if any one will regulate himself herein by supposed real essences, he will, I suppose, be at a loss; and he will never be able to know when anything précisely ceases to be of the species of a horse or lead.

14. *Each distinct abstract Idea is a distinct Essence.*— Nor will any one wonder that I say these essences, or abstract ideas (which are the measures of name, and the boundaries of species), are the workmanship of the understanding, who considers that at least the complex ones are often, in several men, different collections of simple ideas; and therefore that is covetousness to one man, which is not so to another. Nay, even in substances, where their abstract ideas seem to be taken from the things themselves, they are not constantly the same; no, not in that species which is most familiar to us, and with which we have the most intimate acquaintance: it having been more than once doubted whether the foetus born of a woman were a man, even so far as that it hath been debated whether it were or were not to be nourished and baptized; which could not be if the abstract idea or essence to which the name "man" belonged were of nature's making, and were not the uncertain and various collection of simple ideas, which the understanding put together, and then, abstracting it, affixed a name to it. So that in truth every distinct abstract idea is a distinct essence; and the names that stand for such distinct ideas, are the names of things essentially different. Thus, a circle is as essentially different from an oval as a sheep from a goat, and rain is as essentially different from snow as water from earth: that abstract idea which is the essence of one, being impossible to be communicated to the other. And thus any two abstract ideas that in any part vary one from another, with two distinct names annexed to them, constitute two distinct sorts, or,

if you please, species, as essentially different as any two of the most remote or opposite in the world.

15. *Real and nominal Essence.*—But since the essences of things are thought, by some (and not without reason), to be wholly unknown, it may not be amiss to consider the several significations of the word "essence."

First, Essence may be taken for the being of any thing, whereby it is what it is. And thus the real internal, but generally (in substances) unknown, constitution of things, whereon their discoverable qualities depend, may be called their "essence." This is the proper original signification of the word, as is evident from the formation of it; *essentia,* in its primary notation, signifying properly "being." . . .

Secondly, The learning and disputes of the schools having been much busied about genus and species, the word "essence" has almost lost its primary signification: and, instead of the real constitution of things, has been almost wholly applied to the artificial constitution of genus and species. It is true there is ordinarily supposed a real constitution of the sorts of things, and it is past doubt there must be some real constitution, on which any collection of simple ideas coexisting must depend. But it being evident that things are ranked under names into sorts or species only as they agree to certain abstract ideas to which we have annexed those names, the essence of each genus or sort comes to be nothing but that abstract idea which the general or "sortal" (if I may have leave so to call it from "sort," as I do "general" from "genus") name stands for. And this we shall find to be that which the word "essence" imports in its most familiar use. These two sorts of essences, I suppose, may not unfitly be termed, the one the "real," the other "nominal," essence.

17. *Supposition that Species are distinguished by their real Essences, useless.*—Concerning the real essences of corporeal substances—to mention these only—there are, if I mistake not, two opinions. The one is of those who, using the word essence for they know not what, suppose a certain number of those essences according to which all natural things are made, and wherein they do exactly

every one of them partake, and so become of this or that species. The other and more rational opinion is of those who look on all natural things to have a real but unknown constitution of their insensible parts; from which flow those sensible qualities which serve us to distinguish them one from another, according as we have occasion to rank them into sorts under common denominations. The former of these opinions, which supposes these essences as a certain number of forms or moulds wherein all natural things that exist are cast and do equally partake, has, I imagine, very much perplexed the knowledge of natural things. The frequent productions of monsters, in all the species of animals, and of changelings, and other strange issues of human birth, carry with them difficulties not possible to consist with this hypothesis: since it is as impossible that two things partaking exactly of the same real essence should have different properties, as that two figures partaking in the same real essence of a circle should have different properties. But were there no other reason against it, yet the supposition of essences that cannot be known, and the making of them nevertheless to be that which distinguishes the species of things, is so wholly useless and unserviceable to any part of our knowledge, that alone were sufficient to make us lay it by, and content ourselves with such essences of the sorts or species of things as come within the reach of our knowledge; which, when seriously considered, will be found, as I have said, to be nothing else but those abstract complex ideas to which we have annexed distinct general names.

18. *Real and nominal Essence the same in simple Ideas and Modes, different in Substances.*—Essences being thus distinguished into nominal and real, we may further observe, that in the species of simple ideas and modes, they are always the same, but in substances, always quite different. Thus a figure including a space between three lines is the real as well as nominal essence of a triangle; it being not only the abstract idea to which the general name is annexed, but the very *essentia,* or being, of the thing itself—that foundation from which all its properties flow, and to which they are all inseparably annexed. But it is

far otherwise concerning that parcel of matter which makes the ring on my finger, wherein these two essences are apparently different. For it is the real constitution of its insensible parts, on which depend all those properties of colour, weight, fusibility, fixedness, &c., which are to be found in it; which constitution we know not, and, so, having no particular idea of, have no name that is the sign of it. But yet, it is its colour, weight, fusibility, fixedness, &c., which makes it to be gold, or gives it a right to that name, which is therefore its nominal essence: since nothing can be called gold but what has a conformity of qualities to that abstract complex idea to which that name is annexed. But this distinction of essences, belonging particularly to substances, we shall, when we come to consider their names, have an occasion to treat of more fully.

CHAPTER IV. *Of the Names of Simple Ideas*

11. *Simple Ideas, why undefinable, further explained.* —Simple ideas, as has been shown, are only to be got by those impressions objects themselves make on our minds, by the proper inlets appointed to each sort. If they are not received this way, all the words in the world made use of to explain or define any of their names will never be able to produce in us the idea it stands for. For words, being sounds, can produce in us no other simple ideas than of those very sounds; nor excite any in us but by that voluntary connexion which is known to be between them and those simple ideas which common use has made them the signs of. He that thinks otherwise, let him try if any words can give him the taste of a pineapple, and make him have the true idea of the relish of that celebrated delicious fruit. So far as he is told it has a resemblance with any tastes whereof he has the ideas already in his memory, imprinted there by sensible objects not strangers to his palate, so far may he approach that resemblance in his mind. But this is not giving us that idea by a definition, but exciting in us other simple ideas by their known names; which will be still very different from the true taste of that fruit itself. In light and colours, and all other simple ideas, it is the same

thing: for the signification of sounds is not natural, but only imposed and arbitrary. . . .

12. *The contrary shown in complex Ideas, by Instances of a Statue and Rainbow.*—The case is quite otherwise in complex ideas; which consisting of several simple ones, it is in the power of words, standing for the several ideas that make that composition, to imprint complex ideas in the mind which were never there before, and so make their names be understood. In such collections of ideas passing under one name, definition, or the teaching the signification of one word by several others, has place, and may make us understand the names of things which never came within the reach of our senses; and frame ideas suitable to those in other men's minds, when they use those names: provided that none of the terms of the definition stand for any such simple ideas which he to whom the explication is made has never yet had in his thought. Thus the word "statue" may be explained to a blind man by other words, when "picture" cannot, his senses having given him the idea of figure, but not of colours, which therefore words cannot excite in him. . . .

14. *The names of complex Ideas, when to be made intelligible by Words.*—Simple ideas, as has been shown, can only be got by experience from those objects which are proper to produce in us those perceptions. When by this means we have our minds stored with them, and know the names for them, then we are in a condition to define, and by definition to understand, the names of complex ideas that are made up of them. . . .

CHAPTER VI. *Of the Names of Substances*

6. It is true, I have often mentioned a real essence, distinct in substances from those abstract ideas of them, which I call their "nominal essence." By this "real essence," I mean the real constitution of any thing which is the foundation of all those properties that are combined in, and are constantly found to coexist with, the nominal essence; that particular constitution which every thing has within itself, without any relation to any thing without it. But essence,

even in this sense, relates to a sort, and supposes a species: for, being that real constitution on which the properties depend, it necessarily supposes a sort of things, properties belonging only to species, and not to individuals; v.g., supposing the nominal essence of gold to be body of such a peculiar colour and weight, with malleability and fusibility, the real essence is that constitution of the parts of matter on which these qualities and their union depend; and is also the foundation of its solubility in aqua regia, and other properties accompanying that complex idea. Here are essences and properties, but all upon supposition of a sort, or general abstract idea, which is considered as immutable; but there is no individual parcel of matter to which any of these qualities are so annexed as to be essential to it or inseparable from it. That which is essential belongs to it as a condition whereby it is of this or that sort; but take away the consideration of its being ranked under the name of some abstract idea, and then there is nothing necessary to it, nothing inseparable from it. Indeed, as to the real essences of substances, we only suppose their being, without precisely knowing what they are; but that which annexes them still to the species is the nominal essence, of which they are the supposed foundation and cause.

7. *The nominal Essence bounds the Species.*—The next thing to be considered is, by which of those essences it is that substances are determined into sorts or species; and that, it is evident, is by the nominal essence; for it is that alone that the name, which is the mark of the sort, signifies. It is impossible therefore, that any thing should determine the sorts of things which we rank under general names, but that idea which that name is designed as a mark for; which is that, as has been shown, which we call "nominal essence." Why do we say, "This is a horse, and that a mule; this is an animal, that an herb"? How comes any particular thing to be of this or that sort, but because it has that nominal essence, or, which is all one, agrees to that abstract idea that name is annexed to? . . .

9. *Not the real Essence, which we know not.*—Nor, indeed, can we rank and sort things, and consequently

(which is the end of sorting) denominate them, by their real essences, because we know them not. Our faculties carry us no further towards the knowledge and distinction of substances than a collection of those sensible ideas which we observe in them; which, however made with the greatest diligence and exactness we are capable of, yet is more remote from the true internal constitution from which those qualities flow than; as I said, a countryman's idea is from the inward contrivance of that famous clock at Strasburg, whereof he only sees the outward figure and motions. . . .

14. *Difficulties against a certain Number of real Essences.*—To distinguish substantial beings into species, according to the usual supposition, that there are certain precise essences or forms of things whereby all the individuals existing are by nature distinguished into species, these things are necessary:

15. First, To be assured that nature, in the production of things, always designs them to partake of certain regulated, established essences, which are to be the models of all things to be produced. This, in that crude sense it is usually proposed, would need some better explication before it can fully be assented to.

16. Secondly, It would be necessary to know whether nature always attains that essence it designs in the production of things. The irregular and monstrous births that in divers sorts of animals have been observed, will always give us reason to doubt of one or both of these.

17. Thirdly, It ought to be determined whether those we call monsters be really a distinct species, according to the scholastic notion of the word species; since it is certain that everything that exists has its particular constitution: and yet we find that some of these monstrous productions have few or none of those qualities which are supposed to result from and accompany the essence of that species from whence they derive their originals, and to which by their descent they seem to belong.

20. By all which it is clear that our distinguishing substances into species by names, is not at all founded on their real essences; nor can we pretend to range and deter-

mine them exactly into species according to internal essential differences.

21. *But such a Collection as our Name stands for.*— But since, as has been remarked, we have need of general words, though we know not the real essences of things; all we can do is to collect such a number of simple ideas as by examination we find to be united together in things existing, and thereof to make one complex idea. Which, though it be not the real essence of any substance that exists, is yet the specific essence to which our name belongs, and is convertible with it; by which we may at least try the truth of these nominal essences. . . .

28. *But not so arbitrary as mixed Modes.*—But though these nominal essences of substances are made by the mind, they are not yet made so arbitrarily as those of mixed modes. To the making of any nominal essence, it is necessary, First, that the ideas whereof it consists have such a union as to make but one idea, how compounded soever. Secondly, That the particular idea so united be exactly the same, neither more nor less. For if two abstract complex ideas differ either in number or sorts of their component parts, they make two different, and not one and the same, essence. In the first of these, the mind, in making its complex ideas of substances, only follows nature, and puts none together, which are not supposed to have a union in nature. Nobody joins the voice of a sheep with the shape of a horse, nor the colour of lead with the weight and fixedness of gold, to be the complex ideas of any real substances; unless he has a mind to fill his head with chimeras, and his discourse with unintelligible words. Men, observing certain qualities always joined and existing together, therein copied nature; and of ideas so united made their complex ones of substances. For though men may make what complex ideas they please, and give what names to them they will; yet, if they will be understood when they speak of things really existing, they must, in some degree, conform their ideas to the things they would speak of: or else men's language will be like that of Babel; and every man's words, being intelligible only to himself,

would no longer serve to conversation and the ordinary affairs of life, if the ideas they stand for be not some way answering the common appearances and agreement of substances as they really exist.

35. *Men determine the Sorts.*—From what has been said, it is evident that men make sorts of things, for it being different essences alone that make different species, it is plain that they who make those abstract ideas which are the nominal essences, do thereby make the species, or sort.

36. *Nature makes the Similitude.*—This, then, in short, is the case: Nature makes many particular things which do agree.one with another in many sensible qualities, and probably, too, in their internal frame and constitution; but it is not this real essence that distinguishes them into species: it is men, who taking occasion from the qualities they find united in them, and wherein they observe often several individuals to agree, range them into sorts in order to their naming, for the convenience of comprehensive signs; under which, individuals, according to their conformity to this or that abstract idea, come to be ranked as under ensigns; so that this is of the blue, that the red, regiment; this is a man, that a drill; and in this, I think, consists the whole business of "genus" and "species."

*Thus particular ideas are first received and distinguished, and so knowledge got about them; and next to them the less general or specific, which are next to particular: for abstract ideas are not so obvious or easy to children or the yet unexercised mind as particular ones. If they seem so to grown men, it is only because by constant and familiar use they are made so; for when we nicely reflect upon them, we shall find that general ideas are fictions and contrivances of the mind, that carry difficulty with them, and do not so easily offer themselves as we are apt to imagine. For example, does it not require some pains and skill to form the general idea of a triangle? (which is yet none of the most abstract, comprehensive, and difficult), for it must be neither oblique, nor rectangle, neither equilateral, equicrural, nor scalenon; but all and

* The following paragraph is from Book IV, Chapter VIII, No. 9.

none of these at once. In effect, it is something imperfect, that cannot exist; an idea wherein some parts of several different and inconsistent ideas are put together.]

LOCKE'S THEORY OF ABSTRACT GENERAL IDEAS FORMS A chapter in the long history of the philosophical problem of universals. The problem arises in this sort of way. We describe many different things as, say, blue or as men. Why? Because they all possess the common characteristic of blueness or humanity. But then what are blueness and humanity? What is the thing to which such a general word as "blueness" or "humanity" stands in the kind of direct labellike relation in which a proper name—"John" or "Fido"—stands to a particular man or dog? All words, one might suppose, stand for something; what do general words stand for? The blanket answer "universals" is given. And so the catalogue of the entities in the universe comes to include not only all the particular objects there are, but also innumerable entities brought in to correspond to general words, to the names of species or kinds—and these are then called "universals" and are offered as objects of investigation to the natural philosopher as much as the "particulars" into which they "enter" or which they "qualify" or by which they are "instantiated." The answers given to the problem are various, and to some extent the variation is related to the precise question asked. Locke, for example, eschewing metaphysics but deeply involved in his own theory of knowledge, is asking not so much the ontological question "What is blueness? What is humanity?" but rather the epistemological one, "How do we recognize an object as blue? or as a man?"

Some of the traditional answers to this most famous of problems may be summarized as follows:

(1) *Platonic Realism.* "Universals" do not exist in the temporal world. They subsist "outside" it. They can be apprehended by the intellect but not by sense experience. Particular objects in the world of sense experience have universal characteristics by virtue of "partaking in," or "imitating" these timeless patterns, set apart.

(2) *Aristotelian Realism*. Universals in a sense do exist, but only "in" the particular objects that exemplify them. They have no independent reality.

These two answers are obviously related to the ontological question of what there is in the world. The remaining three are more obviously concerned with the epistemological question (of how we know what we do know), and have in common their denial of independent existence to universals outside the minds of men.

(3) *Conceptualism*. Men are able to recognize an entity as blue or as a man by seeing that it "conforms" with, or "fits," a concept or abstract general idea which they have framed in their minds of blueness or humanity.

(4) *Imagism*. Recognition of something as a man or as blue occurs by comparison with a standard or representative image in our minds (or in a book of standard images) of blue or of a man.

(5) *Nominalism*. There is only the general word itself, and the class of particular objects falling under it. These objects are grouped together in the class in virtue of their perceived resemblance to each other, or—the extreme version of this view—in virtue of nothing at all, i.e., arbitrarily.

It seems clear that Locke's views are closest to conceptualism. Observing many particular objects with a certain characteristic or of a certain class, we form an "abstract general idea" of that characteristic or class: this is the idea for which the general word stands. Locke seems, however, to have held several divergent views as to how we form these abstract general ideas:

(a) The abstract general idea is simply the idea of one particular member of the class, the idea being used as "representative of" the whole class.

(b) The abstract general idea is formed by leaving out of the ideas of particular members of the class all those characteristics in which they differ.

(c) The abstract general idea is formed by conflating ideas of all the properties possessed by any member of the class.

Each of these views contradicts the others.

The first is roughly that held by Berkeley, the remaining

two he derides; his treatment of this topic is a vital stage in its history.

Book IV of the Essay ("Of Knowledge and Opinion") is the climax of Locke's enterprise. Here, at last, after the lengthy investigation of "ideas" and words in Books II and III, we are to fulfill his primary aim of determining "the original, certainty and extent of human knowledge." Perhaps no passage in Book IV is more important than the two paragraphs:

"Since the mind in all its thoughts and reasonings, hath no other immediate object but its own *ideas*[6] . . . it is evident that our knowledge is only conversant about them." "Knowledge is the perception of the connection and agreement, or disagreement and repugnancy, of any of our *ideas*."[7]

We shall see how woefully restricted is the "extent" of human knowledge by Locke's "new way of ideas," his representationalism, which ends by creating two worlds— the subjective one, which we are free to investigate and describe but which contains within itself no guarantees of its objective truth; and the external world from which we are divided forever by the screen of our own "ideas." Starting from premises which seem to be those of ordinary common sense, he arrives at a paradoxical dualism, less tenable than that of Descartes, who did at least suppose that he had a priori means of breaking through the delusive data of our senses to a vision of reality. Locke seems to get the worst of both worlds. All the facts we know we derive through the senses: yet they provide truth only if they "correspond" to an outside reality; we think they often do: but we have no evidence for this and cannot justify our optimism, or even explain it.

[CHAPTER I. *Of Knowledge in General*

1. *Our Knowledge conversant about our Ideas.*—Since the mind, in all its thoughts and reasonings, hath no other

---

[6] Editor's italics.
[7] Editor's italics.

immediate object but its own ideas, which it alone does or can contemplate, it is evident that our knowledge is only conversant about them.

2. *Knowledge is the Perception of the Agreement or Disagreement of two Ideas.*—Knowledge then seems to me to be nothing but the perception of the connexion and agreement, or disagreement and repugnancy, of any of our ideas. In this alone it consists. Where this perception is, there is knowledge; and where it is not, there, though we may fancy, guess or believe, yet we always come short of knowledge. For, when we know that white is not black, what do we else but perceive that these two ideas do not agree? When we possess ourselves with the utmost security of the demonstration that the three angles of a triangle are equal to two right ones, what do we more but perceive that equality to two right ones does necessarily agree to, and is inseparable from, the three angles of a triangle?

3. *This Agreement fourfold.*—But, to understand a little more distinctly wherein this agreement or disagreement consists, I think we may reduce it all to these four sorts: (1) Identity, or diversity. (2) Relation. (3) Coexistence, or necessary connexion. (4) Real existence.

4. *First, Of Identity or Diversity.*—First, As to the first sort of agreement or disagreement, viz., identity or diversity. It is the first act of the mind, when it has any sentiments or ideas at all, to perceive its ideas; and, so far as it perceives them, to know each what it is, and thereby also to perceive their difference, and that one is not another. This is so absolutely necessary that without it there could be no knowledge, no reasoning, no imagination, no distinct thoughts at all. By this the mind clearly and infallibly perceives each idea to agree with itself, and to be what it is; and all distinct ideas to disagree, i.e., the one not to be the other: and this it does without pains, labour, or deduction, but at first view, by its natural power of perception and distinction . . . and if there ever happen any doubt about it, it will always be found to be about the names, and not the ideas themselves. . . .

5. *Secondly, Relative.*—Secondly, The next sort of agreement or disagreement the mind perceives in any of its

ideas may, I think, be called "relative," and is nothing but the perception of the relation between any two ideas, of what kind soever, whether substances, modes, or any other. For, since all distinct ideas must eternally be known not to be the same, and so be universally and constantly denied one of another, there could be no room for any positive knowledge at all, if we could not perceive any relation between our ideas, and find out the agreement or disagreement they have one with another, in several ways the mind takes of comparing them.

6. *Thirdly, Of Coexistence.*—Thirdly, The third sort of agreement or disagreement to be found in our ideas, which the perception of the mind is employed about, is coexistence, or non-coexistence in the same subject; and this belongs particularly to substances. Thus when we pronounce concerning gold that it is fixed, our knowledge of this truth amounts to no more but this, that fixedness, or a power to remain in the fire unconsumed, is an idea that always accompanies and is joined with that particular sort of yellowness, weight, fusibility, malleableness and solubility in aqua regia, which make our complex idea, signified by the word "gold."

7. *Fourthly, Of real Existence.*—The fourth and last sort is that of actual and real existence agreeing to any idea. Within these four sorts of agreement or disagreement is, I suppose, contained all the knowledge we have or are capable of: for all the inquiries we can make concerning any of our ideas, all that we know or can affirm concerning any of them, is, that it is or is not the same with some other; that it does or does not always coexist with some other idea in the same subject; that it has this or that relation with some other idea; or that it has a real existence without the mind. Thus, "Blue is not yellow," is of identity; "two triangles upon equal bases between two parallels are equal," is of relation; "iron is susceptible of magnetical impressions," is of coexistence; "God is," is of real existence. Though identity and coexistence are truly nothing but relations, yet they are such peculiar ways of agreement or disagreement of our ideas, that they deserve well to be considered as distinct heads, and not under relation in general:

since they are so different grounds of affirmation and nega-
tion, as will easily appear to any one who will but reflect
on what is said in several places of this *Essay*. . . .

CHAPTER II. *Of the Degrees of our Knowledge*

1. *Intuitive.*—All our knowledge consisting, as I have
said, in the view the mind has of its own ideas, which is
the utmost light and greatest certainty we, with our faculties and in our way of knowledge, are capable of, it may
not be amiss to consider a little the degrees of its evidence.
The different clearness of our knowledge seems to me to
lie in the different way of perception the mind has of the
agreement or disagreement of any of its ideas. For if we will
reflect on our own ways of thinking, we shall find that
sometimes the mind perceives the agreement or disagreement of two ideas immediately by themselves, without the
intervention of any other: and this, I think, we may call
"intuitive knowledge." For in this the mind is at no pains
of proving or examining, but perceives the truth, as the
eye doth light, only by being directed towards it. Thus the
mind perceives that white is not black, that a circle is not
a triangle, that three are more than two, and equal to one
and two. Such kinds of truths the mind perceives at the
first sight of the ideas together, by bare intuition, without
the intervention of any other idea; and this kind of knowledge is the clearest and most certain that human frailty is
capable of. This part of knowledge is irresistible, and, like
bright sunshine, forces itself immediately to be perceived
as soon as ever the mind turns its view that way; and
leaves no room for hesitation, doubt, or examination, but
the mind is presently filled with the clear light of it. It is
on this intuition that depends all the certainty and evidence of all our knowledge; which certainty every one
finds to be so great, that he cannot imagine, and therefore
not require, a greater: for a man cannot conceive himself
capable of a greater certainty than to know that any idea in
his mind is such as he perceives it to be; and that two
ideas wherein he perceives a difference are different, and
not precisely the same. He that demands a greater certainty

than this demands he knows not what, and shows only
that he has a mind to be a sceptic without being able to
be so. Certainty depends so wholly on this intuition that
in the next degree of knowledge, which I call demonstrative, this intuition is necessary in all the connexions of the
intermediate ideas without which we cannot attain knowledge and certainty.

2. *Demonstrative.*—The next degree of knowledge is,
where the mind perceives the agreement or disagreement
of any ideas but not immediately. . . . In this case, then,
when the mind cannot so bring its ideas together as, by
their immediate comparison and, as it were, juxtaposition
or application one to another, to perceive their agreement
or disagreement, it is fain, by the intervention of other
ideas (one or more, as it happens), to discover the agreement or disagreement which it searches; and this is that
which we call "reasoning." Thus the mind, being willing
to know the agreement or disagreement in bigness between
the three angles of a triangle and two right ones, cannot,
by an immediate view and comparing them, do it: because
the three angles of a triangle cannot be brought at once,
and be compared with any other one or two angles; and
so of this the mind has no immediate, no intuitive, knowledge. In this case the mind is fain to find out some other
angles, to which the three angles of a triangle have an
equality; and finding those equal to two right ones, comes
to know their equality to two right ones.

3. *Depends on Proofs.*—Those intervening ideas which
serve to show the agreement of any two others, are called
"proofs"; and where the agreement and disagreement is
by this means plainly and clearly perceived, it is called
"demonstration." . . .

7. *Each Step must have intuitive Evidence.*—Now, in
every step reason makes in demonstrative knowledge, there
is an intuitive knowledge of that agreement or disagreement it seeks with the next intermediate idea, which it
uses as a proof: for if it were not so, that yet would need a
proof; since without the perception of such agreement or
disagreement there is no knowledge produced. If it
be perceived by itself, it is intuitive knowledge: if it can-

not be perceived by itself, there is need of some intervening idea, as a common measure, to show their agreement or disagreement. By which it is plain, that every step in reasoning that produces knowledge has intuitive certainty; which when the mind perceives, there is no more required but to remember it, to make the agreement or disagreement of the ideas, concerning which we inquire, visible and certain. So that to make any thing a demonstration, it is necessary to perceive the immediate agreement of the intervening ideas, whereby the agreement or disagreement of the two ideas under examination (whereof the one is always the first, and the other the last in the account) is found. This intuitive perception of the agreement or disagreement of the intermediate ideas, in each step and progression of the demonstration, must also be carried exactly in the mind, and a man must be sure that no part is left out: which, because in long deductions, and the use of many proofs, the memory does not always so readily and exactly retain: therefore it comes to pass, that this is more imperfect than intuitive knowledge, and men embrace often falsehood for demonstrations.

14. *Sensitive Knowledge of particular Existence.*— These two, viz., intuition and demonstration, are the degrees of our knowledge; whatever comes short of one of these, with what assurance soever embraced, is but faith or opinion, but not knowledge, at least in all general truths. There is, indeed, another perception of the mind employed about the particular existence of finite beings without us; which, going beyond bare probability, and yet not reaching perfectly to either of the foregoing degrees of certainty, passes under the name of "knowledge." There can be nothing more certain than that the idea we receive from an external object is in our minds: this is intuitive knowledge. But whether there be any thing more than barely that idea in our minds, whether we can thence certainly infer the existence of any thing without us which corresponds to that idea, is that whereof some men think there may be a question made; because men may have such ideas in their minds when no such thing exists, no such object affects their senses. But yet here, I think, we are provided with

an evidence that puts us past doubting: for I ask any one whether he be not invincibly conscious to himself of a different perception when he looks on the sun by day and thinks on it by night; when he actually tastes wormwood, or smells a rose, or only thinks on that savour or odour? We as plainly find the difference there is between an idea revived in our minds by our own memory, and actually coming into our minds by our senses, as we do between any two distinct ideas. If any one say, "A dream may do the same thing, and all these ideas may be produced in us without any external objects," he may please to dream that I make him this answer: (1) That it is no great matter whether I remove his scruple or no: where all is but dream, reasoning and arguments are of no use, truth and knowledge nothing. (2) That I believe he will allow a very manifest difference between dreaming of being in the fire, and being actually in it. But yet if he be resolved to appear so sceptical as to maintain that what I call "being actually in the fire" is nothing but a dream, and we cannot thereby certainly know that any such thing as fire actually exists without us, I answer that we certainly, finding that pleasure or pain follows upon the application of certain objects to us, whose existence we perceive, or dream that we perceive, by our senses, this certainty is as great as our happiness or misery, beyond which we have no concernment to know or to be. So that, I think, we may add to the two former sorts of knowledge this also, of the existence of particular external objects by that perception and consciousness we have of the actual entrance of ideas from them, and allow these three degrees of knowledge, viz., intuitive, demonstrative, and sensitive: in each of which there are different degrees and ways of evidence and certainty.

CHAPTER III. *Of the Extent of Human Knowledge*

9. *Of Coexistence, a very little Way.*—Secondly, As to the second sort, which is the agreement or disagreement of our ideas in coexistence, in this our knowledge is very short, though in this consists the greatest and most material

part of our knowledge concerning substances. For our ideas of the species of substances being, as I have showed, nothing but certain collections of simple ideas united in one subject, and so coexisting together, v.g., our idea of flame is a body hot, luminous, and moving upward; of gold, a body heavy to a certain degree, yellow, malleable, and fusible; these, or some such complex ideas as these in men's minds, do these two names of the different substances, "flame" and "gold," stand for. When we would know any thing further concerning these, or any other sort of substances, what do we inquire but what other qualities or powers these substances have or have not? which is nothing else but to know what other simple ideas do or do not coexist with those that make up that complex idea.

10. *Because the Connexion between most simple Ideas is unknown.*—This, how weighty and considerable a part soever of human science, is yet very narrow, and scarce any at all. The reason whereof is, that the simple ideas whereof our complex ideas of substances are made up are, for the most part, such as carry with them, in their own nature, no visible necessary connexion or inconsistency with any other simple ideas, whose coexistence with them we would inform ourselves about.

11. *Especially of secondary qualities.*—The ideas that our complex ones of substances are made up of, and about which our knowledge concerning substances is most employed, are those of their secondary qualities; which, depending all (as has been shown) upon the primary qualities of their minute and insensible parts—or, if not upon them, upon something yet more remote from our comprehension—it is impossible we should know which have a necessary union or inconsistency one with another: for, not knowing the root they spring from, not knowing what size, figure, and texture of parts they are on which depend and from which result those qualities which make our complex idea ot gold, it is impossible we should know what other qualities result from, or are incompatible with, the same constitution of the insensible parts of gold, and so, consequently, must always coexist with that complex idea we have of it, or else are inconsistent with it.

12. *Because all connexion between any secondary and primary Qualities is undiscoverable.*—Besides this ignorance of the primary qualities of the insensible parts of bodies, on which depend all their secondary qualities, there is yet another and more incurable part of ignorance, which sets us more remote from a certain knowledge of the coexistence or incoexistence (if I may so say) of different ideas in the same subject; and that is, that there is no discoverable connexion between any secondary quality and those primary qualities which it depends on.

14. . . . For of all the qualities that are coexistent in any subject, without this dependence and evident connexion of their ideas one with another, we cannot know certainly any two to coexist any further than experience by our senses informs us. Thus, though we see the yellow colour, and upon trial find the weight, malleableness, fusibility, and fixedness that are united in a piece of gold; yet, because no one of these ideas has any evident dependence or necessary connexion with the other, we cannot certainly know that where any four of these are, the fifth will be there also, how highly probable soever it may be: because the highest probability amounts not to certainty; without which there can be no true knowledge. For this coexistence can be no further known than it is perceived; and it cannot be perceived but either in particular subjects by the observation of our senses, or in general by the necessary connexion of the ideas themselves.

21. *Fourthly, Of real existence.* . . .—As to the fourth sort of our knowledge, viz., of the real actual existence of things, we have an intuitive knowledge of our own existence, and a demonstrative knowledge of the existence of a God; of the existence of anything else, we have no other but a sensitive knowledge, which extends not beyond the objects present to our senses.

25. *Because of their Minuteness.*—If a great, nay, far the greatest, part of the several ranks of bodies in the universe escape our notice by their remoteness, there are others that are no less concealed from us by their minute-

ness. These insensible corpuscles, being the active parts of matter, and the great instruments of nature, on which depend not only all their secondary qualities, but also most of their natural operations, our want of precise distinct ideas of their primary qualities keeps us in an incurable ignorance of what we desire to know about them. I doubt not but if we could discover the figure, size, texture, and motion of the minute constituent parts of any two bodies, we should know without trial several of their operations one upon another, as we do now the properties of a square or a triangle. Did we know the mechanical affections of the particles of rhubarb, hemlock, opium, and a man, as a watchmaker does those of a watch, whereby it performs its operations, and of a file, which by rubbing on them will alter the figure of any of the wheels, we should be able to tell beforehand that rhubarb will purge, hemlock kill, and opium make a man sleep; as well as a watchmaker can, that a little piece of paper laid on the balance will keep the watch from going, till it be removed; or that some small part of it being rubbed by a file, the machine would quite lose its motion, and the watch go no more. The dissolving of silver in aqua fortis, and gold in aqua regia, and not vice versa, would be then perhaps no more difficult to know, than it is to a smith to understand why the turning of one key will open a lock, and not the turning of another. But whilst we are destitute of senses acute enough to discover the minute particles of bodies, and to give us ideas of their mechanical affections, we must be content to be ignorant of their properties and ways of operation; nor can we be assured about them any further than some few trials we make are able to reach. But whether they will succeed again another time, we cannot be certain. This hinders our certain knowledge of universal truths concerning natural bodies; and our reason carries us herein very little beyond particular matter of fact.

26. *Hence no Science of Bodies.*—And therefore I am apt to doubt that how far soever human industry may advance useful and experimental philosophy in physical things, scientifical will still be out of our reach; because we want perfect and adequate ideas of those very bodies

which are nearest to us, and most under our command.
. . . Distinct ideas of the several sorts of bodies that fall
under the examination of our senses perhaps we may have:
but adequate ideas, I suspect, we have not of any one
amongst them. And though the former of these will serve
us for common use and discourse, yet whilst we want the
latter, we are not capable of scientifical knowledge; nor
shall ever be able to discover general, instructive, unquestionable, truths concerning them. Certainty and demonstration are things we must not, in these matters, pretend
to. By the colour, figure, taste, and smell, and other sensible
qualities, we have as clear and distinct ideas of sage and
hemlock, as we have of a circle and a triangle; but having
no ideas of the particular primary qualities of the minute
parts of either of these plants, nor of other bodies which
we would apply them to, we cannot tell what effects they
will produce; nor when we see those effects can we so much
as guess, much less know, their manner of production. . . .

CHAPTER IV. *Of the Reality of Knowledge*

3. It is evident the mind knows not things immediately,
but only by the intervention of the ideas it has of them.
Our knowledge therefore is real only so far as there is a
conformity between our ideas and the reality of things.
But what shall be here the criterion? How shall the mind,
when it perceives nothing but its own ideas, know that
they agree with things themselves? This, though it seems
not to want difficulty, yet I think there be two sorts of
ideas that we may be assured agree with things.

4. *As, First, all simple Ideas do*— . . .

5. *Secondly, All complex Ideas, except of substances*
— . . .

6. *Hence the Reality of Mathematical Knowledge.*—I
doubt not but it will be easily granted that the knowledge
we have of mathematical truths is not only certain but
real knowledge; and not the bare empty vision of vain,
insignificant chimeras of the brain: and yet, if we will
consider, we shall find that it is only of our own ideas.
The mathematician considers the truth and properties be-

longing to a rectangle or circle only as they are an idea in his own mind. For it is possible he never found either of them existing mathematically, i.e., precisely true, in his life. But yet the knowledge he has of any truths or properties belonging to a circle, or any other mathematical figure, are never the less true and certain even of real things existing; because real things are no further concerned, nor intended to be meant, by any such propositions, than as things really agree to those archetypes in his mind. Is it true of the idea of a triangle, that its three angles are equal to two right ones? It is true also of a triangle wherever it really exists. . . .

7. *And of Moral.*—And hence it follows that moral knowledge is as capable of real certainty as mathematics: for, certainty being but the perception of the agreement or disagreement of our ideas, and demonstration nothing but the perception of such agreement by the intervention of other ideas or mediums; our moral ideas as well as mathematical being archetypes themselves, and so adequate and complete ideas; all the agreement or disagreement which we shall find in them will produce real knowledge, as well as in mathematical figures.

18. *Recapitulation.*—Wherever we perceive the agreement or disagreement of any of our ideas, there is certain knowledge; and wherever we are sure those ideas agree with the reality of things, there is certain real knowledge. Of which agreement of our ideas with the reality of things having here given the marks, I think I have shown wherein it is that certainty, real certainty, consists, which, whatever it was to others, was, I confess, to me heretofore one of those desiderata which I found great want of.

CHAPTER VI. *Of Universal Propositions, their Truth and Certainty*

6. *The Truth of few universal Propositions concerning Substances is to be known.* . . .

7. *Because Coexistence of Ideas in few Cases is to be known.*—The complex ideas that our names of the species of substances properly stand for, are collections of such

qualities as have been observed to coexist in an unknown substratum which we call substance: but what other qualities necessarily coexist with such combinations we cannot certainly know, unless we can discover their natural dependence; which in their primary qualities we can go but a very little way in; and in all their secondary qualities we can discover no connexion at all, for the reasons mentioned (Ch. 3), viz., (1) Because we know not the real constitutions of substances, on which each secondary quality particularly depends. (2) Did we know that, it would serve us only for experimental (not universal) knowledge; and reach with certainty no further than that bare instance: because our understandings can discover no conceivable connexion between any secondary quality and any modification whatsoever of any of the primary ones.

9. . . . I would gladly meet with one general affirmation concerning any quality of gold that any one can certainly know is true. It will, no doubt, be presently objected, Is not this an universal certain proposition, "all gold is malleable"? To which I answer, It is a very certain proposition, if malleableness is a part of the complex idea the word "gold" stands for. But then here is nothing affirmed of gold, but that that sound stands for an idea in which malleableness is contained: and such a sort of truth and certainty as this it is to say, "A centaur is four-footed." But if malleableness make not a part of the specific essence the name of gold stands for, it is plain "all gold is malleable" is not a certain proposition; because, let the complex idea of gold be made up of whichsoever of its other qualities you please, malleableness will not appear to depend on that complex idea, nor follow from any simple one contained in it: the connexion that malleableness has (if it has any) with those other qualities being only by the intervention of the real constitution of its insensible parts; which since we know not, it is impossible we should perceive that connexion unless we could discover that which ties them together.

11. *The Qualities which make our complex Ideas of Substances depend mostly on external, remote, and unperceived Causes.*—Had we such ideas of substances as to

know what real constitutions produce those sensible qualities we find in them, and how those qualities flowed from
thence, we could, by the specific ideas of their real essences
in our own minds, more certainly find out their properties,
and discover what qualities they had or had not, than we
can know by our senses; and to know the properties of
gold, it would be no more necessary that gold should exist,
and that we should make experiments upon it, than it is
necessary for the knowing the properties of a triangle that
a triangle should exist in any matter; the idea in our minds
would serve for the one as well as the other. . . .

13. *Judgment may reach further, but that is not Knowledge.*—We are not therefore to wonder if certainty be to be
found in very few general propositions made concerning
substances: our knowledge of their qualities and properties goes very seldom further than our senses reach and
inform us. Possibly inquisitive and observing men may, by
strength of judgment, penetrate further; and on probabilities taken from wary observation, and hints well laid together, often guess right at what experience has not yet
discovered to them. But this is but guessing still; it amounts
only to opinion, and has not that certainty which is requisite to knowledge. For all general knowledge lies only
in our own thoughts, and consists barely in the contemplation of our own abstract ideas. Wherever we perceive any
agreement or disagreement amongst them, there we have
general knowledge; and by putting the names of those ideas
together accordingly in propositions, can with certainty
pronounce general truths. But because the abstract ideas
of substances . . . have a discoverable connexion or inconsistency with but a very few other ideas, the certainty
of universal propositions concerning substances is very
narrow and scanty. . . .

15— . . . We cannot with certainty affirm that all men
sleep by intervals, that no man can be nourished by wood
or stones, that all men will be poisoned by hemlock; because these ideas have no connexion nor repugnancy with
this our nominal essence of man, with this abstract idea
that name stands for; we must, in these and the like, appeal
to trial in particular subjects, which can reach but a little

way. We must content ourselves with probability in the rest: but can have no general certainty, whilst our specific idea of man contains not that real constitution which is the root wherein all his inseparable qualities are united, and from whence they flow. . . . As long as we want ideas of those real constitutions of different sorts of animals . . . we must not hope to reach certainty in universal propositions concerning them. Those few ideas only which have a discernible connexion with our nominal essence, or any part of it, can afford us such propositions. But these are so few and of so little moment that we may justly look on our certain general knowledge of substances as almost none at all.

16. *Wherein lies the general Certainty of Propositions.* —To conclude: general propositions, of what kind soever, are then only capable of certainty when the terms used in them stand for such ideas whose agreement or disagreement, as there expressed, is capable to be discovered by us. And we are then certain of their truth or falsehood when we perceive the ideas the terms stand for to agree or not agree, according as they are affirmed or denied one of another. Whence we may take notice, that general certainty is never to be found but in our ideas. Whenever we go to seek it elsewhere, in experiment or observations without us, our knowledge goes not beyond particulars. It is the contemplation of our abstract ideas that alone is able to afford us general knowledge. . . .

CHAPTER VIII. *Of Trifling Propositions*

7. . . . Before a man makes any proposition, he is supposed to understand the terms he uses in it, or else he talks like a parrot, only making a noise by imitation, and framing certain sounds which he has learnt of others; but not as a rational creature, using them for signs of ideas which he has in his mind. The hearer also is supposed to understand the terms as the speaker uses them. . . . And therefore he trifles with words who makes such a proposition, which, when it is made, contains no more than one

of the terms does . . . ; v.g., "A triangle hath three sides," or, "Saffron is yellow." And this is no further tolerable than where a man goes to explain his terms to one who is supposed or declares himself not to understand him.

8. . . . We can know then the truth of two sorts of propositions with perfect certainty: the one is, of those trifling propositions which have a certainty in them, but it is only a verbal certainty, but not instructive. And, secondly, we can know the truth, and so may be certain in propositions which affirm something of another, which is a necessary consequence of its precise complex idea, but not contained in it: as that "the external angle of all triangles is bigger than either of the opposite internal triangles"; which relation of the outward angle to either of the opposite internal angles, making no part of the complex idea signified by the name triangle, this is a real truth, and conveys with it instructive real knowledge.

CHAPTER IX. *Of Our Knowledge of Existence*

1. *General certain Propositions concern not Existence.* —Hitherto we have only considered the essences of things, which, being only abstract ideas, and thereby removed in our thoughts from particular existence (that being the proper operation of the mind in abstraction, to consider an idea under no other existence but what it has in the understanding), give us no knowledge of real existence at all. Where, by the way, we may take notice, that universal propositions, of whose truth or falsehood we can have certain knowledge, concern not existence; and further, that all particular affirmations or negations that would not be certain if they were made general, are only concerning existence; they declaring only the accidental union or separation of ideas in things existing, which in their abstract natures have no known necessary union or repugnancy.

2. *A threefold Knowledge of Existence.*—But, leaving the nature of propositions and different ways of predication to be considered more at large in another place, let us proceed now to inquire concerning our knowledge of the existence of things, and how we come by it. I say, then,

that we have the knowledge of our own existence by intuition; of the existence of God by demonstration; and of other things by sensation.

3. *Our Knowledge of our own Existence is Intuitive.*— As for our own existence, we perceive it so plainly and so certainly that it neither needs nor is capable of any proof. For nothing can be more evident to us than our own existence: I think, I reason, I feel pleasure and pain: can any of these be more evident to me than my own existence? If I doubt of all other things, that very doubt makes me perceive my own existence, and will not suffer me to doubt of that. For, if I know I feel pain, it is evident I have as certain perception of my own existence as of the existence of the pain I feel: or if I know I doubt, I have as certain perception of the existence of the thing doubting, as of that thought which I call "doubt." Experience, then, convinces us that we have an intuitive knowledge of our own existence, and an internal infallible perception that we are. In every act of sensation, reasoning, or thinking, we are conscious to ourselves of our own being; and, in this matter, come not short of the highest degree of certainty.

CHAPTER XI. *Of Our Knowledge of the Existence of Other Things*

13. *Particular Propositions concerning Existence are knowable.*—By which it appears that there are two sorts of propositions. (1) There is one sort of propositions concerning the existence of any thing answerable to such an idea: as having the idea of an elephant, phoenix, motion, or an angel in my mind, the first and natural inquiry is, whether such a thing does any where exist. And this knowledge is only of particulars. No existence of any thing without us, but only of God, can certainly be known further than our senses inform us. (2) There is another sort of propositions, wherein is expressed the agreement or disagreement of our abstract ideas, and their dependence on one another. Such propositions may be universal and certain. So, having the idea of God and myself, of fear and obedience, I cannot but be sure that God is to be feared

and obeyed by me: and this proposition will be certain concerning man in general, if I have made an abstract idea of such a species, whereof I am one particular. But yet this proposition, how certain soever, that men ought to fear and obey God, proves not to me the existence of men in the world, but will be true of all such creatures whenever they do exist: which certainty of such general propositions depends on the agreement or disagreement to be discovered in those abstract ideas.

CHAPTER XV. *Of Probability*

1. *Probability is the Appearance of Agreement upon fallible Proofs.*—As demonstration is the showing the agreement or disagreement of two ideas by the intervention of one or more proofs which have a constant, immutable, and visible connexion one with another; so probability is nothing but the appearance of such an agreement or disagreement by the intervention of proofs whose connexion is not constant and immutable, or at least is not perceived to be so; but is, or appears for the most part to be, so, and is enough to induce the mind to judge the proposition to be true or false, rather than the contrary. For example: in the demonstration of it, a man perceives the certain immutable connexion there is of equality between the three angles of a triangle, and those intermediate ones which are made use of to show their equality to two right ones. . . . But another man, who never took the pains to observe the demonstration, hearing a mathematician, a man of credit, affirm "the three angles of a triangle to be equal to two right ones," assents to it, i.e., receives it for true: in which case the foundation of his assent is the probability of the thing . . . ; the man on whose testimony he receives it not being wont to affirm anything contrary to or besides his knowledge, especially in matters of this kind. . . .

2. *It is to supply the Want of Knowledge.*—Our knowledge, as has been shown, being very narrow . . . most of the propositions we think, reason, discourse—nay, act upon—are such as we cannot have undoubted knowledge

of their truth; yet some of them border so near upon certainty that we make no doubt at all about them; but assent to them as firmly, and act according to that assent as resolutely, as if they were infallibly demonstrated, and that our knowledge of them was perfect and certain. But, there being degrees herein, from the very neighbourhood of certainty and demonstration, quite down to improbability and unlikeliness, even to the confines of impossibility; and also degrees of assent from full assurance and confidence, quite down to conjecture, doubt, and distrust: I shall come now (having, as I think, found out the bounds of human knowledge and certainty), in the next place, to consider the several degrees and grounds of probability, and assent or faith.

3. *Being that which makes us presume Things to be true, before we know them to be so.*—Probability is likeliness to be true; the very notation of the word signifying such a proposition, for which there be arguments or proofs to make it pass, or be received for true. The entertainment the mind gives this sort of propositions is called "belief," "assent," or "opinion," which is the admitting or receiving any proposition for true, upon arguments or proofs that are found to persuade us to receive it as true, without certain knowledge that it is so. And herein lies the difference between probability and certainty, faith and knowledge, that in all the parts of knowledge there is intuition; each immediate idea, each step, has its visible and certain connexion: in belief not so. That which makes me believe is something extraneous to the thing I believe; something not evidently joined on both sides to, and so not manifestly showing the agreement or disagreement, of those ideas that are under consideration.]

IN THE PRECEDING EXPOSITION LOCKE DIVIDES OUR KNOWLedge into groups according to four quite independent canons of division:

(1) Knowledge according to the respect in which the ideas "agree" or "disagree."

(a) Identity or diversity (i.e., incompatibility). This appears to give us knowledge of obvious logical truths, e.g., "white is white" and "black is not white."

(b) Relation. This seems to refer to the logical relations involved in any deductive process whereby the logical connection of different ideas can be established.

(c) Coexistence. This kind of agreement or disagreement is that *de facto* togetherness or apartness which is to be found in the propositions of natural science. To take Locke's example: "All gold is fixed" (i.e., roughly is solid, nonvolatile, stable) asserts the coexistence ("agreement") of the defining properties of gold with the further property of "fixedness."

(d) Real existence. This is the basic relation of ideas to realities: "Actual real existence agreeing to any idea" as Locke expresses it.

As to this, Locke himself admits that both identity (or diversity) and coexistence are in fact themselves relations. Nevertheless he seems to regard them as so peculiar and important as to be singled out for special treatment. Hence we may regard the category of "relations" as comprising relations other than identity or diversity and coexistence; more especially logical relations since Locke regards it as particularly applicable where a deduction is involved. As for the fourth of his categories, it falls wholly outside Locke's scheme of knowledge. He seems to be saying that we can show that some entity "A" exists, by showing that the idea of A and the idea of existence "agree." This is one of the profoundest of all logical fallacies, of crucial importance for philosophy as a form of human thought. Its classical exposure was performed by Kant and again by Russell, who proved that it rests on treatment of such words as "exists," "is real," "is in time and space," and the like, as if they were predicates on a par with "is red" or "is jealous." That this is a fallacy is shown by the fact that otherwise we could cause entities to exist by the arbitrary fiat of our thoughts, by so arranging our ideas, that since the entire process remained mental, we could make any one of them—say the idea of a unicorn or of a man with a head bigger than the sun—"agree" with our "idea" of existence; for ideas at least are in our power. Composers of fairy tales do just this, and, having made them "agree" with "existence," thereby by this means alone make them

literally exist. This is the fallacy on which rests the famous
ontological argument for the existence of God, invented in
the Middle Ages and restated by Descartes; and it is significant that Locke gives as his illustration of knowledge of
the fourth category, "God is." On the other hand, and
perhaps equally significantly, Locke himself seeks to establish the existence of God not by the ontological argument,
but by a causal argument.

But we obviously cannot prove that some entity exists
by showing that the idea of that entity and the idea of existence "agree," but rather by some procedure appropriate
to the type of entity in question (e.g., observation or argument based on observation in the case of material objects).
Locke, having defined knowledge as the agreement or disagreement of ideas, has thereby debarred himself from allowing that we know any existential statements, i.e., those
asserting existence outside the realm of our free thoughts
and free imagination.

(2) The second canon of classification of knowledge is
according to what Locke calls "degree," i.e., degree of
certainty.

(a) Intuitive knowledge, where the mind perceives the
truth of the statement *immediately*.

(b) Demonstrative knowledge, where steps of reasoning are required.

(c) Sensitive knowledge, i.e., knowledge of the existence of particular objects outside us.

With regard to (a) and (b), Locke's criterion of certainty is evidently (like that of Descartes) psychological.

"Demonstration" (i.e., deduction) consists of a series
of steps, each of which must, however, be perceived intuitively. It is therefore inferior to "intuition" only in so
far as we are obliged to rely upon memory in holding together the steps. Intuition itself is utterly incontrovertible.
The metaphor of the infallible inner eye (cf. Introd.
p. 18), as opposed to the poor sense faculties, comes out
particularly clearly in the discussion of intuition; and this
despite the fact that Locke's fame rests, rightly, on his
victories over the great seventeenth-century champions of
infallible rational knowledge.

Sensitive knowledge is, within Locke's terms of reference, simply not knowledge. In the first place he himself admits that it does not reach perfectly to either of the foregoing degrees of certainty; yet he claims that it goes beyond bare probability. It oscillates, as it were, on the borderline between knowledge and opinion. But for Locke this borderline is a line (of no thickness) and not an area. "What I know, that I am certain of; and what I am certain of, that I know." The distinction between knowledge (certainty) and opinion (probability) is an absolute distinction of kind and not a distinction of degree. There is no halfway house. Moreover, this kind of knowledge does not conform to his earlier definition; there is here no question of the "agreement" or "disagreement" of ideas. Locke informs us that "this certainty is as great as our happiness or misery beyond which we have no concern to be," and while this may entitle him to be considered as one of the great exponents of English common sense it will not do in one who claims to inaugurate a new way of thinking. Locke is supposedly concerned with crucial questions of what we can or cannot know, and not with pragmatic questions about what we need to think that we know in order to be happy.

(3) The distinction between "actual" knowledge and "habitual" knowledge.

This valuable dichotomy is almost self-explanatory. I am properly said to know throughout my life many propositions, e.g., of history or mathematics that I learned at school, even though I may subsequently think of such a proposition only very seldom or never at all. I know these propositions in the sense that if occasion arises for me to consider them, then I am quite certain of their truth, but of course I do not hold them constantly before my conscious mind. This sort of knowledge Locke calls "habitual," and it is obvious that at any given moment by far the greatest part of our knowledge is in this sense "habitual." With this Locke contrasts "actual" knowledge, "the present view the mind has of the agreement or disagreement of any of its ideas, or of the relation they have to

one another," i.e., the knowledge that we have at a given
moment of a proposition which we know to be true, and
are at that moment consciously considering.

(4) Two types of knowledge, distinguished according
to whether the proposition known is "real" or "trifling."

Here Locke is, to some degree, anticipating Kant's distinction between synthetic and analytic truths; like Kant he
fails to recognize the extent or the importance of the domain covered by analytic truths.

Locke himself does not see any philosophical problems
in "habitual" knowledge, regarding it as a kind of extension (by means of memory) of "actual" knowledge, in
which he is primarily interested; and he (mistakenly) regards "trifling" propositions as quite insignificant for the
theory of knowledge. Knowledge for him is, in the main, in
his sense of these words, both "actual" and "real."

The gravest objection to Locke's account of knowledge
is that, by his own definition, all knowledge is only of the
relations of *ideas* on our minds. How then can we be sure
that any of our knowledge is knowledge of the real world?
Does it even make sense to ask how we could find out
whether our knowledge is applied to anything beyond our
ideas? or what it means to say that there is such a "beyond"? Locke, by his representationalism, has finally
trapped human knowledge within the circle of the human
mind.

Locke himself is, at times, not unaware of this problem,
which is more than can be said of his uncritical French
disciples. He tries to answer it by declaring that our knowledge is genuine "only so far as there is a conformity between our ideas and the reality of things." And there is
this "conformity" or "agreement" in, for example,

(a) Our simple ideas. For how could they err? Being
without parts, simple, they cannot fail to be authentic
copies of whatever has emitted them, and therefore true.
It is not easy to know what is meant by saying that all
"simple" thoughts, images, etc., are true—cannot mislead.
All "ideas" known to ordinary man can lead astray: and
the chemical metaphor of simple elements is not happily

applied to psychology. In any case the knowledge here referred to is sensitive knowledge, which we have already seen not to be knowledge within Locke's definition of knowledge.

(b) Complex ideas, other than those of substance. Under this head Locke concludes that our mathematical and moral knowledge is in this sense genuine.

About mathematical knowledge Locke shows great acumen. He sees that, for example, geometrical propositions are true of certain ideal constructions of the human mind and not of, e.g., chalk marks or surveyor's chains in the real world. All that pure geometry can tell us is that if objects in the world did conform precisely to Euclid's definition of points, lines and planes (as they could not) and did obey his axioms then Euclid's theorems would be true of such objects; "real things are no further concerned, nor intended to be meant, by any such propositions, than as things really agree to those archetypes in his mind." But his acumen does not extend to seeing that in this case the propositions of pure mathematics are not knowledge about the world in the sense in which "real" propositions differ from "trifling" ones. Indeed, the facts about mathematical propositions to which he draws attention, i.e., that they are not verified or falsified, confirmed or disconfirmed, by events in the "real," empirical world, are the very facts which later induced some philosophers to call mathematical propositions "analytic."

Locke's views on moral philosophy are very strange. In Book IV he claims that the truths of ethics can be rigorously deduced from the ideas of God and of ourselves as rational beings. Though frequently urged, in view of the supreme importance of the issue, to expound such demonstrative ethics, he never did so. What he does produce is two palpably verbal truths, or in his own phrase "trifling" propositions, as examples of the results of such rigorous deduction. "Where there is no property, there is no injustice," he tells us, is a proposition as certain as any demonstration in Euclid: for the idea of property being a right to anything, and the idea to which the name injustice is given being the

invasion or violation of that right, it is evident that these
ideas being thus established, and these names annexed to
them, I can as certainly know this proposition to be true
as that a triangle has three angles equal to two right ones.
On Locke's definitions of "property" and "injustice" I can
indeed certainly know this proposition; for it follows from
the definitions; and illuminates us not at all.

Locke's account of scientific knowledge, or rather of
what scientific knowledge would be like if we had any, is
one of the most interesting things in the *Essay*. The difficulty is this. According to Locke our general words for
kinds of things, e.g., "gold," stand only for "nominal essences" or "abstract general ideas," i.e., for some set of
characteristics which we have always found to be coexistent, although we can provide no *rational* (i.e., for Locke,
demonstrable, as are the truths of mathematics) explanation for this constant conjunction. Hence for him a proposition like "All gold is malleable" belongs to one of two
types. Either malleableness has been specifically included
as part of the definition of gold ("part of the complex idea
the word 'gold' stands for," as Locke puts it) or it has not.
In the first case, the proposition follows *ex vi terminorum*
and is obviously analytic ("trifling"); in the second case,
since, alas, we have no deductively certain knowledge of
the interdependence of characteristics, we cannot know for
certain that the proposition is always true, "nor can we be
assured about them any further than some few trials we
make are able to reach." Consequently, however far "useful and experimental philosophy" may be advanced in
"physical things," yet *"scientifical* will still be out of our
reach." Locke has here stumbled, as it were, by accident,
on the notorious problem of induction.[8] Stumbled by accident, for he does not seem to have realized that the problem is a logical one; on the contrary, he thinks that there
would be no such problem if the world were in certain
respects empirically different.

When Locke took over from scholasticism the idea of a

[8] For a statement and discussion of this problem in connection with
Hume, who first explicitly formulated it, see p. 185ff. below.

"real essence," that which makes a thing what it is, he used the expression very differently from the schoolmen. For them it was a metaphysical notion independent of material properties. But he identified the real essence of substances with the "real internal, but generally in substances unknown, construction of things whereon their discoverable qualities depend," i.e., the primary (physical) qualities of the minute particles. In some passages of Book IV he seems to hold that if the world were empirically different in one respect—namely that we should have "senses acute enough" to detect the primary qualities of the minute particles of substances—we should be able to *deduce* all the properties of those substances; as if primary qualities and these other properties were connected by a species of quasi-logical necessary connections, needing not observation but *deductive* power to trace their subtle paths. Whatever inklings in the matter Hobbes or others may have had, it is not until Hume's revolutionary theses had been put forward, that it was realized that the relation between logically distinct natural entities could not, in principle, be deductive, or knowable a priori; and that the relations between Locke's minute atomic structure, however fine, detected by senses however acute, and other, grosser, "macroscopic," properties of a material object, could only be objects of observation, or inductive reasoning, or inspired conjecture, but not of deductive—quasi-mathematical—inference. At times Locke admits that even if our senses were acute enough to detect the primary qualities of the minute particles we should still be baffled by our ignorance of the connection between these and the macroscopic properties; but here again he seems to think that this ignorance is an empirical fact, and that if it were removed, then again we should have a *deductive* science of nature. In short, the problem of induction is for him not a logical one—about the nature of the reasoning which allows us to move from the known to the less known or unknown—but is due to the complexity of the world which defeats our feeble senses and reasoning powers.

Thus Locke reduces human knowledge to a very meager

sum. All general propositions are only about our ideas, and tell us nothing about the existence of objects in the real world. The most that they can tell us about the world is something hypothetical, e.g., that if an object has certain properties ("answers to a certain idea"), then it must also (the nature of this "must" being left unclear,) have certain other properties; but whether there exist objects with certain properties we cannot know.

To this Locke adds three sorts of propositions which he claims that we can know, which do assert the existence of particular objects in the world:

(a) Each of us has an intuitive knowledge of the existence of his own mind.

(b) We have knowledge by deduction of the existence of God.

(c) We have sensitive knowledge of the existence of particular objects outside us.

We have already seen that Locke should not, by his own definition, have called sensitive knowledge knowledge at all. His deductive proof of the existence of God rests upon obsolete metaphysical premises, which afford no light to a post-mediaeval reader. Our supposed intuitive knowledge of the existence of our own minds (Locke takes over unchanged the famous *Cogito* argument) belongs to the history of Cartesian fallacies. Apart from this last, Locke is left with an assembly of propositions, which, depending as they do on "the agreement and disagreement of our ideas" are not about the real world, and which we should today be inclined to call "analytic." To the confinement of human knowledge within this melancholy compass Locke has been brought by a combination of various doctrines, unplausible in themselves and impossible to combine: insistence on a mathematico-deductive standard of certainty in knowledge; a representative theory of knowledge which excluded the real world from the very start; a mechanical model of the mind; and finally, a non-empiricist belief in the existence of a capacity for intuitive knowledge which, in certain fortunate cases, affords short cuts across territory more slowly and painfully traversed by observation, experiment, memory, inductive reasoning and which could, if only the world were different, do away with these inefficient methods altogether.

These are Locke's faults and errors. His merits are very great: he asked questions the answers to which by philosophers of greater genius created modern empiricism; he established the connection between philosophical criticism and action and scientific processes and thought; and he used intelligible language, destroying the magic of scholastic and rationalist terminology, which was the greatest of all obstacles to intellectual progress.

CHAPTER II

Voltaire

JEAN FRANÇOIS MARIE AROUET (TO WHICH HE HIMSELF added the name of Voltaire) was born in 1694 and became the most famous individual in the eighteenth century. Poet, dramatist, essayist, historian, novelist, philosopher, scientific amateur, his claim to immortality rests on his polemical genius and his power of ridicule in which, to this day, he knows no equal. The friend of kings and the implacable enemy of the Roman Church and indeed, of all institutional Christianity, he was the most admired and dreaded writer of the century, and by his unforgettable and deadly mockery did more to undermine the foundations of the established order than any of its other opponents. He died in 1778, the intellectual and aesthetic dictator of the civilized world of his day. Voltaire was not an original philosopher, but he did more to increase the prestige and the understanding of the new empiricism than any other human being. Locke seemed to him, as to so many of his most enlightened contemporaries, the genius who, in his tentative and modest fashion, had done for the human mind what Newton had done for nature. He, and the generation which he had done so much to educate and liberate, believed that by the scrupulous use of genetic psychology—although they did not call it that—the functioning of everything in man and in nature could be explained, and an end put to all those dark mysteries and grotesque fairy tales (the fruit of indolence, blindness and deliberate chicanery) which went by the names of theology, metaphysics and other brands of concealed dogma or superstition, with which unscrupulous knaves had for so long befuddled the stupid and benighted multitudes whom they murdered, enslaved,

113

oppressed and exploited. The passage which follows is a characteristic testimonial to Locke as the great spreader of light, and expresses the simple faith in the new genetic science common to the entire European Enlightenment. The growth of science would not only provide knowledge of all there was in the world and in the mind, and of how it worked. It would also tell men what their natures—part of the vast harmonious whole called "nature"—needed; how to obtain it by the most painless and efficient means; and therefore how to be wise, rational, happy and good. Some of the virtues and shortcomings of this noble, in part true, in part utopian, vision have been examined in the commentaries on specific texts by Locke.

[FROM *Philosophical Letters*

Many a philosopher has written the tale of the soul's adventures, but now a sage has appeared who has, more modestly, written its history. Locke has developed human reason before men, as an excellent anatomist unfolds the mechanism of the human body. Aided everywhere by the torch of physics, he dares at times to affirm, but he also dares to doubt. Instead of collecting in one sweeping definition what we do not know, he explores by degrees what we desire to know. He takes a child at the moment of its birth, step by step he follows the progress of its understanding; he sees what it has in common with the beasts, and wherein it is set above them; he is guided throughout by the testimony that is in himself, consciousness of his own thought.]

CHAPTER III

George Berkeley

GEORGE BERKELEY (1685-1753) WAS BORN AND EDUCATED in Ireland, where he spent the greater part of his life. He displayed his brilliant gifts in his early twenties; the works which secured his immortality were all published before the age of thirty. He taught at Trinity College, Dublin, until, in 1725, he conceived the project of founding a college in Bermuda for the training of missionaries. Such were his extraordinary natural goodness and charm, to the fascination of which almost all who met him bore testimony, that he very nearly succeeded in extracting funds for his various benevolent schemes from Walpole's unsentimental government. In pursuit of his educational and missionary purposes, he settled for three years in Newport, Rhode Island, and was one of the benefactors of Yale University. He returned to England in 1731, and in 1734 was appointed Bishop of Cloyne, in Ireland, where he remained writing and administering his diocese until 1752, when he settled in Oxford. He died in that city a year later, widely loved and universally mourned.

Berkeley is usually regarded as being at the same time the acutest critic and the legitimate successor of Locke, and his views are represented as a unique contribution to, and an essential link in, the development of British Empiricism—the "natural" bridge between the "common sense" doctrines of Locke and the "skepticism" of Hume. But this is at most a half truth. Berkeley was certainly in one sense an empiricist: he tried to give an intelligible and coherent account of the "outer" and the "inner" worlds the truth of which could be established by direct verification

115

in normal everyday experience without recourse to special
metaphysical devices or reference to occult entities beyond
the bounds of the senses. And he went further in this direction, and attacked the ontologies both of the seventeenth-
century rationalists and of their scholastic predecessors in
a more radical fashion than Locke, or indeed anyone before
him. In this sense he is an even more fanatical empiricist
than Hobbes. But his outlook was wholly different from
that of either Hobbes or Locke—indeed, in one sense, directly opposed to theirs. Both Hobbes and Locke were
wholly under the spell of the scientific revolution of their
day. Hobbes set himself to extend its methods directly to
the fields of ethics and politics, and more cursorily to logic
and psychology. Locke, more cautiously and tentatively,
also attempted this task, as well as that of an interpretation
of the doctrines of the new physical sciences which made
them both intelligible to, and compatible with the findings
of, ordinary common sense. He is, among other things, the
father of all those interpreters and popularizers of the sciences who try to represent them as saying, in their own
technical terminologies, something which not only does
not contradict common sense, but can, less precisely but
still not inaccurately, be conveyed in ordinary prose; and,
in the course of such expositions, in fact themselves cast
alternate light and darkness on the subject, invent their
own special vocabularies, and propagate their own mythol-
ogies, which in their turn demand—and breed—interpreters and specialists, until the needs of ordinary men and of
their allegedly simple minds are all but forgotten.

Berkeley's approach is totally opposed to this. His position is that of a Christian believer (he was bishop of
Cloyne) with an inclination to mysticism. The world is
for him a spectacle of continuous spiritual life, in the first
place, in the mind of God, and secondarily in the minds
of His creatures, men. This is not, for him, a philosophical
theory or hypothesis, but a direct vision. He is principally
concerned to deny what is to him, oddly enough, at once
atheistical and unintelligible—the assertion that there exists something called matter perceptible neither to the

senses nor to the imagination, independent of minds either divine or human, the properties of which cause the world to behave as it does and are the proper study of rational men. This is to Berkeley a genuine chimera, and the source of all our confusions, intellectual and spiritual. His philosophy is directed to the demonstration that nothing exists save spiritual activity, that is, the creative process of spirits —God's infinite spirit and men's finite souls—and, dependent upon them, as their content or modification, human experience—imagination, memory, thoughts, expectations, dreams, feelings, and above all the sensations, the combinations and procession of which *are* the external world.

This vision of the universe is at once more ruthlessly empirical than Locke's, with no room in it for material objects independent of experience—ultimate lumps of stuff, mysterious substrata in which the data of the senses "inhere," which Locke cannot either explain or eliminate— and one that is rooted in a pre-Renaissance, medieval spiritualism which conceives of all there is as consisting of spirits and what they create or enjoy. This is the positive content of Berkeley's metaphysics. As for the paradoxes which caused so much stir and incredulity, they are his polemical weapon designed to eliminate the figments with which philosophers have, in his view, peopled the world: first and foremost among them, inanimate matter, uncreated and existing by itself, dependent on nothing; and secondly, attributes—universals or properties of objects, whether mathematical magnitudes or sense qualities and relations, which have been accorded similarly independent status not only by Platonists or Aristotelians of all periods, but by Cartesians, Leibnizians, and, however uncertainly and halfheartedly, by Locke himself. The celebrated and cogent pages in which Berkeley tries to explode these, for him, central myths and confusions of rationalism and materialism, and to explain how words and symbols relate to things, possess a classical lucidity and beauty of expression never again attained in Western philosophy. The following selections are from *A Treatise Concerning the Principles of Human Knowledge.*

[*Introduction*

6. In order to prepare the mind of the reader for the easier conceiving what follows, it is proper to premise somewhat, by way of introduction, concerning the nature and abuse of Language. But the unravelling this matter leads me in some measure to anticipate my design, by taking notice of what seems to have had a chief part in rendering speculation intricate and perplexed, and to have occasioned innumerable errors and difficulties in almost all parts of knowledge. And that is the opinion that the mind hath a power of framing *abstract* ideas or notions of things. He who is not a perfect stranger to the writings and disputes of philosophers, must needs acknowledge that no small part of them are spent about abstract ideas. These are, in a more especial manner, thought to be the object of those sciences which go by the name of logic and metaphysics, and of all that which passes under the notion of the most abstracted and sublime learning; in all which one shall scarce find any question handled in such a manner, as does not suppose their existence in the mind, and that it is well acquainted with them.

7. It is agreed on all hands that the *qualities* or *modes* of things do never really exist each of them apart by itself, and separated from all others, but are mixed, as it were, and blended together, several in the same object. But, we are told, the mind being able to consider each quality singly, or abstracted from those other qualities with which it is united, does by that means frame to itself *abstract ideas*. For example, there is perceived by sight an object extended, coloured, and moved: this mixed or compound idea the mind resolving into its simple, constituent parts, and viewing each by itself, exclusive of the rest, does frame the abstract ideas of extension, colour, and motion. Not that it is possible for colour or motion to exist without extension; but only that the mind can frame to itself by abstraction the idea of colour exclusive of extension, and of motion exclusive of both colour and extension.

8. Again, the mind having observed that in the particular extensions perceived by sense, there is something *common* and alike in *all,* and some other things peculiar, as this or that figure or magnitude, which distinguish them one from another; it considers apart or singles out by itself that which is common; making thereof a most abstract idea of extension, which is neither line, surface, nor solid, nor has any figure of magnitude, but is an idea entirely prescinded from all these. So likewise the mind, by leaving out of the particular colours perceived by sense, that which distinguishes them one from another, and retaining that only which is common to all, makes an idea of colour in abstract; which is neither red, nor blue, nor white, nor any other determinate colour. And in like manner, by considering motion abstractedly not only from the body moved, but likewise from the figure it describes, and all particular directions and velocities, the abstract idea of motion is framed; which equally corresponds to all particular motions whatsoever that may be perceived by sense.

9. And as the mind frames to itself abstract ideas of *qualities* or *modes,* so does it, by the same precision or mental separation, attain abstract ideas of the more compounded *beings,* which include several coexistent qualities. For example, the mind having observed that Peter, James, and John resemble each other, in certain common agreements of shape and other qualities, leaves out of the complex or compound idea it has of Peter, James, and any other particular man, that which is peculiar to each, retaining only what is common to all; and so makes an abstract idea wherein all the particulars equally partake, abstracting entirely from and cutting off all those circumstances and differences, which might determine it to any particular existence. And after this manner it is said we come by the abstract idea of *man,* or, if you please, humanity or human nature; wherein it is true there is included colour, because there is no man but has some colour, but then it can be neither white, nor black, nor any particular colour, because there is no one particular colour wherein all men partake. So likewise there is included stature, but then it

is neither tall stature nor low stature, nor yet middle stature, but something abstracted from all these. And so of the rest. Moreover, there being a great variety of other creatures that partake in some parts, but not all, of the complex idea of man, the mind leaving out those parts which are peculiar to men, and retaining those only which are common to all the living creatures, frames the idea of *animal*, which abstracts not only from all particular men, but also all birds, beasts, fishes and insects. The constituent parts of the abstract idea of animal are body, life, sense and spontaneous motion. By *body* is meant body without any particular shape or figure, there being no one shape or figure common to all animals, without covering, either of hair or feathers, or scales, &c., nor yet naked: hair, feathers, scales. and nakedness, being the distinguishing properties of particular animals, and for that reason left out of the abstract idea. Upon the same account the spontaneous motion must be neither walking, nor flying, nor creeping; it is nevertheless a motion, but what that motion is, it is not easy to conceive.

10. Whether others have this wonderful faculty of abstracting their ideas, they best can tell. For myself, I find indeed I have a faculty of imagining, or representing to myself, the ideas of those particular things I have perceived, and of variously compounding and dividing them. I can imagine a man with two heads, or the upper parts of a man joined to the body of a horse. I can consider the hand, the eye, the nose, each by itself abstracted or separated from the rest of the body. But then whatever hand or eye I imagine, it must have some particular shape and colour. Likewise the idea of man that I frame to myself, must be either of a white, or a black, or a tawny, a straight, or a crooked, a tall, or a low, or a middle-sized man. I cannot by any effort of thought conceive the abstract idea above described. And it is equally impossible for me to form the abstract idea of motion distinct from the body moving, and which is neither swift nor slow, curvilinear nor rectilinear; and the like may be said of all other abstract general ideas whatsoever. To be plain, I own myself

able to abstract in one sense, as when I consider some particular parts or qualities separated from others, with which though they are united in some object, yet it is possible they may really exist without them. But I deny that I can abstract one from another, or conceive separately, those qualities which it is impossible should exist so separated; or that I can frame a general notion by abstracting from particulars in the manner aforesaid—which two last are the proper acceptations of *abstraction*. And there is ground to think most men will acknowledge themselves to be in my case. The generality of men which are simple and illiterate never pretend to abstract notions. It is said they are difficult, and not to be attained without pains and study. We may therefore reasonably conclude that, if such there be, they are confined only to the learned.

11. I proceed to examine what can be alleged in defence of the doctrine of abstraction, and try if I can discover what it is that inclines the men of speculation to embrace an opinion so remote from common sense as that seems to be. There has been a late deservedly esteemed philosopher who, no doubt, has given it very much countenance by seeming to think the having abstract general ideas is what puts the widest difference in point of understanding betwixt man and beast. "The having of general ideas," saith he, "is that which puts a perfect distinction betwixt man and brutes, and is an excellency which the faculties of brutes do by no means attain unto. For it is evident we observe no foot-steps in them of making use of general signs for universal ideas; from which we have reason to imagine that they have not the faculty of abstracting, or making general ideas, since they have no use of words or any other general signs." And a little after: "Therefore, I think, we may suppose that it is in this that the species of brutes are discriminated from man: and it is that proper difference wherein they are wholly separated, and which at last widens to so wide a distance. For if they have any ideas at all, and are not bare machines (as some would have them), we cannot deny them to have some reason. It seems as evident to me that they do, some of them, in

certain instances, reason as that they have sense; but it is only in particular ideas, just as they receive them from their senses. They are the best of them tied up within those narrow bounds, and have not (as I think) the faculty to enlarge them by any kind of abstraction." (*Essay on Human Understanding,* B.II., ch. XI., §§ 10 and 11.) I readily agree with this learned author that the faculties of brutes can by no means attain to abstraction. But then if this be made the distinguishing property of that sort of animals, I fear a great many of those that pass for men must be reckoned into their number. The reason that is here assigned why we have no grounds to think brutes have abstract general ideas, is that we observe in them no use of words or any other general signs: which is built on this supposition, to wit, that the making use of words implies the having general ideas. From which it follows that men who use language are able to abstract or generalize their ideas. That this is the sense and arguing of the author will further appear by his answering the question he in another place puts: "Since all things that exist are only particulars, how come we by general terms?" His answer is, "Words become general by being made the signs of general ideas." (Ibid., B.III., ch. III., § 6.) But it seems that a word becomes general by being made the sign, not of an abstract general idea, but of several particular ideas, any one of which it indifferently suggests to the mind. For example, when it is said "the change of motion is proportional to the impressed force," or that "whatever has extension is divisible," these propositions are to be understood of motion and extension in general; and nevertheless it will not follow that they suggest to my thoughts an *idea* of motion without a body moved, or any determinate direction and velocity; or that I must conceive an *abstract general idea* of extension, which is neither line, surface, nor solid, neither great nor small, black, white, nor red, nor of any other determinate colour. It is only implied that whatever particular motion I consider, whether it be swift or slow, perpendicular, horizontal, or oblique, or in whatever object, the axiom concerning it holds equally true.

As does the other of every particular extension, it matters not whether line, surface, or solid, whether of this or that magnitude or figure.

12. By observing how ideas become general, we may the better judge how words are made so. And here it is to be noted that I do not deny absolutely there are *general ideas,* but only that there are any *abstract general ideas.* For in the passages above quoted, wherein there is mention of general ideas, it is always supposed that they are formed by abstraction, after the manner set forth in §§ 8 and 9. Now if we will annex a meaning to our words, and speak only of what we can conceive, I believe we shall acknowledge that an idea which, considered in itself, is particular, becomes general by being made to represent or stand for all other particular ideas of the same sort. To make this plain by an example. Suppose a geometrician is demonstrating the method of cutting a line in two equal parts. He draws, for instance, a black line of an inch in length; this, which in itself is a particular line, is nevertheless *with regard to its signification* general; since, as it is there used, it represents all particular lines whatsoever; so that what is demonstrated of it, is demonstrated of all lines, or, in other words, of a line in general. And, as *that particular line* becomes general, by being made a sign, so the *name* "line," which, taken absolutely, is particular, by being a sign is made general. And as the former owes its generality, not to its being the sign of an abstract or general line, but of all particular right lines that may possibly exist, so the latter must be thought to derive its generality from the same cause, namely, the various particular lines which it indifferently denotes.

13. To give the reader a yet clearer view of the nature of abstract ideas, and the uses they are thought necessary to, I shall add one more passage out of the *Essay on Human Understanding,* which is as follows: "Abstract ideas are not so obvious or easy to children or the yet unexercised mind as particular ones. If they seem so to grown men, it is only because by constant and familiar use they are made so. For when we nicely reflect upon them, we

shall find that general ideas are fictions and contrivances of the mind that carry difficulty with them, and do not so easily offer themselves as we are apt to imagine. For example, does it not require some pains and skill to form the general idea of a triangle (which is yet none of the most abstract, comprehensive and difficult); for it must be neither oblique nor rectangle, neither equilateral, equicrural, nor scalenon; but *all and none* of these at once. In effect, it is something imperfect that cannot exist; an idea wherein some parts of several different and *inconsistent* ideas are put together. It is true the mind in this imperfect state has need of such ideas, and makes all the haste to them it can, for the *conveniency of communication and enlargement of knowledge,* to both which it is naturally very much inclined. But yet one has reason to suspect such ideas are marks of our imperfection; at least this is enough to show that the most abstract and general ideas are not those that the mind is first and most easily acquainted with, nor such as its earliest knowledge is conversant about." (Book IV., ch. VII., § 9.) If any man has the faculty of framing in his mind such an idea of a triangle as is here described, it is in vain to pretend to dispute him out of it, nor would I go about it. All I desire is, that the reader would fully and certainly inform himself whether he has such an idea or no. And this, methinks, can be no hard task for any one to perform. What more easy than for any one to look a little into his own thoughts, and there try whether he has, or can attain to have, an idea that shall correspond with the description that is here given of the general idea of a triangle which is "neither oblique, nor rectangle, equilateral, equicrural, nor scalenon, but all and none of these at once"?

16. But here it will be demanded, how can we know any proposition to be true of all particular triangles, except we have first seen it demonstrated of the abstract idea of a triangle which equally agrees to all? For, because a property may be demonstrated to agree to some one particular triangle, it will not thence follow that it equally belongs to any other triangle, which in all re-

spects is not the same with it. For example, having demonstrated that the three angles of an isosceles rectangular triangle are equal to two right ones, I cannot therefore conclude this affection agrees to all other triangles which have neither a right angle, nor two equal sides. It seems therefore that, to be certain this proposition is universally true, we must either make a particular demonstration for every particular triangle, which is impossible, or once for all demonstrate it of the abstract idea of a triangle, in which all the particulars do indifferently partake, and by which they are all equally represented. To which I answer, that though the idea I have in view whilst I make the demonstration, be, for instance, that of an isosceles rectangular triangle, whose sides are of a determinate length, I may nevertheless be certain it extends to all other rectilinear triangles, of what sort or bigness soever. And that, because neither the right angle, nor the equality, nor determinate length of the sides, are at all concerned in the demonstration. It is true, the diagram I have in view includes all these particulars; but then there is not the least mention made of *them* in the proof of the proposition. It is not said the three angles are equal to two right ones because one of them is a right angle, or because the sides comprehending it are of the same length. Which sufficiently shows that the right angle might have been oblique, and the sides unequal, and for all that the demonstration have held good. And for this reason it is, that I conclude that to be true of any obliquangular or scalenon, which I had demonstrated of a particular right-angled equicrural triangle, and not because I demonstrated the proposition of the abstract idea of a triangle. And here it must be acknowledged that a man may *consider* a figure merely as triangular, without attending to the particular qualities of the angles, or relations of the sides. *So far he may abstract.* But this will never prove that he can frame an abstract general inconsistent *idea* of a triangle. In like manner we may consider Peter so far forth as man, or so far forth as animal, without framing the forementioned abstract idea, either of man or of animal; inasmuch as all that is perceived is not considered.

18. I come now to consider the *source* of this prevailing notion, and that seems to me to be *language*. And surely nothing of less extent than reason itself could have been the source of an opinion so universally received. The truth of this appears, as from other reasons, so also from the plain confession of the ablest patrons of abstract ideas, who acknowledge that they are made in order to naming; from which it is clear consequence, that if there had been no such thing as speech or universal signs, there never had been any thought of abstraction. See Book III, Ch. VI, § 39, and elsewhere, of the *Essay on Human Understanding*. Let us therefore examine the manner wherein Words have contributed to the origin of that mistake.—First, then, it is thought that every name has, or ought to have, one only precise and settled signification; which inclines men to think there are certain abstract, determinate ideas, that constitute the true and only immediate signification of each general name; and that it is by the mediation of these abstract ideas that a general name comes to signify any particular thing. Whereas, in truth, there is no such thing as one precise and definite signification annexed to any general name, they all signifying indifferently a great number of particular ideas. All which does evidently follow from what has been already said, and will clearly appear to any one by a little reflection. To this it will be objected, that every name that has a definition is thereby restrained to one certain signification. For example, a triangle is defined to be "a plain surface comprehended by three right lines"; by which that name is limited to denote one certain idea and no other. To which I answer, that in the definition it is not said whether the surface be great or small, black or white, nor whether the sides are long or short, equal or unequal, nor with what angles they are inclined to each other; in all which there may be great variety, and consequently there is no one settled idea which limits the signification of the word triangle. It is one thing to keep a name constantly to the same *definition,* and another to make it stand every where for the same *idea:* the one is necessary, the other useless and impracticable.

19. But, to give a farther account how words came to produce the doctrine of abstract ideas, it must be observed that it is a received opinion that language has no other end but the communicating ideas, and that every significant name stands for an idea. This being so, and it being withal certain that names, which yet are not thought altogether insignificant, do not always mark out particular conceivable ideas, it is straightway concluded that they stand for abstract notions. That there are many names in use amongst speculative men which do not always suggest to others determinate particular ideas, or, in truth, any thing at all, is what nobody will deny. And little attention will discover that it is not necessary (even in the strictest reasonings) that significant names which stand for ideas should, every time they are used, excite in the understanding the ideas they are made to stand for: in reading and discoursing, names being, for the most part, used as letters are in Algebra, in which, though a particular quantity be marked by each letter, yet to proceed right it is not requisite that in every step each letter suggest to your thoughts that particular quantity it was appointed to stand for.

20. Besides, the communicating of ideas marked by words is not the chief and only end of language, as is commonly supposed. There are other ends, as the raising of some passion, the exciting to, or deterring from an action, the putting the mind in some particular disposition; to which the former is, in many cases, barely subservient, and sometimes entirely omitted, when these can be obtained without it, as I think doth not infrequently happen in the familiar use of language. I entreat the reader to reflect with himself, and see if it doth not often happen, either in hearing or reading a discourse, that the passions of fear, love, hatred, admiration, and disdain, and the like, arise immediately in his mind upon the perception of certain words, without any ideas coming between. At first, indeed, the words might have occasioned ideas that were fitting to produce those emotions; but, if I mistake not, it will be found that when language is once grown familiar, the hearing of the sounds or sight of the characters is oft

immediately attended with those passions, which at first were wont to be produced by the intervention of ideas, that are now quite omitted. May we not, for example, be affected with the promise of a *good thing,* though we have not an idea of what it is? Or is not the being threatened with danger sufficient to excite a dread, though we think not of any particular evil likely to befall us, nor yet frame to ourselves an idea of danger in abstract? If any one shall join ever so little reflection of his own to what has been said, I believe that it will evidently appear to him, that general names are often used in the propriety of language without the speaker's designing them for marks of ideas in his own which he would have them raise in the mind of the hearer. Even proper names themselves do not seem always spoken with a design to bring into our view the ideas of those individuals that are supposed to be marked by them. For example, when a schoolman tells me, "Aristotle hath said it," all I conceive he means by it is to dispose me to embrace his opinion with the deference and submission which custom has annexed to that name. And this effect may be so instantly produced in the minds of those who are accustomed to resign their judgment to the authority of that philosopher, as it is impossible any idea either of his person, writings, or reputation, should go before. Innumerable examples of this kind may be given, but why should I insist on those things which every one's experience will, I doubt not, plentifully suggest unto him?]

BERKELEY'S ATTACK ON LOCKE'S DOCTRINE OF ABSTRACT general ideas is another famous chapter in the history of the problem of universals. As we have seen, Locke seems to have held three different and inconsistent views as to how abstract general ideas are formed. In this passage Berkeley attacks the latter two of these, namely: (1) The view that abstract general ideas of, e.g., color or humanity, are formed by *leaving out* of the "ideas" of various colors or of various human beings all those qualities which are not common to all colors or to all human beings. (2) The view that an abstract general idea, e.g., of a triangle, is formed by *conflating* all the properties possessed by any triangle whatsoever.

Berkeley does not distinguish these two radically different theories; nor is he required to, since he regards them both as false on exactly the same grounds, namely that it is totally impossible to form any such ideas. He destroys the first doctrine by pointing out that any idea that we form of color must be of some particular color; to take a particular shade of blue and one of red, and then to think away their hues altogether, leaves us with nothing at all before the mind's eye; so, too, any idea of man must be of some particular man, i.e., must be of a determinate height, determinate color, etc.; as to the other doctrine, the conflated idea, e.g., of a triangle proposed by Locke, is self-contradictory, for it contains within itself inconsistent properties, e.g., of being at once equilateral and rectangular, scalene, etc.

This refutation is echoed even more convincingly in the relevant passage in the *Principles*. Berkeley is relying on the doctrine of the "inner eye." The only "ideas" (other than those of introspection) that can be in the mind, are ideas of sense, or else images which are compounded out of ideas of sense. The "inner eye" can perceive only such entities as can be perceived by the normal outer eye, namely, objects with absolutely *determinate* properties—a specific shade of blue, a specific oval shape, a particular fluty sound, etc. So far so good. But those who hold that the problem of universals is a problem as to the mental machinery by which we recognize an object as belonging to a certain kind or type (or think in general terms about all the members of a particular class) tend to find Berkeley's own positive answer to the problem no better than Locke's. According to Berkeley we do form an image of a particular triangle, or of man, say, Peter, but consider that image not for what it is in itself, but as representing all triangles, or all men. But how can we do this unless we already know which characteristics are possessed by all triangles or men as such, and which are merely peculiar to this sample, that is to say, unless we already possess a general idea of triangle or man? How can we do what Berkeley commands us—to "consider Peter so far forth as man,"—without already having a general idea of man distinguishable from Peter?

Berkeley's positive doctrine about the function of general words and universals is open to objections, and his refutation looks more convincing than it is. For it seems to be the case that most people's images are *not* always fully determinate, but often thin, vague and schematic; and that we can in fact form blurred composite images in which many inconsistent properties coexist in a confused fashion. And it might further be added that the role of images—for this is what "ideas" in Berkeley seem to denote—is much exaggerated. In order to recognize an object as being of a certain type, we do not have to carry about a mental sample, a piece of mental furniture, either a concept or a representative image, with which real objects have to be matched. Comparison with some standard sample "in the mind" is not necessary, and indeed such processes are seldom carried out. If it were necessary each time we identified an object to match it against the standard object we carry about with us, then in order to recognize the standard itself as the relevant one, while we rummaged in our minds to extract it, we would have to match it, in its turn, with another standard, and so on ad infinitum. The problem of recognition and classification is not to be resolved in this way. The problem of universals is a logical problem. How do general words mean? Do they mean in a fashion different from proper names, or from other kinds of words? Such a logical problem is not to be solved by appeal to introspection to determine whether we do or do not form schematic or composite images.

But in the course of discussing the problem in apparently psychological terms, Berkeley does expose one of the great sources of the philosophical puzzle about universals, namely the so-called *unum nomen, unum nominatum* fallacy. And this is a major achievement in the history of philosophy, one for which alone he would deserve eternal fame. It is a naïve, but very natural, assumption that in order to have a meaning a word must "stand for" or designate an object in the real world. This is true of some words, for instance of proper names: "George Berkeley" is only significant because it designates a particular being. But do general terms designate in this "one-to-one" way? The word "bishop" obviously does not designate one unique being; what then does it stand for? It is clear that general terms do not designate particular objects; hence entities called "universals" are invented to be the objective counterparts of general words. But this will not work. Proper names may be like caps designed to fit particular heads, but they are not typical of words in general. General words do not *name* at all. Their function in language is different. Certainly they have meanings; but to have a meaning is not to stand in a one-to-one relation to any entity—whether a real object or a more shadowy one called "a meaning."

And Berkeley's genius is further shown in this: philosophers have been constantly misled by the assumption that the descriptive (and its most exact species, the scientific) use of language is its primary, if not only, use. They are constantly tempted to construe mathematical, ethical or aesthetic judgments as descriptions. Descriptions of what? While they may ultimately turn out to be descriptive, in some sense, they obviously do not resemble typical scientific descriptions of the everyday world; so they are taken to be descriptions of some other world, populated by "pure mathematical concepts," or "values," or the like. And this leads to the assumption of many strange worlds. Berkeley is one of the first philosophers to point out that language is used for many purposes besides that of describing; and that to look for objective counterparts in the same sense, to all varieties of sentences, leads to many fertile inventions of fictional entities, and conceals plain facts under a rich mythology. This too is an intellectual service of the first order.

The following is from *Of the Principles of Human Knowledge;* Part I.

{ 1. It is evident to any one who takes a survey of the *objects of human knowledge*, that they are either *ideas* actually imprinted on the senses, or else such as are perceived by attending to the passions and operations of the mind; or lastly, *ideas* formed by help of memory and imagination, either compounding, dividing, or barely representing those originally perceived in the aforesaid ways. By sight I have the ideas of light and colours with their several degrees and variations. By touch I perceive hard and soft, heat and cold, motion and resistance; and of all these more and less either as to quantity or degree. Smelling furnishes me with odours; the palate with tastes; and hearing conveys sounds to the mind in all their variety of tone and composition. And as several of these are observed to accompany each other, they come to be marked by one name, and so to be reputed as one *thing*. Thus, for example, a certain colour, taste, smell, figure, and consistence having been observed to go together, are accounted one distinct thing, signified by the name "apple"; other collections of ideas constitute a stone, a tree, a book, and the like sensible things; which, as they are pleasing or disagreeable, excite the passions of love, hatred, joy, grief, and so forth.

2. But besides all that endless variety of ideas or objects of knowledge, there is likewise *something* which knows or perceives them, and exercises divers operations, as willing, imagining, remembering, about them. This perceiving, active being is what I call *mind, spirit, soul,* or *myself.* By which words I do not denote any one of my ideas, but a thing entirely distinct from them, wherein they exist, or, which is the same thing, whereby they are perceived; for the existence of an idea consists in being perceived.

3. That neither our thoughts, nor passions, nor ideas formed by the imagination, exist without the mind, is what every body will allow. And to me it seems no less evident that the various sensations or ideas imprinted on the Sense, however blended or combined together (that is, whatever objects they compose), cannot exist otherwise than in a mind perceiving them. I think an intuitive knowledge may be obtained of this, by any one that shall attend to what is

meant by the term "exist," when applied to sensible things. The table I write on, I say, exists; that is, I see and feel it: and if I were out of my study I should say it existed; meaning thereby that if I was in my study I might perceive it, or that some other spirit actually does perceive it. There was an odour, that is, it was smelt; there was a sound, that is, it was heard; a colour or figure, and it was perceived by sight or touch. This is all that I can understand by these and the like expressions. For as to what is said of the *absolute* existence of unthinking things without any relation to their being perceived, that is to me perfectly unintelligible. Their *esse* is *percipi;* nor is it possible they should have any existence out of the minds or thinking things which perceive them.

4. It is indeed an opinion strangely prevailing amongst men that houses, mountains, rivers, and in a word all sensible objects have an existence natural or real, distinct from their being perceived by the understanding. But with how great an assurance and acquiescence soever this Principle may be entertained in the world, yet whoever shall find in his heart to call it in question, may, if I mistake not, perceive it to involve a manifest contradiction. For what are the forementioned objects but the things we perceive by sense? and what do we perceive besides our own ideas or sensations? and is it not plainly repugnant that any one of these or any combination of them should exist unperceived?

5. If we thoroughly examine this tenet, it will, perhaps, be found at bottom to depend on the doctrine of *abstract ideas*. For can there be a nicer strain of abstraction than to distinguish the existence of sensible objects from their being perceived, so as to conceive them existing unperceived? Light and colours, heat and cold, extension and figures—in a word the things we see and feel—what are they but so many sensations, notions, ideas, or impressions on the sense? and is it possible to separate, even in thought, any of these from perception? For my part I might as easily divide a thing from itself. I may indeed divide in my thoughts or conceive apart from each other those things which, perhaps, I never perceived by sense so divided.

Thus I imagine the trunk of a human body without the limbs, or conceive the smell of a rose without thinking on the rose itself. So far I will not deny I can abstract; if that may properly be called "abstraction," which extends only to the conceiving separately such objects as it is possible may really exist or be actually perceived asunder. But my conceiving or imagining power does not extend beyond the possibility of real existence or perception. Hence as it is impossible for me to see or feel any thing without an actual sensation of that thing, so is it impossible for me to conceive in my thoughts any sensible thing or object distinct from the sensation or perception of it.

6. Some truths there are so near and obvious to the mind that a man need only open his eyes to see them. Such I take this important one to be, viz., that all the choir of heaven and furniture of the earth, in a word all those bodies which compose the mighty frame of the world, have not any subsistence without a mind; that their being is to be perceived or known; that consequently so long as they are not actually perceived by me, or do not exist in my mind or that of any other created spirit, they must either have no existence at all, or else subsist in the mind of some Eternal Spirit: it being perfectly unintelligible and involving all the absurdity of abstraction to attribute to any single part of them an existence independent of a spirit. To be convinced of which, the reader need only reflect and try to separate in his own thoughts the *being* of a sensible thing from its *being perceived*.

7. From what has been said it is evident there is not any other Substance than Spirit, or that which perceives. But for the fuller proof of this point, let it be considered the sensible qualities are colour, figure, motion, smell, taste, and such like, that is the ideas perceived by sense. Now for an idea to exist in an unperceiving thing is a manifest contradiction; for to have an idea is all one as to perceive: that therefore wherein colour, figure, and the like qualities exist, must perceive them; hence it is clear there can be no unthinking substance or *substratum* of those ideas.

8. But, say you, though the ideas themselves do not exist without the mind, yet there may be things like them whereof they are copies or resemblances; which things exist without the mind, in an unthinking substance. I answer, an idea can be like nothing but an idea; a colour or figure can be like nothing but another colour or figure. If we look but never so little into our thoughts, we shall find it impossible for us to conceive a likeness except only between our ideas. Again, I ask whether those supposed *originals* or external things, of which our ideas are the pictures or representations, be themselves perceivable or no? If they are, then *they* are ideas, and we have gained our point: but if you say they are not, I appeal to any one whether it be sense, to assert a colour is like something which is invisible; hard or soft, like something which is intangible; and so of the rest.

9. Some there are who make a distinction betwixt *primary* and *secondary* qualities: by the former, they mean extension, figure, motion, rest, solidity or impenetrability, and number; by the latter they denote all other sensible qualities, as colours, sounds, tastes, and so forth. The ideas we have of these last they acknowledge not to be the resemblances of any things existing without the mind or unperceived; but they will have our ideas of the *primary qualities* to be patterns or images of things which exist without the mind, in an unthinking substance which they call Matter. By Matter therefore we are to understand an inert, senseless substance, in which extension, figure, and motion do actually subsist. But it is evident, from what we have already shown, that extension, figure, and motion are only ideas existing in the mind, and that an idea can be like nothing but another idea; and that consequently neither they nor their archetypes can exist in an unperceiving substance. Hence it is plain that the very notion of what is called *Matter,* or *corporeal substance,* involves a contradiction in it.

10. They who assert that figure, motion, and the rest of the primary or original qualities do exist without the mind, in unthinking substances, do at the same time ac-

knowledge that colours, sounds, heat, cold, and such like secondary qualities, do not; which they tell us are sensations existing in the mind alone, that depend on and are occasioned by the different size, texture, and motion of the minute particles of matter. This they take for an undoubted truth, which they can demonstrate beyond all exception. Now if it be certain, that those *original* qualities are inseparably united with the other sensible qualities, and not, even in thought, capable of being abstracted from them, it plainly follows that *they* exist only in the mind. But I desire any one to reflect and try whether he can, by any abstraction of thought, conceive the extension and motion of a body without all other sensible qualities. For my own part, I see evidently that it is not in my power to frame an idea of a body extended and moving but I must withal give it some colour or other sensible quality which is acknowledged to exist only in the mind. In short, extension, figure, and motion, abstracted from all other qualities, are inconceivable. Where therefore the other sensible qualities are, there must these be also, to wit, in the mind and nowhere else.

14. I shall further add that after the same manner as modern philosophers prove certain sensible qualities to have no existence in Matter, or without the mind, the same thing may be likewise proved of all other sensible qualities whatsoever. Thus, for instance, it is said that heat and cold are affections only of the mind, and not at all patterns of real beings, existing in the corporeal substances which excite them; for that the same body which appears cold to one hand, seems warm to another. Now why may we not as well argue that figure and extension are not patterns or resemblances of qualities existing in Matter, because to the same eye at different stations, or eyes of a different texture at the same station, they appear various, and cannot therefore be the images of any thing settled and determinate without the mind? Again, it is proved that sweetness is not really in the sapid thing, because, the thing remaining unaltered, the sweetness is changed into

bitter, as in case of a fever or otherwise vitiated palate. Is it not as reasonable to say that motion is not without the mind; since if the succession of ideas in the mind becomes swifter, the motion, it is acknowledged, shall appear slower without any alteration in any external object.

18. But though it were possible that solid, figured, moveable substances may exist without the mind, corresponding to the ideas we have of bodies, yet how is it possible for us to know this? Either we must know it by Sense, or by Reason. As for our senses, by them we have the knowledge only of our sensations, ideas, or those things that are immediately perceived by sense, call them what you will: but they do not inform us that things exist without the mind, or unperceived, like to those which are perceived. This the materialists themselves acknowledge.—It remains therefore that if we have any knowledge at all of external things, it must be by reason inferring their existence from what is immediately perceived by sense. But (I do not see) what reason can induce us to believe the existence of bodies without the mind, from what we perceive, since the very patrons of Matter themselves do not pretend there is any necessary connexion betwixt them and our ideas. I say, it is granted on all hands (and what happens in dreams, frenzies, and the like, puts it beyond dispute) that it is possible we might be affected with all the ideas we have now, though no bodies existed without, resembling them. Hence it is evident the supposition of external bodies is not necessary for the producing our ideas; since it is granted they are produced sometimes, and might possibly be produced always, in the same order we see them in at present, without their concurrence.

19. But though we might possibly have all our sensations without them, yet perhaps it may be thought easier to conceive and explain the manner of their production by supposing external bodies in their likeness rather than otherwise; and so it might be at least probable there are such things as bodies that excite their ideas in our minds. But neither can this be said. For though we give the ma-

terialists their external bodies, they, by their own confession, are never the nearer knowing how our ideas are produced; since they own themselves unable to comprehend in what manner body can act upon spirit, or how it is possible it should imprint any idea in the mind. Hence it is evident the production of ideas or sensations in our minds can be no reason why we should suppose Matter or corporeal substances; since that is acknowledged to remain equally inexplicable with or without this supposition. If therefore it were possible for bodies to exist without the mind, yet to hold they do so must-needs be a very precarious opinion; since it is to suppose, without any reason at all, that God has created innumerable beings that are entirely useless, and serve to no manner of purpose.

20. In short, if there were external bodies, it is impossible we should ever come to know it; and if there were not, we might have the very same reasons to think there were that we have now. Suppose—what no one can deny possible—an intelligence, without the help of external bodies, to be affected with the same train of sensations or ideas that you are, imprinted in the same order and with like vividness in his mind. I ask whether that intelligence hath not all the reason to believe the existence of Corporeal Substances, represented by his ideas, and exciting them in his mind, that you can possibly have for believing the same thing? Of this there can be no question. Which one consideration were enough to make any reasonable person suspect the strength of whatever arguments he may think himself to have for the existence of bodies without the mind.

24. It is very obvious, upon the least inquiry into our own thoughts, to know whether it be possible for us to understand what is meant by the *absolute existence of sensible objects in themselves* or *without the mind*. To me it is evident those words mark out either a direct contradiction, or else nothing at all. And to convince others of this, I know no readier or fairer way than to entreat they

would calmly attend to their own thoughts; and if by this attention the emptiness or repugnancy of those expressions does appear, surely nothing more is requisite for their conviction. It is on this therefore that I insist, to wit, that the *absolute existence of unthinking things* are words without a meaning, or which include a contradiction. This is what I repeat and inculcate, and earnestly recommend to the attentive thoughts of the reader.

25. All our ideas, sensations, notions, or the things which we perceive, by whatsoever names they may be distinguished, are visibly inactive: there is nothing of power or agency included in them. So that one idea or object of thought cannot produce, or make any alteration in another. To be satisfied of the truth of this, there is nothing else requisite but a bare observation of our ideas. For since they and every part of them exist only in the mind, it follows that there is nothing in them but what is perceived: but whoever shall attend to his ideas, whether of sense or reflection, will not perceive in them any power or activity; there is therefore no such thing contained in them. A little attention will discover to us that the very being of an idea implies passiveness and inertness in it; insomuch that it is impossible for an idea to do any thing, or, strictly speaking, to be the cause of any thing: neither can it be the resemblance or pattern of any active being, as is evident from sect. 8. Whence it plainly follows that extension, figure and motion, cannot be the cause of our sensations. To say, therefore, that these are the effects of powers resulting from the configuration, number, motion, and size of corpuscles, must certainly be false.

26. We perceive a continual succession of ideas; some are anew excited, others are changed or totally disappear. There is, therefore, *some* cause of these ideas whereon they depend, and which produces and changes them. That this cause cannot be any quality or idea or combination of *ideas,* is clear from the preceding section. It must therefore be a *substance;* but it has been shown that there is no corporeal or material substance: it remains therefore that the cause of ideas is an incorporeal active substance or Spirit.

29. But whatever power I may have over my own thoughts, I find the ideas actually perceived by Sense have not a like dependence on *my* will. When in broad daylight I open my eyes, it is not in my power to choose whether I shall see or no, or to determine what particular objects shall present themselves to my views: and so likewise as to the hearing and other senses; the ideas imprinted on them are not creatures of *my* will. There is therefore some other Will or Spirit that produces them.

30. The ideas of Sense are more strong, lively, and distinct than those of the Imagination; they have likewise a steadiness, order and coherence, and are not excited at random, as those which are the effects of human wills often are, but in a regular train or series—the admirable connexion whereof sufficiently testifies the wisdom and benevolence of its Author. Now the set rules or established methods, wherein the Mind we depend on excites in us the ideas of Sense, are called *the laws of nature;* and these we learn by experience, which teaches us that such and such ideas are attended with such and such other ideas, in the ordinary course of things.

33. The ideas imprinted on the Senses by the Author of nature are called *real things:* and those excited in the imagination, being less regular, vivid, and constant, are more properly termed *ideas,* or *images of* things, which they copy and represent. But then our *sensations,* be they never so vivid and distinct, are nevertheless ideas: that is, they exist in the mind, or are perceived by it, as truly as the ideas of its own framing. The ideas of Sense are allowed to have more reality in them, that is, to be more strong, orderly, and coherent than the creatures of the mind; but this is no argument that they exist without the mind. They are also less dependent on the spirit, or thinking substance which perceives them, in that they are excited by the will of another and more powerful Spirit: yet still they are *ideas,* and certainly no idea, whether faint or strong, can exist otherwise than in a mind perceiving it.

35. I do not argue against the existence of any one thing that we can apprehend, either by sense or reflection. That the things I see with my eyes and touch with my hands do exist, really exist, I make not the least question. The only thing whose existence we deny, is that which *philosophers* call Matter or corporeal substance. And in doing of this, there is no damage done to the rest of mankind, who, I dare say, will never miss it. The Atheist indeed will want the colour of an empty name to support his impiety; and the Philosophers may possibly find they have lost a great handle for trifling and disputation.

36. If any man thinks this detracts from the existence or reality of things, he is very far from understanding what hath been premised in the plainest terms I could think of. Take here an abstract of what has been said:—There are spiritual substances, minds, or human souls, which will or excite ideas in themselves at pleasure; but these are faint, weak and unsteady in respect of others they perceive by sense: which being impressed upon them according to certain rules or laws of nature, speak themselves the effects of a Mind more powerful and wise than human spirits. These latter are said to have *more reality* in them than the former;—by which is meant that they are affecting, orderly, and distinct, and that they are not fictions of the mind perceiving them. And in this sense the sun that I see by day is the real sun, and that which I imagine by night is the idea of the former. In the sense here given of *reality,* it is evident that every vegetable, star, mineral, and in general each part of the mundane system, is as much a *real being* by our principles as by any other. Whether others mean any thing by the term *reality* different from what I do, I entreat them to look into their own thoughts and see.

37. It will be urged that thus much at least is true, to wit, that we take away all *corporeal substances.* To this my answer is, that if the word *substance* be taken in the vulgar sense, for a *combination* of sensible qualities, such as extension, solidity, weight, and the like—this we cannot be accused of taking away: but if it be taken in a philosophic

sense, for the support of accidents or qualities without the mind—then indeed I acknowledge that we take it away, if one may be said to take away that which never had an existence, not even in the imagination.

38. But, after all, say you, it sounds very harsh to say we eat and drink ideas, and are clothed with ideas. I acknowledge it does so—the word *idea* not being used in common discourse to signify the several combinations of sensible qualities, which are called *things;* and it is certain that any expression which varies from the familiar use of language will seem harsh and ridiculous. But this doth not concern the truth of the proposition, which in other words is no more than to say we are fed and clothed with those things which we perceive immediately by our senses. The hardness or softness, the colour, taste, warmth, figure, and such like qualities, which combined together constitute the several sorts of victuals and apparel, have been shown to exist only in the mind that perceives them: and this is all that is meant by calling them *ideas;* which word, if it was as ordinarily used as *thing,* would sound no harsher nor more ridiculous than it. I am not for disputing about the propriety, but the truth of the expression. If therefore you agree with me that we eat, and drink, and are clad with the immediate objects of sense, which cannot exist unperceived or without the mind, I shall readily grant it is more proper or conformable to custom that they should be called *things* rather than *ideas.*

39. If it be demanded why I make use of the word *idea,* and do not rather in compliance with custom call them *things,* I answer, I do it for two reasons:—First because the term *thing,* in contradistinction to *idea,* is generally supposed to denote somewhat existing without the mind: Secondly, because *thing* hath a more comprehensive signification than *idea,* including spirits, or thinking things, as well as ideas. Since therefore the objects of sense exist only in the mind, and are withal thoughtless and inactive, I chose to mark them by the word *idea;* which implies those properties.

40. But, say what we can, some one perhaps may be

apt to reply, he will still believe his senses, and never suffer
any arguments, how plausible soever, to prevail over the
certainty of them. Be it so; assert the evidence of sense as
high as you please, we are willing to do the same. That
what I see, hear, and feel doth exist, that is to say, is perceived by me, I no more doubt than I do of my own being.
But I do not see how the testimony of sense can be alleged
as a proof for the existence of any thing which is *not*
perceived by sense. We are not for having any man turn
sceptic, and disbelieve his senses; on the contrary, we give
them all the stress and assurance imaginable; nor are there
any principles more opposite to Scepticism than those we
have laid down, as shall be hereafter clearly shown.

52. In the ordinary affairs of life, any phrases may be
retained, so long as they excite in us proper sentiments, or
dispositions to act in such a manner as is necessary for our
well-being, how false soever they may be, if taken in a
strict and speculative sense. Nay, this is unavoidable, since
propriety being regulated by custom, language is suited to
the received opinions, which are not always the truest.
Hence it is impossible—even in the most rigid philosophic
reasonings—so far to alter the bent and genius of the
tongue we speak, as never to give a handle for cavillers to
pretend difficulties and inconsistencies. But a fair and in-
genuous reader will collect the sense from the scope and
tenor and connexion of a discourse, making allowances for
those inaccurate modes of speech which use has made inevitable.

140. In a large sense indeed, we may be said to have
an idea, or rather a notion of *spirit,* that is we understand
the meaning of the word, otherwise we could not affirm
or deny any thing of it. Moreover, as we conceive the
ideas that are in the minds of other spirits by means of
our own, which we suppose to be resemblances of them, so
we know other spirits by means of our own soul; which in
that sense is the image or idea of them; it having a like
respect to other spirits that blueness or heat by me perceived has to those ideas perceived by another.]

BERKELEY'S REFUTATION OF LOCKE'S VIEWS OF PERCEP-
tion, of material objects, of universals, and of the general
function of language, have become a permanent element in
the development of European philosophy. Yet taken literally, at its face value, what Berkeley here says about "our
knowledge of the external world" seemed to his readers
quite absurd; it seemed (despite his constant protestations
to the contrary) to lead to an ontology about as far removed as it is possible to be from the ontology of common sense. For Berkeley appears to deny the existence in
the universe of anything except minds and "ideas" in those
minds. What we ordinarily call apples and trees and desks
are not objects existing in their own right, external to and
independent of minds; rather they are certain sorts of collections of ideas in minds.

Berkeley's "idealist" theory of perception is the logical
terminus to which a combination of the subjectivist and
"egocentric" starting point of Descartes's theory of knowledge with the empiricism of Locke, must lead. Locke had
arrived at an impasse with regard to our knowledge of the
external world, a combination of two mutually inconsistent
and individually untenable theories of perception, the
"causal" and the "representative." According to Locke we
are acquainted only with our own ideas, which are "in"
our minds. Some of these are ideas of secondary qualities,
some of primary qualities. The former have only a causal
relation to anything "in" external bodies; they are caused
by the primary qualities of the minute particles of these
bodies. The latter are also caused by qualities in those
bodies; but, more than this, they resemble qualities in those
bodies. But if all that we can ever come to be acquainted
with are ideas, how can we know anything at all about
qualities in bodies, which are not ideas? How can we know
either that they cause our ideas, or that in some cases
they resemble them? Once Berkeley pointed out that this
was impossible, it became plain to everyone: the existence
of external bodies and their qualities was seen to be a
hypothesis, for or against which we could not—logically

could not, on Locke's empiricist premises—have any means of collecting evidence.

Locke in fact, like every "representationalist," is forever penned within the circle of his own ideas—a fact which comes out clearly in his account of knowledge in Book IV. But there is yet another facet of his theory of the external world which excites Berkeley to violent attack, namely the supposed existence of material substance, the substratum, the "something-I-know-not-what" totally devoid of qualities underlying each material object; this also, Berkeley rightly claims, is a hypothesis in principle unverifiable (and unjustifiable).

Berkeley's arguments are of very unequal merit.[1] For example, the arguments in the beginning of the *Principles*, which appear to lead directly to the paradoxical ontology discussed above, rest upon a misleading use of the phrases "to perceive," "to *have* an idea," "to be *in* the mind," and some others. Berkeley talks of "in the mind" and "without the mind" as if these were two distinct but co-ordinate regions in which entities could be located (only it so happens that none are located in the latter), much as a point on the surface óf the earth can be located in the northern or the southern hemisphere. At the same time, the argument is further bedeviled by the old metaphysical dogma, which had been taken for granted by Locke, that a quality must exist "in" a substance, like a pin in a pincushion. The preposition "in" has proved exceedingly treacherous in the history of philosophy: in this case the combination of an unperceived false analogy with the spatial use of "in" plus an uncriticized metaphysical use of the same word, leads to a perpetuation of the confusions which Berkeley's arguments are meant to eliminate. Nevertheless the crucial point

[1] The very number and variety of his arguments (of which only some are quoted in the text above), all used to prove, if not exactly the same point, very closely related points, is, in itself, suspicious. If a philosophical question of the sort with which Berkeley is dealing is clearly formulated, then, to demonstrate conclusively the truth of one answer to it, we should not require a string of different arguments, any more than we need a string of different proofs for one theorem in mathematics.

—that some of the most frustrating perplexities of philosophy can be traced to ambiguities and false analogies in the use of apparently innocent words—owes much to Berkeley's new approach; the word "in" is among the worst offenders: and the unconscious assumption that "in the mind" is somehow similar to "in the box" or "in the country" (and not "in my view" or "in general") has brought about some of the darkest hours of philosophy.

On the other hand, the arguments, both in the *Principles* and in the *First Dialogue,* against Locke's representationalism are certainly valid. Berkeley disposes without difficulty of what seems to be Locke's position, in his doctrine of primary and secondary qualities, namely that the observed sizes, shapes, etc., of bodies do not vary with the condition and place of the observer, the intervening medium, etc., (which is untrue), whereas the sensed colors, smells, sounds and tastes alone do so; and that therefore the "ideas of the primary qualities" are copies of those qualities as they exist in bodies, while the "ideas of the secondary qualities" are not. Berkeley further points out that Locke's hypothesis of the existence of material substance is such that it is logically impossible that any evidence could be found for or against it, and that, consequently, the hypothesis itself is "words without a meaning." This has a very modern ring.

Having reduced objects to collections of ideas which exist only "in" (i.e., when perceived by) minds, Berkeley is now committed to saying either that objects go in and out of existence, according to whether a mind is perceiving the appropriate ideas or not, or else that all ideas are perceived at all times by some mind or minds. He chooses the latter alternative. The continued existence of objects is ensured by the continuous perceptions of God. If Berkeley's God were brought in solely to save his theory of the material world, He would constitute a hypothesis no better than Locke's material substratum. Berkeley claims that we can have no "idea" of such a chimera as Locke's "substance": but neither, according to him, have we any "idea" of a spirit; only "notions." What these are he does not clearly explain. But it is evident that God is the center of Berkeley's metaphysical vision: the universe depends on Him as Shakespeare's characters and their lives depend on Shakespeare. But this is not compatible with Berkeley's professed empiricism, and the introduction of God to rescue an otherwise untenable view of what material objects are, is illegitimate. Berkeley's empiricism is in any case not consistent. God not merely perceives all ideas: He is the *cause* of them. They are kept in being by God's volitions; and the regularity of events in nature is the regularity of the patterns of His volitions. Berkeley leaves the notion of cause and effect unanalyzed; it obtains its first empirical examination at the hands of Hume. For Berkeley, cause, as for many medieval philosophers, and indeed the ancients too, is construed by analogy with an act of the will.

The following is from *Three Dialogues Between Hylas and Philonous in Opposition to Sceptics and Atheists.*

[First Dialogue

Hyl. I frankly own, Philonous, that it is in vain to stand out any longer. Colours, sounds, tastes, in a word, all those termed *secondary qualities*, have certainly no existence without the mind. But by this acknowledgment I must not be supposed to derogate any thing from the reality of Matter or external objects; seeing it is no more than several philosophers maintain, who nevertheless are the farthest imaginable from denying Matter. For the clearer understanding of this, you must know sensible qualities are by philosophers divided into *Primary* and *Secondary*. The former are Extension, Figure, Solidity, Gravity, Motion, and Rest; and these they hold exist really in bodies. The latter are those above enumerated; or, briefly, *all sensible qualities beside the Primary*, which they assert are only so many sensations or ideas existing nowhere but in the mind. But all this, I doubt not, you are apprised of. For my part, I have been a long time sensible there was such an opinion current among philosophers, but was never thoroughly convinced of its truth until now.

Phil. You are still then of opinion that *extension* and *figure* are inherent in external unthinking substances?

Hyl. I am.

Phil. But what if the same arguments which are brought against Secondary Qualities will hold good against these also?

Hyl. Why then I shall be obliged to think they too exist only in the mind.

Phil. Is it your opinion, the very figure and extension which you perceive by sense exist in the outward object or material substance?

Hyl. It is.

Phil. Have all other animals as good grounds to think the same of the figure and extension which they see and feel?

Hyl. Without doubt, if they have any thought at all.

Phil. Answer me, Hylas. Think you the senses were bestowed upon all animals for their preservation and well-being in life? or were they given to men alone for this end?

Hyl. I make no question but they have the same use in all other animals.

Phil. If so, is it not necessary they should be enabled by them to perceive their own limbs, and those bodies which are capable of harming them?

Hyl. Certainly.

Phil. A mite therefore must be supposed to see his own foot, and things equal or even less than it, as bodies of some considerable dimension; though at the same time they appear to you scarce discernible, or at best as so many visible points?

Hyl. I cannot deny it.

Phil. And to creatures less than the mite they will seem yet large?

Hyl. They will.

Phil. Insomuch that what you can hardly discern will to another extremely minute animal appear as some huge mountain?

Hyl. All this I grant.

Phil. Can one and the same thing be at the same time in itself of different dimensions?

Hyl. That were absurd to imagine.

Phil. But from what you have laid down it follows that both the extension by you perceived, and that perceived by the mite itself, as likewise all those perceived by lesser animals, are each of them the true extension of the mite's foot; that is to say, by your own principles you are led into an absurdity.

Hyl. There seems to be some difficulty in the point.

Phil. Again, have you not acknowledged that no real inherent property of any object can be changed without some change in the thing itself?

Hyl. I have.

Phil. But as we approach to or recede from an object, the visible extension varies, being at one distance ten or a hundred times greater than at another. Doth it not therefore follow from hence likewise that it is not really inherent in the object?

Hyl. I own I am at a loss what to think.

Phil. Your judgment will soon be determined, if you will venture to think as freely concerning this quality as you have done concerning the rest. Was it not admitted as a good argument that neither heat nor cold was in the water, because it seemed warm to one hand and cold to the other?

Hyl. It was.

Phil. Is it not the very same reasoning to conclude there is no extension or figure in an object, because to one eye it shall seem little, smooth and round, when at the same time it appears to the other great, uneven and angular?

Hyl. The very same. But does this latter fact ever happen?

Phil. You may at any time make the experiment, by looking with one eye bare, and with the other through a microscope.

Hyl. I know not how to maintain it, and yet I am loath to give up *extension,* I see so many odd consequences following upon such a concession.

Phil. Odd, say you? After the concessions already made,

I hope you will stick at nothing for its oddness. But, on the other hand, should it not seem very odd, if the general reasoning which includes all other sensible qualities did not also include extension? If it be allowed that no idea nor any thing like an idea can exist in an unperceiving substance, then surely it follows that no figure or mode of extension which we can either perceive or imagine, or have any idea of, can be really inherent in Matter; not to mention the peculiar difficulty there must be in conceiving a material substance prior to and distinct from extension to be the *substratum* of extension. Be the sensible quality what it will—figure or sound, or colour; it seems alike impossible it should subsist in that which doth not perceive it.

Hyl. I give up the point for the present, reserving still a right to retract my opinion, in case I shall hereafter discover any false step in my progress to it.

Phil. That is a right you cannot be denied. Figures and extension being despatched, we proceed next to *motion*. Can a real motion in any external body be at the same time both very swift and very slow?

Hyl. It cannot.

Phil. Is not the motion of a body swift in a reciprocal proportion to the time it takes up in describing any given space? Thus a body that describes a mile in an hour moves three times faster than it would in case it described only a mile in three hours.

Hyl. I agree with you.

Phil. And is not time measured by the succession of ideas in our minds?

Hyl. It is.

Phil. And is it not possible ideas should succeed one another twice as fast in your mind as they do in mine, or that of some spirit of another kind?

Hyl. I own it.

Phil. Consequently the same body may to another seem to perform its motion over any space in half the time that it doth to you. And the same reasoning will hold as to any other proportion: that is to say, according to your principles (since the motions perceived are both really in the

object) it is possible one and the same body shall be really
moved the same way at once, both very swift and very
slow. How is this consistent either with common sense, or
with what you just now granted?

Hyl. I have nothing to say to it.

Phil. Then as for *solidity*; either you do not mean any
sensible quality by that word, and so it is beside our inquiry: or if you do, it must be either hardness or resistance. But both the one and the other are plainly relative
to our senses: it being evident that what seems hard to
one animal may appear soft to another, who hath greater
force and firmness of limbs. Nor is it less plain that the
resistance I feel is not in the body.

Hyl. I own the very *sensation* of resistance, which is
all you immediately perceive, is not in the body; but the
cause of that sensation is.

Phil. But the causes of our sensations are not things
immediately perceived, and therefore are not sensible. This
point I thought had been already determined.

Hyl. I own it was; but you will pardon me if I seem a
little embarrassed: I know not how to quit my old notions.

Phil. To help you out, do but consider that if *extension*
be once acknowledged to have no existence without the
mind, the same must necessarily be granted of motion,
solidity and gravity; since they all evidently suppose extension. It is therefore superfluous to inquire particularly
concerning each of them. In denying extension, you have
denied them all to have any real existence. . . .

. . . . . .

Phil. . . . if I understand you rightly, you say our ideas
do not exist without the mind, but that they are copies,
images, or representations of certain originals that do?

Hyl. You take me right.

Phil. They are then like external things?

Hyl. They are.

Phil. Have those things a stable and permanent nature
independent of our senses; or are they in a perpetual
change, upon our producing any motions in our bodies—
suspending, exerting, or altering our faculties or organs of
sense?

Hyl. Real things, it is plain, have a fixed and real nature, which remains the same, notwithstanding any change in our senses, or in the posture and motion of our bodies; which, indeed, may affect the ideas in our minds, but it were absurd to think they had the same effect on things existing without the mind.

Phil. How then is it possible that things perpetually fleeting and variable as our ideas should be copies or images of any thing fixed and constant? Or, in other words, since all sensible qualities, as size, figure, colour, &c., that is, our ideas, are continually changing upon every alteration in the distance, medium, or instruments of sensation; how can any determinate material objects be properly represented or painted forth by several distinct things each of which is so different from and unlike the rest? Or, if you say it resembles some one only of our ideas, how shall we be able to distinguish the true copy from all the false ones?

Hyl. I profess, Philonous, I am at a loss. I know not what to say to this.

Phil. But neither is this all. Which are material objects in themselves—perceptible or imperceptible?

Hyl. Properly and immediately nothing can be perceived but ideas. All material things therefore are in themselves insensible, and to be perceived only by our ideas.

Phil. Ideas then are sensible, and their archetypes or originals insensible?

Hyl. Right.

Phil. But how can that which is sensible be *like* that which is insensible? Can a real thing in itself *invisible* be like a *colour;* or a real thing which is not *audible,* be like a *sound?* In a word, can any thing be like a sensation or idea, but another sensation or idea?

Hyl. I must own, I think not.

Phil. Is it possible there should be any doubt on the point? Do you not perfectly know your own ideas?

Hyl. I know them perfectly; since what I do not perceive or know can be no part of my idea.

Phil. Consider therefore and examine them, and then tell me if there be any thing in them which can exist without the mind: or if you can conceive any thing like them existing without the mind.

Hyl. Upon inquiry, I find it is impossible for me to conceive or understand how any thing but an idea can be like an idea. And it is most evident that *no idea can exist without the mind.*

Phil. You are therefore by your principles forced to deny the *reality* of sensible things; since you made it to consist in an absolute existence exterior to the mind. That is to say, you are a downright sceptic. So I have gained my point, which was to show your principles led to Scepticism.

Hyl. For the present I am, if not entirely convinced, at least silenced.

The Third Dialogue

Phil. I assure you, Hylas, I do not pretend to frame any hypothesis at all. I am of a vulgar cast, simple enough to believe my senses, and leave things as I find them. To be plain, it is my opinion that the real things are those very things I see and feel, and perceive by my senses. These I know; and finding they answer all the necessities and purposes of life, have no reason to be solicitous about any other unknown beings. A piece of sensible bread, for instance, would stay my stomach better than ten thousand times as much of that insensible, unintelligible, real bread you speak of. It is likewise my opinion that colours and other sensible qualities are on the objects. I cannot for my life help thinking that snow is white and fire hot. You indeed, who by *snow* and *fire* mean certain external, unperceived, unperceiving substances, are in the right to deny whiteness or heat to be affections inherent in *them.* But I, who understand by those words the things I see and feel, am obliged to think like other folks. And, as I am no sceptic with regard to the nature of things, so neither am I as to their existence. That a thing should be really perceived by my senses, and at the same time not really exist, is to me a plain contradiction; since I cannot prescind or abstract, even in thought, the existence of a sensible thing from its being perceived. Wood, stones, fire-water, flesh, iron, and the like things, which I name and discourse of, are things that I know. And I should not have known them but that I perceived them by my senses; and things perceived by the senses are immediately perceived; and things immediately perceived are ideas; and ideas cannot exist without the mind; their existence therefore consists in being perceived; when therefore they are actually perceived, there can be no doubt of their existence. Away then with all that scepticism, all those ridiculous philosophical doubts. What a jest is it for a philosopher to question the existence of sensible things till he hath it proved to him from the veracity of God; or to pretend our knowledge in this point falls short of intuition or demonstration! I might as well doubt of my own being, as of the being of those things I actually see and feel.

Hyl. Not so fast, Philonous: you say you cannot conceive how sensible things should exist without the mind. Do you not?

Phil. I do.

Hyl. Supposing you were annihilated, cannot you conceive it possible that things perceivable by sense may still exist?

Phil. I can; but then it must be in another mind. When I deny sensible things an existence out of the mind, I do not mean my mind in particular, but all minds. Now, it is plain they have an existence exterior to my mind; since I find them by experience to be independent of it. There is therefore some other Mind wherein they exist, during the intervals between the times of my perceiving them: as likewise they did before my birth, and would do after my supposed annihilation. And as the same is true with regard to all other finite created spirits, it necessarily follows there is an *omnipresent, eternal Mind,* which knows and comprehends all things, and exhibits them to our view in such a manner, and according to such rules, as He Himself hath ordained, and are by us termed the *laws of nature.*

. . . . . .

Phil. I say in the first place that I do not deny the existence of material substance merely because I have no notion of it, but because the notion of it is inconsistent; or, in other words, because it is repugnant that there should be a notion of it. Many things, for aught I know, may exist, whereof neither I nor any other man hath or can have any idea or notion whatsoever. But then those things must be possible, that is, nothing inconsistent must be included in their definition. I say, secondly, that although we believe things to exist which we do not perceive, yet we may not believe that any particular thing exists without some reason for such belief: but I have no reason for believing the existence of Matter. I have no immediate intuition thereof: neither can I mediately from my sensations, ideas, notions, actions or passions, infer an unthinking, unperceiving, inactive Substance—either by probable deduction or necessary consequence. Whereas the being of Myself, that is, my own soul, mind, or thinking principle, I evidently know by reflection. You will forgive me if I repeat the same things in answer to the same objections. In the very notion or definition of *Material Substance,* there is included a manifest repugnance and inconsistency. But this cannot be said of the notion of Spirit. That ideas should exist in what doth not perceive, or be produced by what doth not act, is repugnant. But it is no repugnancy to say that a perceiving thing should be the subject of ideas, or an active thing the cause of them. It is granted we have neither an immediate evidence nor a demonstrative knowledge of the existence of other finite spirits; but it will not thence follow that such spirits are on a foot with material substances: if to suppose the one be inconsistent, and it be not inconsistent to suppose the other; if the one can be inferred by no argument, and there is a probability for the other; if we see signs and effects indicating distinct finite agents like ourselves, and see no sign or symptom whatever that leads to a rational belief of Matter. I say, lastly, that I have a notion of Spirit, though I have not, strictly speaking, an idea of it. I do not perceive it as an idea, or by means of an idea, but know it by reflection.

· · · · · ·

Phil. The ideas formed by the imagination are faint and indistinct; they have, besides, an entire dependence on the will. But the ideas perceived by sense, that is, real things, are more vivid and clear; and being imprinted on the mind by a spirit distinct from us, have not the like dependence on our will. There is therefore no danger of confounding these with the foregoing: and there is as little of confounding them with the visions of a dream, which are dim, irregular and confused. And though they should happen to be never so lively and natural, yet by their not being connected, and of a piece with the preceding and subsequent transactions of our lives, they might easily be distinguished from realities. In short, by whatever method you distinguish *things* from *chimeras* on your scheme, the same, it is evident, will hold also upon mine. For it must be, I presume, by some perceived difference; and I am not for depriving you of any one thing that you perceive.

Hyl. But still, Philonous, you hold, there is nothing in the world but spirits and ideas. And this, you must needs acknowledge, sounds very oddly.

Phil. I own the word *idea,* not being commonly used for *thing,* sounds something out of the way. My reason for using it was because a necessary relation to the mind is understood to be implied by that term; and it is now commonly used by philosophers to denote the immediate objects of the understanding. But however oddly the proposition may sound in words, yet it includes nothing so very strange or shocking in its sense; which in effect amounts to no more than this, to wit, that there are only things perceiving and things perceived; or that every unthinking being is necessarily, and from the very nature of its existence, perceived by some mind; if not by a finite created mind, yet certainly by the infinite mind of God, in whom "we live and move, and have our being." Is this as strange as to say the sensible qualities are not on the objects: or, that we cannot be sure of the existence of things, or know any thing of their real natures—though we both see and feel them, and perceive them by all our senses? . . .

. . . .

Hyl. What say you to this? Since, according to you, men judge of the reality of things by their senses, how can a man be mistaken in thinking the moon a plain lucid surface, about a foot in diameter; or a square tower, seen at a distance, round; or an oar, with one end in the water, crooked?

Phil. He is not mistaken with regard to the ideas he actually perceives, but in the inferences he makes from his present perceptions. Thus in the case of the oar, what he immediately perceives by sight is certainly crooked; and so far he is in the right. But if he thence conclude that upon taking the oar out of the water he shall perceive the same crookedness; or that it would affect his touch as crooked things are wont to do: in that he is mistaken. In like manner, if he shall conclude from what he perceives in one station that, in case he advances towards the moon or tower, he should still be affected with the like ideas, he is mistaken. But his mistake lies not in what he perceives immediately and at present (it being a manifest contradiction to suppose he should err in respect of that), but in the wrong judgment he makes concerning the ideas he apprehends to be connected with those immediately perceived: or concerning the ideas that, from what he perceives at present, he imagines would be perceived in other circumstances. The case is the same with regard to the Copernican system. We do not here perceive any motion of the earth: but it were erroneous thence to conclude that in case we were placed at as great a distance from that as we are now from the other planets, we should not then perceive its motion.

.   .   .   .   .   .

Phil. With all my heart: retain the word *Matter,* and apply it to the objects of sense, if you please, provided you do not attribute to them any subsistence distinct from their being perceived. I shall never quarrel with you for an expression. *Matter,* or *material substance,* are terms introduced by philosophers; and, as used by them, imply a sort of independency, or a subsistence distinct from being perceived by a mind: but are never used by common people; or, if ever, it is to signify the immediate objects of sense. One would think, therefore, so long as the names of all particular things, with the terms *sensible, substance, body, stuff,* and the like, are retained, the word *Matter* should be never missed in common talk. And in philosophical discourses it seems the best way to leave it quite out: since there is not perhaps any one thing that hath more favoured and strengthened the depraved bent of the mind towards Atheism, than the use of that general confused term.}

THERE ARE SEVERAL DOCTRINES OF IMPORTANCE, IN ADDI-tion to those discussed earlier, put forward in the crucial passages cited above—some fully developed, some merely adumbrated. There is the effective refutation of Locke's attempt to find a basis in empiricism for the distinction between primary and secondary qualities—the quantitative versus the qualitative aspect of objects. The distinction is evidently embedded in the thought of the great physicists: therefore it must be kept, and even made central. But the empirical evidence for all qualities is the same, namely sense perception: and the difference of status—the dualism —is not compatible with the identical nature and "source" of the experience. Locke makes a brave attempt to recon-cile this contradiction; Berkeley, who wished not to inter-pret but to confute materialistic physics or non-empirical mathematics, easily knocks over Locke's rickety structure. Furthermore he offers a new basis for differentiating be-tween on the one hand subjective impressions, created by imagination or memory working consciously or uncon-sciously, and on the other, objective reality, namely, vivid-ness, compulsive force, unalterable order and regularity, as determining what we call "objective," as opposed to ideas and images which we generate and manipulate more or less at will. This doctrine is open to objections, e.g., that delu-sions, false memories, and other obsessive but not neces-sarily misleading experiences, are at times just as strong, vivid, persistent, and internally orderly as that which we call veridical perception—yet we classify them as sub-

jective. But Berkeley's suggestion has always strongly
tempted empiricists: Hume, Mill, Mach, Russell, have all
made some use of it; and it has respectable adherents
today. Still more interesting is Berkeley's adumbration of
what Russell, borrowing a term from mathematical philosophy, called "logical constructions." Berkeley is replying
to those who complain that, since, according to him, nothing exists save ideas, we must be eating ideas, drinking
ideas, clothing ourselves in ideas, etc., which is surely
absurd. Berkeley points out that this is a verbal, not a
philosophical, absurdity, committed because we substitute
"ideas" for "material objects" without making corresponding substitutions for the other factors involved. To say
that bread is only an idea in my head, and that therefore
when I eat bread I am eating an idea, is to forget that my
body and my eating are similarly ideas: "I am eating bread"
becomes equivalent to "an experience (ideas) is (are)
occurring which is described as 'I am eating bread'; and if
this experience (these ideas) were not occurring, 'I am
eating bread' would not be true." The absurdity is due to
"reducing" bread to "ideas" while leaving my body and
my eating "unreduced" and "real," in contrast to the now
illusory bread.[2]

From this sprang the modern doctrine of "logical fictions," or "logical constructions," which maintained that
all statements about apparently experience-independent
entities—from political "entities" like France, or the British Constitution, or the Stock Exchange, or American de-
mocracy, or the Russian Revolution, to things and events
like tables or rainbows or earthquakes or heart disease or
pistol shots—could be translated completely into statements not involving any entities save the experience, actual

---

[2] The eminent Russian Marxist Georgi Plekhanov in his introduction to a textbook on dialectical materialism once argued that the
"old idealist Berkeley said that everything was a child of our
brains: ergo our parents were children of our brains: ergo our
parents were our children; but anyone who produced absurdities
of this order was not worth bothering about." To this silly and
entertaining attempt at a mate in four moves, Berkeley's (and later
Mach's and Russell's) answers are sufficient refutation. Lenin later
repeats the argument in an even cruder form.

or possible, of empirical observers. Thus all philosophies which assumed that material objects, or political "patterns," or "organic wholes" and the like, were ultimate constituents of the world, and could not be eliminated, and that this was a fatal obstacle to out-and-out empiricism, were themselves exploded by this uniquely powerful deflationary weapon. This doctrine, while itself no longer as formidable as it used to seem, has played a crucial role in modern empiricism.

Finally, Berkeley's point that our knowledge of other selves is not based on "ideas" (which would be compatible with solipsism), but rests on analogy—the notion that observers other than ourselves, and similar to us, could exist, which is not an "idea" as defined by him—is an insight of cardinal importance and originality, by which Hume and Russell, who regard it (rightly) as an inconsistency in Berkeley, failed to profit, to their own cost.

Berkeley's contribution to logic, and to what is today called "linguistic analysis," is very great. But his abiding importance in the history of philosophy still lies in his unequivocal insistence that any statement purporting to be about physical objects in the external world must, if it is to be meaningful, be somehow "reducible to," or "analyzable into," statements about the contents of immediate sense experience. This has been the main thesis of empiricist theories of perception until the present day. Among the difficulties of the thesis—and they have led to much obscure empiricist metaphysics—are failures to agree about what is meant by analysis (or reduction) or by speaking of the contents of immediate sense experience. The word "analysis" has a precise meaning in, say, chemistry or mathematics; its use by philosophers has, as often as not, rested on some ill-defined analogy.

More particularly, one widely held modern philosophical theory of sense perception, phenomenalism, owes much to a sentence in the *Principles*: "The table I write on, I say, exists, that is, I see and feel it; and if I were out of my study I should say it existed, *meaning thereby that if I was in my study I might perceive it*,[3] or that some other

* Editor's italics.

spirit actually does perceive it." In other words, to say that something not now perceived exists, is to say that *if* an observer were suitably situated, he *would* perceive it. Berkeley himself does not pursue this line of thought. For him, as we have seen, the continued existence of unperceived objects is secured by recourse to God. But the suggestion was taken up by J. S. Mill, who described physical objects as "permanent possibilities of sensation," and it is of this analysis that phenomenalism is a development. According to phenomenalism, all meaningful statements about physical objects can be translated into sets of hypothetical statements about the "sense data" that observers would have *if* they were suitably situated (whether any observers are in fact so situated or not). In this way phenomenalists hope to render secure Berkeley's empiricist thesis of the complete "reducibility" of statements about physical objects to statements about immediate sense experience. This hope has not yet been fulfilled: efforts of varying degrees of plausibility to "reduce" either still continue to be made, or else have led to the formulation of elaborate explanations of why, although in practice such reduction is not feasible, this is nevertheless (in theory at least) not fatal to the doctrine. The issue is still in hot dispute.

CHAPTER IV

David Hume

DAVID HUME WAS BORN IN 1711 INTO A GOOD SCOTTISH family at Edinburgh. He was not rich, but possessed sufficient means to abandon the pursuit of the law for which his father had intended him, and apply himself, in a somewhat desultory fashion, to the study of philosophy and general learning. In 1734, after unsuccessfully trying to be a merchant in Bristol, he went through an intellectual crisis and in a moment of illumination found his true vocation. He went to France, and there composed his philosophical masterpiece, the *Treatise of Human Nature*. It was published in the next year, and in his own words, "fell dead born from the press."

Not discouraged by the chilliness of the learned world and the public alike, he published his first essays in 1742. He became tutor to Lord Allandale, accompanied General St. Clair on a military expedition against France, visited the courts of Vienna and Turin, and after that returned to Scotland and lived in the country. In 1752 he moved to Edinburgh, published several political essays and began the publication of his celebrated *History of England*. The celebrity which had eluded him as a philosopher came to him as an historian, and by the time he had finished his history—in 1761—he had become world famous. Two years later he accepted a post in the British Embassy in Paris, and was there warmly welcomed by the brilliant and enlightened intellectual society which made that city the center of the civilized world. He returned to Edinburgh in 1766, became an Under-Secretary of State in the following year, retired two years later, and lived in his native city for the rest of his life, by this time widely recognized as one of the foremost men of genius of his time. An *Enquiry*

Concerning the Principles of Morals, published fourteen years after the *Treatise,* had finally secured Hume's claim to be one of the greatest and most iconoclastic philosophers of his own or any age. In 1776 he died, as he had lived, an atheist, loved by his friends, being, (so he describes himself) "a man of mild dispositions, command of temper, of an open social and cheerful humour, capable of attachment, but little susceptible of enmity, and of great moderation in all my passions. Even my love of literary fame, my ruling passion, never sorrowed my humour, notwithstanding my frequent disappointments. My company was not unacceptable to the young and careless as well as to the studious and literary." Adam Smith said of him "that gaiety of temper so agreeable in society that was so often accompanied with frivolous and superficial qualities, was in him certainly attended with a most severe application, the most intensive learning, the greatest depth of thought and of capacity to be in every respect the most comprehensive. Upon the whole I have always considered him both in his lifetime and in his death as approaching as nearly to the idea of a perfectly wise and virtuous man as perhaps the nature of human frailty will admit." Rousseau alone contrived to pick a quarrel with this most delightful and generous of men. His philosophical writings have remained controversial to this day, not least the *Dialogues upon Natural Religion,* perhaps the most remarkable treatise upon this topic ever composed. No man has influenced the history of philosophical thought to a deeper and more disturbing degree.

Hume's philosophical writings need little interpretation. He is, with the possible exception of Berkeley, the clearest philosophical writer in an age of exceptional clarity, and he may claim to be the greatest and most revolutionary (in the history of ideas these are almost synonymous terms) of British philosophers. His particular conception of philosophy as an empirical "science of man" is the true beginning of modern philosophy, which, in essence, is the history of the development of, and opposition to, his thought. The "science of man" is to be conducted by the methods of the natural sciences: observation and generalization. Philosophy to become properly scientific must dispense with methods of its own; these are to be exposed as shams and illusions.

The "observations" required for Hume's theory of knowledge are, apparently, to be conducted mainly in the field of introspective psychology, from which indeed his philosophizing is often scarcely distinguishable. "Men's behaviour in company, in affairs and in their pleasures" is more relevant to the account of "The Passions" and to moral philosophy, as discussed in Books II and III of the Treatise, than to Hume's theory of knowledge and criticism of metaphysics.

The following extracts are from *A Treatise of Human Nature*.

〔 *Introduction*

. . . As the science of man is the only solid foundation for the other sciences, so, the only solid foundation we can give to this science itself must be laid on experience and observation. It is no astonishing reflection to consider that the application of experimental philosophy to moral subjects should come after that to natural, at the distance of above a whole century; since we find in fact that there was about the same interval betwixt the origins of these sciences; and that, reckoning from Thales to Socrates, the space of time is nearly equal to that betwixt my Lord Bacon and some late philosophers in England, who have begun to put the science of man on a new footing, and have engaged the attention, and excited the curiosity, of the public. So true it is, that however other nations may rival us in poetry, and excel us in some other agreeable arts, the improvements in reason and philosophy can only be owing to a land of toleration and of liberty.

Nor ought we to think that this latter improvement in the science of man will do less honour to our native country than the former in natural philosophy, but ought rather to esteem it a greater glory, upon account of the greater importance of that science, as well as the necessity it lay under of such a reformation. For to me it seems evident that the essence of the mind being equally unknown to us with that of external bodies, it must be equally impossible to form any notion of its powers and qualities otherwise than from careful and exact experiments, and the observation of those particular effects which result from its different circumstances and situations. And though we must endeavour to render all our principles as universal as possible, by tracing up our experiments to the utmost, and explaining all effects from the simplest and fewest causes, it is still certain we cannot go beyond experience; and any hypothesis that pretends to discover the ultimate original qualities of human nature ought at first to be rejected as presumptuous and chimerical. . . .

Moral philosophy has, indeed, this peculiar disadvantage, which is not found in natural, that in collecting its experiments it cannot make them purposely, with premeditation, and after such a manner as to satisfy itself concerning every particular difficulty which may arise. When I am at a loss to know the effects of one body upon another in any situation, I need only put them in that situation, and observe what results from it. But should I endeavour to clear up after the same manner any doubt in moral philosophy, by placing myself in the same case with that which I consider, it is evident this reflection and premeditation would so disturb the operation of my natural principles as must render it impossible to form any just conclusion from the phaenomenon. We must, therefore, glean up our experiments in this science from a cautious observation of human life, and take them as they appear in the common course of the world, by men's behaviour in company, in affairs, and in their pleasures. Where experiments of this kind are judiciously collected and compared, we may hope to establish on them a science which will not be inferior in certainty, and will be much superior in utility, to any other of human comprehension.]

HUME DIVIDES "THE CONTENTS OF THE MIND," ALL labeled indiscriminately "ideas" by Locke and Berkeley, into two classes, "impressions" and "ideas." The impressions are intended to be the immediately given data of sense and of introspection, while the ideas are the images of memory and imagination. Hume avoids the trap, into which Locke falls, of distinguishing impressions (of sense) from ideas by their respective sources, the impressions "coming from bodies without us." Rather he distinguishes them—and indeed, having once adopted a strictly epistemological approach (i.e. that of giving an inventory of mental data, not of some unknown external reality), he must do so if he is to avoid a vicious circle—by an intrinsic quality of impressions that is not shared by ideas, namely force and liveliness. The distinction is, as Hume himself notes, unsatisfactory; images seen in a hallucination or in the dreams of delirium may be far more "forceful" and "lively" than any sense-experience.

Next he establishes that every simple idea that we have is a copy of a simple impression, and that, while we may form complex ideas which do not copy any impression, these are built up from simple ideas which are copies of impressions. Finally he proves that the impressions are temporally prior to the ideas which resemble them: first, by the simple fact of observation that they come earlier in time; and, secondly, by the argument that, while we may have impressions without subsequently having any resembling idea, we never have a (simple) idea without having previously had a resembling impression. This is Hume's statement of the empiricist thesis. It is a piece of descriptive psychology: all complex ideas are built up of simple ideas; all simple ideas are copies of previously experienced simple impressions; thus all our ideas are ultimately derived from impressions. It is characteristic of the genetic approach of the time that Hume should prove not (what would seem to be required) that sense experience and introspection are logically necessary for the existence of our ideas, but rather that they are temporally prior.

The famous case of the intermediate shade of blue—where, contrary to this doctrine, I can imagine a new shade (i.e., one not previously given in sense experience) if the two shades adjacent to it in a continuous scale of colours have been seen by me—is a symptom of the weakness both of Hume's atomistic sensationalism and more generally of the whole psychological and genetic approach to philosophy.

Hume's treatment of philosophy as if it were a none too precise natural science, the results of which are established by observation and induction, is very noticeable in the passage that follows. This is, no doubt, why he is so unconcerned at the exception to his general law, and also about the unsatisfactoriness of distinguishing impressions from ideas by the criterion of "liveliness." He does not expect to be able to prove his generalizations to be irrefutably true as one proves a theorem in mathematics. The world is a rich amalgam, not a Cartesian system; it has no precise frontiers; the lines we draw over it must be our own invention: propositions about it cannot be expected to be more than correct-on-the-whole.

The following is from Book I, "Of the Understanding," Part I, "Of Ideas, their Origin, Composition, Connexion and Abstraction."

[SECTION I. *Of the Origin of our Ideas*

All the perceptions of the human mind resolve themselves into two distinct kinds, which I shall call Impressions and Ideas. The difference betwixt these consists in the degrees of force and liveliness with which they strike upon the mind, and make their way into our thought or consciousness. Those perceptions which enter with most force and violence we may name *impressions*; and, under this name, I comprehend all our sensations, passions, and emotions, as they make their first appearance in the soul. By *ideas,* I mean the faint images of these in thinking and reasoning; such as, for instance, are all the perceptions excited by the present discourse, excepting only those which arise from the sight and touch, and excepting the immediate pleasure or uneasiness it may occasion. I believe it will not be very necessary to employ many words in explaining this distinction. Every one of himself will readily perceive the difference betwixt feeling and thinking. The common degrees of these are easily distinguished; though it is not impossible but, in particular instances, they may very nearly approach to each other. Thus, in sleep, in a fever, in madness, or in any very violent emotions of the soul, our ideas may approach to our impressions: As, on the other hand, it sometimes happens that our impressions are so faint and low that we cannot distinguish them from our ideas. But, notwithstanding this near resemblance in a few instances, they are in general so very different that no-one can make a scruple to rank them under distinct heads, and assign to each a peculiar name to mark the difference.

There is another division of our perceptions which it will be convenient to observe, and which extends itself both to our impressions and ideas. This division is into Simple and Complex. Simple perceptions, or impressions and ideas, are such as admit of no distinction nor separation. The complex are the contrary to these, and may be distinguished into parts. Though a particular colour, taste, and smell, are qualities all united together in this apple, it is easy to perceive they are not the same, but are at least distinguishable from each other.

Having, by these divisions, given an order and arrangement to our objects, we may now apply ourselves to consider, with more accuracy, their qualities and relations. The first circumstance that strikes my eye, is the great resemblance betwixt our impressions and ideas in every other particular except their degree of force and vivacity. The one seem to be, in a manner, the reflexion of the other; so that all the perceptions of the mind are double, and appear both as impressions and ideas. When I shut my eyes and think of my chamber, the ideas I form are exact representations of the impressions I felt; nor is there any circumstance of the one which is not to be found in the other. In running over my other perceptions, I find still the same resemblance and representation. Ideas and impressions appear always to correspond to each other. This circumstance seems to me remarkable, and engages my attention for a moment.

Upon a more accurate survey I find I have been carried away too far by the first appearance, and that I must make use of the distinction of perceptions into *simple* and *com-*

plex, to limit this general decision, *that all our ideas and impressions are resembling.* I observe that many of our complex ideas never had impressions that corresponded to them, and that many of our complex impressions never are exactly copied in ideas. I can imagine to myself such a city as the New Jerusalem, whose pavement is gold, and walls are rubies, though I never saw any such. I have seen Paris; but shall I affirm I can form such an idea of that city as will perfectly represent all its streets and houses in their real and just proportions?

I perceive, therefore, that though there is, in general, a great resemblance betwixt our *complex* impressions and ideas, yet the rule is not universally true that they are exact copies of each other. We may next consider how the case stands with our *simple* perceptions. After the most accurate examination of which I am capable, I venture to affirm that the rule here holds without any exception, and that every simple idea has a simple impression which resembles it, and every simple impression a correspondent idea. That idea of red which we form in the dark, and that impression which strikes our eyes in sun-shine, differ only in degree, not in nature. That the case is the same with all our simple impressions and ideas it is impossible to prove by a particular enumeration of them. Every one may satisfy himself in this point by running over as many as he pleases. But if any one should deny this universal resemblance, I know no way of convincing him but by desiring him to show a simple impression that has not a correspondent idea, or a simple idea that has not a correspondent impression. If he does not answer this challenge, as it is certain he cannot, we may, from his silence, and our own observation, establish our conclusion.

Thus we find that all simple ideas and impressions resemble each other; and, as the complex are formed from them, we may affirm in general that these two species of perception are exactly correspondent. Having dis-covered this relation, which requires no farther examination, I am curious to find some other of their qualities. Let us consider how they stand with regard to their existence, and which of the impressions and ideas are causes and which effects.

The *full* examination of this question is the subject of the present treatise; and, therefore, we shall here content ourselves with establishing one general proposition, *That all our simple ideas in their first appearance are derived from simple impressions, which are correspondent to them, and which they exactly represent.*

In seeking for phaenomena to prove this proposition, I find only those of two kinds; but, in each kird the phaenomena are obvious, numerous, and conclusive. I first make myself certain, by a new review, of what I have already asserted, that every simple impression is attended with a correspondent idea, and every simple idea with a correspondent impression. From this constant conjunction of resembling perceptions I immediately conclude that there is a great connexion betwixt our correspondent impressions and ideas, and that the existence of the one has a considerable influence upon that of the other. Such a constant conjunction, in such an infinite number of instances, can never arise from chance; but clearly proves a dependence of the impressions on the ideas, or of the ideas on the impressions. That I may know on which side this dependence lies, I consider the order of their *first appearance*; and find, by constant experience, that the simple impressions always take the precedence of their correspondent ideas, but never appear in the contrary order. To give a child an idea of scarlet or orange, of sweet or bitter, I present the objects, or, in other words, convey to him these impressions; but proceed not so absurdly as to endeavour to produce the impressions by exciting the ideas. Our ideas, upon their appearance, produce not their correspondent impressions, nor do we perceive any colour, or feel any sensation merely upon thinking of them. On the other hand, we find that any impression, either of the mind or body, is constantly followed by an idea which resembles it, and is only different in the degrees of force and liveliness. The constant conjunction of our resembling perceptions is a convincing proof that the one are the causes of the other; and this priority of the impressions is an equal proof that our impressions are the causes of our ideas, not our ideas of our impressions.

To confirm this, I consider another plain and convincing phaenomenon; which is, that wherever, by any accident, the faculties which give rise to any impressions are obstructed in their operations, as when one is born blind or deaf, not only the impressions are lost, but also their correspondent ideas; so that there never appear in the mind the least traces of either of them. Nor is this only true where the organs of sensation are entirely destroyed, but likewise where they have never been put in action to produce a particular impression. We cannot form to ourselves a just idea of the taste of a pine-apple without having actually tasted it.

There is, however, one contradictory phaenomenon which may prove, that it is not absolutely impossible for ideas to go before their correspondent impressions. I believe it will readily be allowed that the several distinct ideas of colours, which enter by the eyes, or those of sounds, which are conveyed by the hearing, are really different from each other, though, at the same time, resembling. Now, if this be true of different colours, it must be no less so of the different shades of the same colour, that each of them produces a distinct idea, independent of the rest. For, if this should be denied, it is possible, by the continual gradation of shades, to run a colour insensibly into what is most remote from it; and if you will not allow any of the means to be different, you cannot, without absurdity, deny the extremes to be the same. Suppose, therefore, a person to have enjoyed his sight for thirty years, and to have become perfectly well acquainted with colours of all kinds, excepting one particular shade of blue, for instance, which it never has been his fortune to meet with. Let all the different shades of that colour except that single one be placed before him, descending gradually from the deepest to the lightest; it is plain that he will perceive a blank where that shade is wanting, and will be sensible that there is a greater distance in that place betwixt the contiguous colours than in any other. Now, I ask, whether it is possible for him, from his own imagination, to supply this deficiency, and raise up to himself the idea of that particular shade, though it had never been conveyed to him by his senses? I believe there are few but will be of opinion that he can; and this may serve as a proof that the simple ideas are not always derived from the correspondent impressions; though the instance is so particular and singular that it is scarce worth our observing, and does not merit that, for it alone, we should alter our general maxim.

But, besides this exception, it may not be amiss to remark, on this head, that the principle of the priority of impressions to ideas must be understood with another limitation, viz., that as our ideas are images of our impressions, so we can form secondary ideas, which are images of the primary; as appears from this very reasoning concerning them. This is not, properly speaking, an exception to the rule so much as an explanation of it. Ideas produce the images of themselves in new ideas; but as the first ideas are supposed to be derived from impressions, it still remains true that all our simple ideas proceed either mediately or immediately from their correspondent impressions.

This, then is the first principle I establish in the science of human nature; nor ought we to despise it because of the simplicity of its appearance. For it is remarkable that the present question concerning the precedency of our impressions or ideas is the same with what has made so much noise in other terms, when it has been disputed whether there be any *innate ideas,* or whether all ideas be derived from sensation and reflexion. We may observe that in order to prove the ideas of extension and colour not to be innate, philosophers do nothing but show that they are conveyed by our senses. To prove the ideas of passion and desire not to be innate, they observe that we have a preceding experience of these emotions in ourselves. Now, if we carefully examine these arguments, we shall find that they prove nothing but that ideas are preceded by other more lively perceptions, from which they are derived, and which they represent. I hope this clear stating of the question will remove all disputes concerning it, and will render this principle of more use in our reasonings, than it seems hitherto to have been. }

HUME'S DOCTRINE OF THE ASSOCIATION OF IDEAS, DERIVED from Hartley, and the basis of the new psychological science of the eighteenth century, with its mechanical and chemical models, especially in the dominant schools of the French *philosophes,* is discussed in the Introduction.

Hume subscribed to the current idiom of "faculties of the mind." It is noticeable in the passage which follows how much of what we should call ordinary thinking he ascribes to the "faculty" of imagination, "in" which the chemistry of association of ideas takes place.

The penultimate paragraph is a good example of Hume's consciously scientific approach. With the tentativeness, and dislike of metaphysics, of the natural scientist, he proposes to describe *how* things happen, not to look for hidden causes of their happening as they do.

[SECTION IV. *Of the Connexion or Association of Ideas*

As all simple ideas may be separated by the imagination, and may be united again in what form it pleases, nothing would be more unaccountable than the operations of that faculty, were it not guided by some universal principles, which render it, in some measure, uniform with itself in all times and places. Were ideas entirely loose and unconnected, chance alone would join them; and it is impossible the same simple ideas should fall regularly into complex ones (as they commonly do), without some bond of union among them, some associating quality, by which one idea naturally introduces another. This uniting principle among ideas is not to be considered as an inseparable connexion; for that has been already excluded from the imagination: nor yet are we to conclude that without it the mind cannot join two ideas; for nothing is more free than that faculty: but we are only to regard it as a gentle force, which commonly prevails, and is the cause why, among other things, languages so nearly correspond to each other; nature, in a manner, pointing out to every one those simple ideas which are most proper to be united into a complex one. The qualities from which this association arises, and by which the mind is, after this manner, conveyed from one idea to another, are three, viz., Resemblance, Contiguity in time or place, and Cause and Effect.

I believe it will not be very necessary to prove that these qualities produce an association among ideas, and upon the appearance of one idea naturally introduce another. It is plain, that, in the course of our thinking, and in the constant revolution of our ideas, our imagination runs easily from one idea to any other that *resembles* it, and that this quality alone is to the fancy a sufficient bond and association. It is likewise evident that as the senses in changing their objects are necessitated to change them regularly, and take them as they lie *contiguous* to each other, the imagination must, by long custom, acquire the same method of thinking, and run along the parts of space and time in conceiving its objects. As to the connexion that is made by the relation of *cause and effect,* we shall have occasion afterwards to examine it to the bottom, and therefore shall not at present insist upon it. It is sufficient to observe that there is no relation which produces a stronger connexion in the fancy, and makes one idea more readily recall another, than the relation of cause and effect betwixt their objects.

That we may understand the full extent of these relations, we must consider that two objects are connected together in the imagination, not only when the one is immediately resembling, contiguous to, or the cause of, the other, but also when there is interposed betwixt them a third object which bears to both of them any of these relations. This may be carried on to a great length; though at the same time we may observe that each remove considerably weakens the relation. Cousins in the fourth degree are connected by *causation,* if I may be allowed to use that term; but not so closely as brothers, much less as child and parent. In general, we may observe that all the relations of blood depend upon cause and effect, and are esteemed near or remote, according to the number of connecting causes interposed betwixt the persons.

Of the three relations above-mentioned, this of causation is the most extensive. Two objects may be considered as placed in this relation. as well when one is the cause of any of the actions or motions of the other, as when the former is the cause of the existence of the latter. For as that action or motion is nothing but the object itself, considered in a certain light, and as the object continues the same in all its different situations, it is easy to imagine how such an influence of objects upon one another may connect them in the imagination.

We may carry this farther, and remark not only that two objects are connected by the relation of cause and effect when the one produces a motion or any action in the other, but also when it has a power of producing it. And this we may observe to be the source of all the relations of interest and duty, by which men influence each other in society, and are placed in the ties of government and subordination. A master is such a one as, by his situation, arising either from force or agreement, has a power of directing in certain particulars the actions of another, whom we call servant. A judge is one who, in all disputed cases, can fix by his opinion the possession or property of anything betwixt any members of the society. When a person is possessed of any power there is no more required to convert it into action, but the exertion of the will; and *that* in every case is considered as possible, and in many as probable; especially in the case of authority, where the obedience of the subject is a pleasure and advantage to the superior.

These are, therefore, the principles of union or cohesion among our simple ideas, and in the imagination supply the place of that inseparable connexion, by which they are united in our memory. Here is a kind of Attraction, which in the mental world will be found to have as extraordinary effects as in the natural, and to show itself in as many and as various forms. Its effects are everywhere conspicuous; but, as to its causes, they are mostly unknown, and must be resolved into *original* qualities of human nature, which I pretend not to explain. Nothing is more requisite for a true philosopher than to restrain the intemperate desire of searching into causes, and, having established any doctrine upon a sufficient number of experiments, rest contented with that, when he sees a farther examination would lead him into obscure and uncertain speculations. In that case his inquiry would be much better employed in examining the effects than the causes of his principle.

Amongst the effects of this union or association of ideas, there are none more remarkable than those complex ideas which are the common subjects of our thoughts and reasoning, and generally arise from some principle of union among our simple ideas. These complex ideas may be divided into *Relations, Modes,* and *Substances.* We shall briefly examine each of these in order, and shall subjoin some considerations concerning our *general* and *particular* ideas, before we leave the present subject, which may be considered as the elements of this philosophy.]

HUME ACCEPTS COMPLETELY BERKELEY'S VIEW THAT what we ordinarily call a physical object—in Hume's words "what any common man means by a hat, or shoe, or stone"—is no more than a collection and succession in time of sensible qualities. He does not, of course, believe in the need for, or the existence of, the "unknown something" (Locke's "substratum") or, rather, he would have said that discussion of the question of its existence— there being no human experience capable of throwing light upon it—was without any sense. Indeed, in the passage below he calls our practice of referring the qualities to an unknown something a "fiction." In Part IV we shall find him investigating a closely related "fiction," namely our belief in the continuous existence of bodies, independent of, and external to, ourselves.

[SECTION VI. *Of Modes and Substances*

. . . The idea of a substance as well as that of a mode is nothing but a collection of simple ideas that are united by the imagination, and have a particular name assigned them by which we are able to recall, either to ourselves or

others, that collection. But the difference betwixt these
ideas consists in this, that the particular qualities which
form a substance are commonly referred to an unknown
something, in which they are supposed to inhere; or, granting this fiction should not take place, are at least supposed
to be closely and inseparably connected by the relations
of contiguity and causation. The effect of this is that whatever new simple quality we discover to have the same connexion with the rest, we immediately comprehend it among
them, even though it did not enter into the first conception
of the substance. Thus our idea of gold may at first be a
yellow colour, weight, malleableness, fusibility; but upon
the discovery of its dissolubility in aqua regia, we join
that to the other qualities, and suppose it to belong to the
substance as much as if its idea had from the beginning
made a part of the compound one. The principle of union
being regarded as the chief part of the complex idea, gives
entrance to whatever quality afterwards occurs, and is
equally comprehended by it as are the others which first
presented themselves. . . .}

THE PASSAGE WHICH FOLLOWS EMBODIES A MOST IM-
portant principle for Hume, and one which often acts as
a psychological substitute for the notion of logical entailment, or rather non-entailment. Thus where we should say
that what he really wants to prove is, e.g., that the occurrence of an event A does not logically entail the occurrence
of an event B, he will in fact assert that the idea of A is
different from that of B, and hence, by this principle, the
two ideas are distinguishable, and therefore separable.

{ SECTION VII. *Of Abstract Ideas*

. . . First, We have observed that whatever objects are
different are distinguishable, and that whatever objects are
distinguishable are separable by the thought and imagination. And we may here add that these propositions are
equally true in the *inverse,* and that whatever objects are
separable are also distinguishable, and that whatever objects are distinguishable are also different. For how is it

possible we can separate what is not distinguishable, or distinguish what is not different? . . .}

MOREOVER THE OBVERSE OF THIS RULE SEEMS TO HIM to settle the problem of universals along lines not dissimilar from those of Berkeley. He believed that the fallacy of ascribing independent being to characteristics springs from the fact that they can be distinguished from that which they characterize, and whatever is distinguishable can exist separately. He argues against this that this distinguishing is one of "reason" only—that if we distinguish its characteristics from an object, nothing is left. In this sense we cannot, therefore, even distinguish. But we can compare objects—"view them in different aspects, according to the resemblances of which they are susceptible"—without distinguishing, i.e., splitting them into separate "ideas." These inseparable "aspects" and "resemblances" without which an object is nothing—which in a sense *are* the object—are symbolized by general terms, and are mistakenly conceived as having existence—or some sort of being—in their own right. This doctrine, with various modifications and refinements, is held by many modern empiricists. Russell and others regard it as unsatisfactory and complain that universals cannot be exorcised by being called "aspects" or "resemblances," a mere change of nomenclature which leaves us where we were. The question is by no means dead today.

{ Before I leave this subject, I shall employ the same principles to explain that *distinction of reason* which is so much talked of, and is so little understood, in the schools. Of this kind is the distinction betwixt figure and the body figured; motion and the body moved. The difficulty of explaining this distinction arises from the principle above explained, *that all ideas which are different are separable.* For it follows from thence that if the figure be different from the body, their ideas must be separable as well as distinguishable; if they be not different, their ideas can neither be separable nor distinguishable. What then is meant by a distinction of reason, since it implies neither a difference nor separation?

To remove this difficulty, we must have recourse to the foregoing explication of abstract ideas. It is certain that the mind would never have dreamed of distinguishing a figure from the body figured, as being in reality neither distinguishable, nor different, nor separable, did it not observe, that even in this simplicity there might be contained many different resemblances and relations. Thus, when a globe of white marble is presented, we receive only the impression of a white colour disposed in a certain form, nor are we able to separate and distinguish the colour from the form. But observing afterwards a globe of black marble and a cube of white, and comparing them with our former object, we find two separate resemblances in what formerly seemed, and really is, perfectly inseparable. After a little more practice of this kind, we begin to distinguish the figure from the colour by a *distinction of reason;* that is, we consider the figure and colour together, since they are, in effect, the same and undistinguishable; but still view them in different aspects, according to the resemblances of which they are susceptible. When we would consider only the figure of the globe of white marble, we form in reality an idea both of the figure and colour, but tacitly carry our eye to its resemblance with the globe of black marble: And in the same manner, when we would consider its colour only, we turn our view to its resemblance with the cube of white marble. By this means we accompany our ideas with a kind of reflexion, of which custom renders us, in a great measure, insensible. A person who desires us to consider the figure of a globe of white marble without thinking on its colour, desires an impossibility; but his meaning is that we should consider the colour and figure together, but still keep in our eye the resemblance to the globe of black marble, or that to any other globe of whatever colour or substance.}

HAVING FOR THE MOMENT DISPOSED OF THE PROBLEMS of substance and universals, Hume turns to Knowledge. He takes over the fundamental rationalist distinction between indubitable truths: those of reason, the a priori *vérités de raison* of Leibniz; and truths of fact, *vérités de fait,* which are at best only probable. But true to his "scientific" empirical method, he distinguishes them by their sources or origins, not their logical character or content; and introduces the view that was destined to awaken Kant from his "dogmatic slumber" and transform philosophy in the West—that the indubitably knowable, a priori, truths are based on our own, ultimately arbitrary, rules or habits of using words and symbols, and give no information about the world. Propositions are either certain and uninformative, or informative and not certain. Metaphysical knowledge which claims to be both certain and informative is therefore in principle not possible.

The following is from Part III, *"Of Knowledge and Probability."*

{ SECTION I. *Of Knowledge*

There are seven different kinds of philosophical relation, viz., *resemblance, identity, relations of time and place, proportion in quantity or number, degrees in any quality, contrariety, and causation.* These relations may be divided into two classes: into such as depend entirely on the ideas which we compare together, and such as may be changed without any change in the ideas. It is from the idea of a triangle that we discover the relation of equality, which its three angles bear to two right ones; and this relation is invariable, as long as our idea remains the same. On the contrary, the relations of *contiguity* and *distance* betwixt two objects may be changed merely by an alteration of their place, without any change on the objects themselves or on their ideas; and the place depends on a hundred different accidents, which cannot be foreseen by the mind. It is the same case with *identity* and *causation.* Two objects, though perfectly resembling each other, and even appearing in the same place at different times, may be numerically different: and as the power, by which one object produces another, is never discoverable merely from their idea, it is evident *cause* and *effect* are relations of which we receive information from experience, and not from any abstract reasoning or reflexion. There is no single phaenomenon, even the most simple, which can be accounted for from the qualities of the objects as they appear to us; or which we could foresee without the help of memory and experience.

It appears therefore that of these seven philosophical relations there remain only four, which, depending solely upon ideas, can be the objects of knowledge and certainty. These four are *resemblance, contrariety, degrees in quality, and proportions in quantity or number.* Three of these relations are discoverable at first sight, and fall more properly under the province of intuition than demonstration. When any objects *resemble* each other, the resemblance will at first strike the eye, or rather the mind; and seldom requires a second examination. The case is the same with *contrariety,* and with the *degrees* of any *quality.* No one can once doubt but existence and non-existence destroy each other, and are perfectly incompatible and contrary. And though it be impossible to judge exactly of the degrees of any quality, such as colour, taste, heat, cold, when the difference betwixt them is very small; yet it is easy to decide that any of them is superior or inferior to another when their difference is considerable. And this decision we always pronounce at first sight, without any enquiry or reasoning.

We might proceed, after the same manner, in fixing the *proportions* of *quantity* or *number,* and might at one view observe a superiority, or inferiority, betwixt any numbers or figures, especially where the difference is very great and remarkable. As to equality, or any exact proportion, we can only guess at it from a single consideration; except in very short numbers, or very limited portions of extension; which are comprehended in an instant, and where we perceive an impossibility of falling into any considerable error. In all other cases we must settle the proportions with some liberty, or proceed in a more *artificial* manner.

I have already observed that geometry, or the *art* by which we fix the proportions of figures, though it much excels both in universality and exactness, the loose judge-

ments of the senses and imagination; yet never attains a
perfect precision and exactness. Its first principles are still
drawn from the general appearance of the objects; and
that appearance can never afford us any security, when we
examine the prodigious minuteness of which nature is susceptible. Our ideas seem to give a perfect assurance that
no two right lines can have a common segment; but if
we consider these ideas we shall find that they always suppose a sensible inclination of the two lines, and that where
the angle they form is extremely small, we have no standard of a right line so precise as to assure us of the truth of
this proposition. It is the same case with most of the primary decisions of the mathematics.

There remain therefore algebra and arithmetic as the
only sciences in which we can carry on a chain of reasoning to any degree of intricacy, and yet preserve a perfect
exactness and certainty. We are possessed of a precise
standard by which we can judge of the equality and proportion of numbers; and according as they correspond or
not to that standard we determine their relations, without
any possibility of error. When two numbers are so combined as that the one has always an unit answering to every
unit of the other, we pronounce them equal; and it is for
want of such a standard of equality in extension that
geometry can scarce be esteemed a perfect and infallible
science.

But here it may not be amiss to obviate a difficulty,
which may arise from my asserting that though geometry
falls short of that perfect precision and certainty which are
peculiar to arithmetic and algebra, yet it excels the imperfect judgments of our senses and imagination. The reason
why I impute any defect to geometry is because its original and fundamental principles are derived merely from
appearances; and it may perhaps be imagined that this
defect must always attend it and keep it from ever reaching
a greater exactness in the comparison of objects or ideas
than what our eye or imagination alone is able to attain. I
own that this defect so far attends it as to keep it from
ever aspiring to a full certainty: But since these fundamental principles depend on the easiest and least deceitful

appearances, they bestow on their consequences a degree of exactness of which these consequences are singly incapable. It is impossible for the eye to determine the angles of a chiliagon to be equal to 1996 right angles, or make any conjecture, that approaches this proportion; but when it determines that right lines cannot concur; that we cannot draw more than one right line between two given points; its mistakes can never be of any consequence. And this is the nature and use of geometry, to run us up to such appearances, as, by reason of their simplicity, cannot lead us into any considerable error.

I shall here take occasion to propose a second observation concerning our demonstrative reasonings, which is suggested by the same object of the mathematics. It is usual with mathematicians to pretend that those ideas which are their objects are of so refined and spiritual a nature that they fall not under the conception of the fancy, but must be comprehended by a pure and intellectual view, of which the superior faculties of the soul are alone capable. The same notion runs through most parts of philosophy, and is principally made use of to explain our abstract ideas, and to show how we can form an idea of a triangle, for instance, which shall neither be an isosceles nor scalenum, nor be confined to any particular length and proportion of sides. It is easy to see why philosophers are so fond of this notion of some spiritual and refined perceptions; since by that means they cover many of their absurdities, and may refuse to submit to the decisions of clear ideas by appealing to such as are obscure and uncertain. But, to destroy this artifice, we need but reflect on that principle so oft insisted on, *that all our ideas are copied from our impressions.* For from thence we may immediately conclude that since all impressions are clear and precise, the ideas which are copied from them must be of the same nature, and can never, but from our fault, contain anything so dark and intricate. An idea is by its very nature weaker and fainter than an impression; but being in every other respect the same, cannot imply any very great mystery. If its weakness render it obscure, it is our business to remedy that defect, as much as possible, by keeping the idea steady and precise; and till we have done so, it is in vain to pretend to reasoning and philosophy.]

THE FOUR RELATIONS ENUMERATED ABOVE WHICH "DE- pend entirely on the ideas"—sometimes called "relations of reason"—are, for Hume the relations which give rise to a priori truths. The perception of these relations, by in- tuition and demonstration, is the sole power possessed by the faculty of reason; and it is only of propositions re- porting these relations between ideas that we can have *knowledge* as opposed to probable opinion. All other prop- ositions are arrived at by the imagination proceeding by habit in accordance with the principle of association.

As was remarked above, Hume, in common with all other pre-Kantian empiricists, confounds logic with genetic psychology, and distinguishes a priori from other truths by a supposed psychological fact about the way in which we come to know them.

He correctly places the propositions of arithmetic and algebra amongst a priori truths, giving as his reason that these are strictly deduced from intuitively known truths. What intuition is, is left obscure.

In the *Treatise,* Hume does not regard geometry as a priori. The matter is discussed at length in Part II, where he comes to the conclusions summarized in the extract above: the steps of deductive reasoning by which we prove a theorem from the axioms of geometry are indeed infalli- ble; but the axioms, themselves being "drawn from the appearances of things," are not, particularly because we have not (as we have in arithmetic and algebra for num- bers) a precise standard of equality for extension in space. Nevertheless, geometry is much superior to the rest of our empirical knowledge because these axioms, though not fully certain, "depend on the easiest and least deceitful appearances."

Hume is absolutely correct so far as applied geometry, i.e., geometry regarded as describing the properties of ac- tual objects in space, is concerned. We have no absolutely precise criterion of equality, say, of length in two real lines; indeed it is doubtful whether it makes sense to talk of absolute equality without reference to measuring instruments and their degrees of error. Pure geometry, however, is not a description of empirical properties of space; it has nothing to do with the behavior of foot rules, surveyor's chains or theodolites. It is a system of purely abstract relations—a logical pattern applicable to a range of utterly heterogeneous subject matter, as is shown by the fact that "interpretations" (i.e. uses or applications) other than the spatial can be found for it. In an obscure passage in Hume's later work *The Enquiry into Human Understanding* there is a hint that he realized this distinction, and was prepared to assign pure geometry where it belongs, namely to the region of the a priori.

Hume's analysis of causation, and his consequent posing of the problem of induction,[1] is his most important, as it is his most celebrated, contribution to the theory of knowledge. It occupies almost the whole of the long Part III of the *Treatise*. Kant's stupendous effort to deal with its consequences inaugurated modern philosophy. The failure to provide an answer to Hume's problem (attempts to do so have filled many volumes) has been called a scandal to philosophy.

Hume begins by stressing the importance of the relation of cause and effect. It is the only relation that enables us to reason to the existence of any object, or the occurrence of any event, beyond our present immediate impressions; but for it, we should have no ground for believing in anything beyond our own present immediate experience.[2] He then proceeds to examine a single instance of cause and effect. The example which he uses, and which we may as well keep in mind, is that of one billiard ball striking another and thereby causing the second ball to move. In such a case, where we say that an event A has caused an

[1] Locke had vaguely appreciated the existence of this problem, but mentions it only in passing; its importance in modern philosophy dates from Hume.

[2] This may go a little too far. Some few inferences to the past may be based upon memory; but even with this we should still be confined to a minute collection of beliefs, compared with the beliefs and assumptions that we actually do hold. And in any case reliance on the causal relations may well be involved in establishing the trustworthiness of memory.

event B, what do we mean? In the first place, says Hume, that A and B were spatially contiguous; secondly, that A occurred immediately before B. But these, though necessary, are not sufficient, conditions of causation; obviously we do not say of every pair of spatially contiguous events of which one occurs immediately before the other that the one is the cause of the other. If you touch a table with your finger and immediately after feel a pain in it, you do not assume that the first event is necessarily the cause of the second, which might well have occurred without it. A third condition must be fulfilled: there must be a necessary connection.

Having analyzed the idea of causation into its component ideas, those of contiguity, priority in time, and necessary connection, Hume devotes the rest of Part III to an investigation of the most obscure and by far the most important of the three, the idea of necessary connection.

As always, when an obscure idea is being clarified, Hume's investigation is dominated by the genetic question: "From what impression is the idea derived?" The argument is complex and pursues a sinuous course, as Hume "beats about all the neighbouring fields." Accordingly it seems to me best to give a summary of it in modern language.[3]

Let us consider a particular instance of "A causes B." First, says Hume, the connection is not one of logical entailment; for "There is no object which implies the existence of any other." Hume tends to substitute a psychological criterion for logical entailment, and asks whether we can conceive of an A not followed by a B; but this is not the point he means to make: whether or not A and B are psychologically distinct (this may differ from one individual to another), they either are or are not so used that the proposition "An A has occurred not immediately followed

---

[3] The reader will find it easier to follow the relation between this account and the text if he bears in mind Hume's technique for proving that a given proposition is not "analytic," i.e. logically true—"established by reason." He employs not the logical criterion that the contradictory of such a proposition is not self-contradictory but, as we should expect, the more psychological criterion—that we can conceive the contradictory.

by a B" is self-contradictory. If it is not, then what makes us think that it states a *necessary* relation? Now, no doubt, we do sometimes utter propositions of the form "A causes B" where the contradictory of "A causes B" is self-contradictory, i.e., where the proposition "A causes B" is analytic; but this is neither the most frequent nor the historically basic use of the word "cause." And, of course if all our causal propositions were analytic in this way, and followed from definitions and the like, then, taken as a whole, tracing connections between them would become a sort of lexicographical game like exchanging counters for each other according to fixed rules; and such games give us no information about the world. Hence Hume's point remains: there are many, and those the most important, causal propositions where the connection between A and B is *not* logical.

But if the connection is not logical, then it must be empirical. But, as Hume emphasizes, there is nothing observable in any one instance except the mere sequence of events. The one billiard ball rolls up to the other, the two are in contact, the second moves on; there is nothing observable here that can be called a necessary connection. And to talk of one event being "produced" by the other is merely to coin a synonym for being "caused"—the very matter under discussion; nor do such other words as "power," "efficacy," "creation," "agency," etc., advance the inquiry. (It may be observed that words like "force," as used in mechanics, do not denote *unobservable* links between objects; they are shorthand ways of referring to the observed or observable regularities of *observed* phenomena. The anthropomorphic overtones of such terms may indeed be misleading, and have led to various forms of the "pathetic fallacy," but they are not relevant to mechanics.) In a word, the idea of a non-logical necessary connection—a link between two events at once observable and necessary—is unintelligible.

Hume goes on to note a third characteristic which distinguishes the cases of spatial contiguity and temporal succession where we call the sequence causal, from those where we do not: in the former the sequence is *regular,* i.e., has often been observed to occur and *never* been observed to fail. This Hume calls "constant conjunction." According to Hume this is not, of course, a "real," external, necessary connection between events—an item in the world; but it provides the key to the psychological explanation of why we think of some events as necessarily connected, although this thought turns out to embody an illusion. (Today we should, if we accepted Hume's analysis of causation,[4] be more inclined to say that constant conjunction, together with contiguity and temporal succession, constituted the criterion for the correct use of the word "cause".) Hume's explanation is this: When events of type A have been constantly observed without fail to be conjoined with events of type B, a habitual association is set up in the imagination so that whenever we observe a new A, the idea of a B arises in the mind with an overwhelming force, this force being itself an introspectively observable feeling. This feeling of force we now illegitimately project into the external world, and imagine a "force" or "power" as pushing and pulling events or objects in the world. As for the psychological machinery— irresistible association, liability to externalize inner compulsions which themselves seem, prima facie, forms of causation, psychological rather than physical, Hume does not analyze these concepts. If we are to escape a vicious circle whereby external causation is explained away by internal causation, we must assume that Hume regards such processes as themselves merely regularities, themselves observable, "brute facts,"—the ultimate terminus at which enquiry must, of necessity, stop.

Hume's analysis of our use of the word "cause" is inadequate also in other ways. We do not use the word "cause" in the description of every regularity to be found in the world; for example, in statements of the laws of astronomy or modern physics, the word "cause" may never appear. It is only in cases which fulfill certain specifiable conditions that we feel inclined to talk of one event as causing another. Moreover, observed constant conjunction is not always the main ground for detecting "causal

[4] Which is in tact defective.

influence"—it is often reinforced and overshadowed by our deductions from accepted scientific theories; and these theories are often accepted not on the basis of regularities alone. Finally Hume's psychological explanation of the illusion of "real" binding connections in the world is certainly not the whole truth. Such an idea seems traceable no less to animistic projections on to the inanimate world, e.g., the sensation of effort of will, and, perhaps most of all, of muscular effort.

But this criticism does not detract from the crucial importance of Hume's discovery, which consists in the uncovering of the problem of induction. If all our general statements about the world were causal (and they are not), and if the word "cause" stood for some metaphysically binding cement between events, such that the one not merely never did, but *could not,* happen without the other in any circumstances, there would be no problem of induction. Our general statements would be "metaphysically" guaranteed to the hilt for unobserved as for observed cases. But Hume shows that the word "cause" does not stand for any such impalpable entity, and thus reveals to the view a hitherto largely unnoticed problem, namely that we seem to claim to know, yet never in principle do know for certain, that any generalization based upon observed instances of phenomena remains true when extrapolated to cover unobserved instances, whether in the past or the future.

If we are to know facts which we do not observe with a certainty resembling that of our deductive—say mathematical—knowledge; if the statements of physics are to be impregnable like those of, say, geometry, what we need is an absolute guarantee for the principle of induction "that unobserved instances resemble observed instances." Hume rightly concludes that we cannot obtain this guarantee anywhere—that we neither know, nor can know, any principle which makes induction as certain as deduction. Nor—and here he shows more perspicacity than many of his successors in this field—can we without circularity show such a principle to be even probable: "probability is founded on the presumption of a resemblance betwixt those objects of which we have had experience and those of which we have had none; and therefore it is impossible this presumption can arise from probability." Probability rests on the unbolsterable principle of induction, and cannot itself be used to bolster it up. This is the basis of the notorious "skepticism" of Hume and later philosophers. This attitude has either been accepted with pessimistic resignation or else attacked as craven or fallacious. Yet it is difficult to see good reason for either attitude: for the skepticism in question is skeptical only of the possibility of turning induction into a species of precisely what it is not—deduction; and this is not a rational ambition. Hume himself is largely to blame: in common with his contemporaries, he regarded deduction as the only authentic form of true reasoning; and therefore attributed our inferences from cause to effect to the "imagination," the source of irrational processes. If we are to be wholly rational we must have a "justification" of induction. But what could "justify" it? The search for a guarantee is a demand for a world in which events or objects are linked by "objective" necessary connections; if Hume has shown anything he has shown that this notion is not intelligible, and rests on a confusion of logical machinery with the facts of experience, a wish that the symbols of logic or mathematics or grammar should possess objective counterparts. This craving for a metaphysical system is one of the most obsessive of all the fantasies which have dominated human minds.[5]

[SECTION II. *Of Probability; and of the idea of Cause and Effect*

This is all I think necessary to observe concerning those four relations which are the foundation of science; but as to the other three, which depend not upon the idea, and may be absent or present even while *that* remains the same, it will be proper to explain them more particularly.

[5]This applies strictly only to attempts to justify induction *with certainty*. Many philosophers, recognizing this to be hopeless, have tried to establish what is apparently a weaker thesis, namely that induction can be justified *with probability*. This is a mistake of the same sort, but the argument is too complex to be entered into here.

These three relations are *identity, the situations in time and place, and causation.*

All kinds of reasoning consist in nothing but a *comparison,* and a discovery of those relations, either constant or inconstant, which two or more objects bear to each other. This comparison we may make, either when both the objects are present to the senses, or when neither of them is present, or when only one. When both the objects are present to the senses along with the relation, we call *this* perception rather than reasoning; nor is there in this case any exercise of the thought, or any action, properly speaking, but a mere passive admission of the impressions through the organs of sensation. According to this way of thinking, we ought not to receive as reasoning any of the observations we may make concerning *identity* and *the relations* of *time* and *place;* since in none of them the mind can go beyond what is immediately present to the senses, either to discover the real existence or the relations of objects. It is only *causation* which produces such a connexion as to give us assurance from the existence or action of one object that it was followed or preceded by any other existence or action; nor can the other two relations be ever made use of in reasoning except so far as they either affect or are affected by it. There is nothing in any objects to persuade us that they are either always *remote* or always *contiguous;* and when from experience and observation we discover that their relation in this particular is invariable, we always conclude there is some secret *cause* which separates or unites them. The same reasoning extends to *identity.* We readily suppose an object may continue individually the same though several times absent from and present to the senses; and ascribe to it an identity notwithstanding the interruption of the perception, whenever we conclude that if we had kept our eye or hand constantly upon it it would have conveyed an invariable and uninterrupted perception. But this conclusion beyond the impressions of our senses can be founded only on the connexion of *cause and effect;* nor can we otherwise have any security that the object is not changed upon us, however much the new object may resemble that which was formerly present to the senses. Whenever we discover such a perfect resemblance, we consider whether it be common in that species of objects; whether possibly or probably any cause could operate in producing the change and resemblance; and according as we determine concerning these causes and effects, we form our judgment concerning the identity of the object.

Here then it appears that, of those three relations which depend not upon the mere ideas, the only one that can be traced beyond our senses, and informs us of existences and objects which we do not see or feel, is *causation*. This relation, therefore, we shall endeavour to explain fully before we leave the subject of the understanding.

To begin regularly, we must consider the idea of *causation,* and see from what origin it is derived. It is impossible to reason justly without understanding perfectly the idea concerning which we reason; and it is impossible perfectly to understand any idea without tracing it up to its origin, and examining that primary impression from which it arises. The examination of the impression bestows a clearness on the idea; and the examination of the idea bestows a like clearness on all our reasoning.

Let us therefore cast our eye on any two objects which we call cause and effect, and turn them on all sides, in order to find that impression which produces an idea of such prodigious consequence. At first sight I perceive that I must not search for it in any of the particular *qualities* of the objects; since, whichever of these qualities I pitch on, I find some object that is not possessed of it, and yet falls under the denomination of cause or effect. And indeed there is nothing existent, either externally or internally, which is not to be considered either as a cause or an effect; though it is plain there is no one quality which universally belongs to all beings, and gives them a title to that denomination.

The idea then of causation must be derived from some *relation* among objects; and that relation we must now endeavour to discover. I find in the first place that whatever objects are considered as causes or effects are *contiguous;* and that nothing can operate in a time or place which is ever so little removed from those of its existence. Though distant objects may sometimes seem productive of each other, they are commonly found upon examination to be linked by a chain of causes which are contiguous among themselves, and to the distant objects; and when in any particular instance we cannot discover this connexion, we still presume it to exist. We may therefore consider the relation of *contiguity* as essential to that of causation; at least may suppose it such, according to the general opinion, till we can find a more proper occasion to clear up this matter, by examining what objects are or are not susceptible of juxtaposition and conjunction.

The second relation I shall observe as essential to causes and effects, is not so universally acknowledged, but is liable to some controversy. It is that of *priority* of time in the cause before the effect. Some pretend that it is not absolutely necessary a cause should precede its effect; but that any object or action, in the very first moment of its existence, may exert its productive quality, and give rise to another object or action, perfectly contemporary with itself. But beside that experience in most instances seems to contradict this opinion, we may establish the relation of priority by a kind of inference or reasoning. It is an established maxim, both in natural and moral philosophy, that an object which exists for any time in its full perfection without producing another is not its sole cause; but is assisted by some other principle which pushes it from its state of inactivity, and makes it exert that energy of which it was secretly possessed. Now if any cause may be perfectly contemporary with its effect, it is certain, according to this maxim, that they must all of them be so; since any one of them which retards its operation for a single moment exerts not itself at that very individual time in which it might have operated; and therefore is no proper cause. The consequence of this would be no less than the destruction of that succession of causes which we observe in the world; and indeed the utter annihilation of time. For if one cause were contemporary with its effect, and this effect with *its* effect, and so on, it is plain there would be no such thing as succession, and all objects must be coexistent.

If this argument appear satisfactory, it is well. If not, I beg the reader to allow me the same liberty which I have used in the preceding case of supposing it such. For he shall find that the affair is of no great importance.

Having thus discovered or supposed the two relations of *contiguity* and *succession* to be essential to causes and effects, I find I am stopped short, and can proceed no farther in considering any single instance of cause and effect. Motion in one body is regarded upon impulse as the cause of motion in another. When we consider these objects with the utmost attention, we find only that the one body approaches the other; and that the motion of it precedes that of the other, but without any sensible interval. It is in vain to rack ourselves with farther thought and reflection upon this subject. We can go no farther in considering this particular instance.

Should any one leave this instance, and pretend to define a cause by saying it is something productive of another, it is evident he would say nothing. For what does he mean by *production?* Can he give any definition of it that will not be the same with that of causation? If he can, I desire it may be produced. If he cannot, he here runs in a circle, and gives a synonymous term instead of a definition.

Shall we then rest contented with these two relations of contiguity and succession, as affording a complete idea of causation? By no means. An object may be contiguous and prior to another, without being considered as its cause. There is a *necessary connexion* to be taken into consideration; and that relation is of much greater importance than any of the other two above-mentioned.

Here again I turn the object on all sides, in order to discover the nature of this necessary connexion, and find the impression, or impressions, from which its idea may be derived. When I cast my eye on the *known qualities* of objects, I immediately discover that the relation of cause and effect depends not in the least on *them*. When I consider their *relations,* I can find none but those of contiguity and succession; which I have already regarded as imperfect and unsatisfactory. Shall the despair of success make me assert that I am here possessed of an idea, which is not preceded by any similar impression? This would be too strong a proof of levity and inconstancy; since the contrary principle has been already so firmly established as to admit of no farther doubt; at least, till we have more fully examined the present difficulty.

We must therefore proceed like those who, being in search of anything that lies concealed from them, and not finding it in the place they expected, beat about all the neighbouring fields, without any certain view or design, in hopes their good fortune will at last guide them to what they search for. It is necessary for us to leave the direct survey of this question concerning the nature of that *necessary connexion* which enters into our idea of cause and effect; and endeavour to find some other questions, the examination of which will perhaps afford a hint that may serve to clear up the present difficulty. Of these questions there occur two which I shall proceed to examine, viz.,

First, For what reason we pronounce it *necessary* that everything whose existence has a beginning, should also have a cause?

Secondly, Why we conclude, that such particular causes must *necessarily* have such particular effects; and what is the nature of that *inference* we draw from the one to the other, and of the *belief* we repose in it?

I shall only observe before I proceed any farther, that though the ideas of cause and effect be derived from the impressions of reflexion as well as from those of sensation, yet for brevity's sake, I commonly mention only the latter as the origin of these ideas; though I desire that whatever I say of them may also extend to the former. Passions are connected with their objects and with one another; no less than external bodies are connected together. The same relation then of cause and effect which belongs to one, must be common to all of them.

SECTION III. *Why a Cause Is Always Necessary*

To begin with the first question concerning the necessity

of a cause: It is a general maxim in philosophy that *whatever begins to exist must have a cause of existence*. This is commonly taken for granted in all reasonings, without any proof given or demanded. It is supposed to be founded on intuition, and to be one of those maxims which, though they may be denied with the lips, it is impossible for men in their hearts really to doubt of. But if we examine this maxim by the idea of knowledge above-explained, we shall discover in it no mark of any such intuitive certainty; but on the contrary shall find that it is of a nature quite foreign to that species of conviction.

All certainty arises from the comparison of ideas, and from the discovery of such relations as are unalterable, so long as the ideas continue the same. These relations are *resemblance, proportions in quantity and number, degrees of any quality, and contrariety;* none of which are implied in this proposition, *Whatever has a beginning has also a cause of existence.* That proposition therefore is not intuitively certain. At least, any one who would assert it to be intuitively certain must deny these to be the only infallible relations, and must find some other relation of that kind to be implied in it; which it will then be time enough to examine.

But here is an argument which proves at once that the foregoing proposition is neither intuitively nor demonstrably certain. We can never demonstrate the necessity of a cause to every new existence, or new modification of existence, without showing at the same time the impossibility there is that anything can ever begin to exist without some productive principle; and where the latter proposition cannot be proved, we must despair of ever being able to prove the former. Now, that the latter proposition is utterly incapable of a demonstrative proof, we may satisfy ourselves by considering that as all distinct ideas are separable from each other, and as the ideas of cause and effect are evidently distinct, it will be easy for us to conceive any object to be non-existent this moment and existent the next, without conjoining to it the distinct idea of a cause or productive principle. The separation therefore of the idea of a cause from that of a beginning of existence, is plainly possible for the imagination; and consequently the actual separation of these objects is so far possible, that it implies no contradiction nor absurdity; and is therefore incapable of being refuted by any reasoning from mere ideas; without which it is impossible to demonstrate the necessity of a cause.

Accordingly, we shall find upon examination that every demonstration which has been produced for the necessity of a cause is fallacious and sophistical. All the points of time and place, say some philosophers, in which we can suppose any object to begin to exist, are in themselves equal; and unless there be some cause which is peculiar to one time and to one place, and which by that means determines and fixes the existence, it must remain in eternal suspense; and the object can never begin to be, for want of something to fix its beginning. But, I ask, Is there any more difficulty in supposing the time and place to be fixed without a cause, than to suppose the existence to be determined in that manner? The first question that occurs on this subject is always, *whether* the object shall exist or not: The next, *when* and *where* it shall begin to exist. If the removal of a cause be intuitively absurd in the one case, it must be so in the other: And if that absurdity be not clear without a proof in the one case, it will equally require one in the other. The absurdity then of the one supposition can never be a proof of that of the other; since they are both upon the same footing, and must stand or fall by the same reasoning.

The second argument which I find used on this head, labours under an equal difficulty. Everything, it is said, must have a cause; for if anything wanted a cause, *it* would produce *itself;* that is, exist before it existed, which is impossible. But this reasoning is plainly unconclusive; because it supposes that, in our denial of a cause, we still grant what we expressly deny, viz., that there must be a cause; which therefore is taken to be the object itself; and *that,* no doubt, is an evident contradiction. But to say that anything is produced, or, to express myself more properly, comes into existence, without a cause, is not to affirm that it is itself its own cause; but, on the contrary, in excluding all external causes, excludes a fortiori the thing itself which is created. An object that exists absolutely without any cause certainly is not its own cause; and when you assert that the one follows from the other, you suppose the very point in question, and take it for granted that it is utterly impossible anything can ever begin to exist without a cause, but that, upon the exclusion of one productive principle, we must still have recourse to another.

It is exactly the same case with the third argument which has been employed to demonstrate the necessity of a cause. Whatever is produced without any cause, is produced by *nothing;* or, in other words, has nothing for its cause. But nothing can never be a cause, no more than it can be something, or equal to two right angles. By the same intuition that we perceive nothing not to be equal to two right angles, or not to be something, we perceive that it can never be a cause; and consequently must perceive that every object has a real cause of its existence.

I believe it will not be necessary to employ many words in showing the weakness of this argument, after what I have said of the foregoing. They are all of them founded on the same fallacy, and are derived from the same turn of thought. It is sufficient only to observe that when we exclude all causes we really do exclude them, and neither suppose nothing nor the object itself to be the cause of the existence; and consequently can draw no argument from the absurdity of these suppositions to prove the absurdity of that exclusion. If everything must have a cause, it follows that, upon the exclusion of other causes, we must accept of the object itself or of nothing as causes. But it is the very point in question, whether everything must have a cause or not; and therefore, according to all just reasoning, it ought never to be taken for granted.

They are still more frivolous who say that every effect must have a cause because it is implied in the very idea of effect. Every effect necessarily presupposes a cause; effect being a relative term, of which cause is the correlative. But this does not prove that every being must be preceded by a cause; no more than it follows because every husband must have a wife, that therefore every man must be married. The true state of the question is, whether every object which begins to exist must owe its existence to a cause; and this I assert neither to be intuitively nor demonstratively certain, and hope to have proved it sufficiently by the foregoing arguments.

Since it is not from knowledge or any scientific reasoning that we derive the opinion of the necessity of a cause to every new production, that opinion must necessarily arise from observation and experience. The next question, then, should naturally be, *how experience gives rise to such a principle?* But as I find it will be more convenient to sink this question in the following, *Why we conclude that such particular causes must necessarily have such particular effects, and why we form an inference from one to another?* we shall make that the subject of our future enquiry. It will, perhaps, be found in the end that the same answer will serve for both questions. . . .

SECTION VI. *Of the Inference from the Impression to the Idea*

It is easy to observe that, in tracing this relation, the inference we draw from cause to effect is not derived merely from a survey of these particular objects, and from such a penetration into their essences as may discover the dependence of the one upon the other. There is no object which implies the existence of any other, if we consider these objects in themselves, and never look beyond the ideas which we form of them. Such an inference would amount to knowledge, and would imply the absolute contradiction and impossibility of conceiving anything different. But as all distinct ideas are separable, it is evident there can be no impossibility of that kind. When we pass from a present impression to the idea of any object, we might possibly have separated the idea from the impression, and have substituted any other idea in its room.

It is therefore by *experience* only that we can infer the existence of one object from that of another. The nature of experience is this. We remember to have had frequent instances of the existence of one species of objects; and also remember that the individuals of another species of objects have always attended them, and have existed in a regular order of contiguity and succession with regard to them. Thus we remember to have seen that species of object we call *flame,* and to have felt that species of sensation we call *heat.* We likewise call to mind their constant conjunction in all past instances. Without any farther ceremony, we call the one *cause,* and the other *effect,* and infer the existence of the one from that of the other. In all those instances from which we learn the conjunction of particular causes and effects, both the causes and effects have been perceived by the senses, and are remembered: But in all cases wherein we reason concerning them, there is only one perceived or remembered, and the other is supplied in conformity to our past experience.

Thus, in advancing, we have insensibly discovered a new relation betwixt cause and effect when we least expected it, and were entirely employed upon another subject. This relation is their *constant conjunction.* Contiguity and succession are not sufficient to make us pronounce any two objects to be cause and effect, unless we perceive that these two relations are preserved in several instances. We may now see the advantage of quitting the direct survey of this relation in order to discover the nature of that *necessary connexion* which makes so essential a part of it. There are hopes that by this means we may at last arrive at our proposed end; though, to tell the truth, this new-discovered relation of a constant conjunction seems to advance us but very little in our way. For it implies no more than this, that like objects have always been placed in like relations of contiguity and succession; and it seems evident, at least at first sight, that by this means we can never discover any new idea, and can only multiply, but not enlarge, the objects of our mind. It may be thought, that what we learn not from one object, we can never learn from a hundred, which are all of the same kind, and are perfectly resembling in every circumstance. As our senses show us in one instance two bodies, or motions, or qualities, in certain relations of succession and contiguity; so our memory presents us only with a multitude of instances wherein we always

find like bodies, motions, or qualities, in like relations.
From the mere repetition of any past impression, even to
infinity, there never will arise any new original idea, such
as that of a necessary connexion; and the number of impressions has in this case no more effect than if we confined
ourselves to one only. But though this reasoning seems just
and obvious, yet, as it would be folly to despair too soon,
we shall continue the thread of our discourse; and, having
found that after the discovery of the constant conjunction
of any objects we always draw an inference from one object to another, we shall now examine the nature of that
inference, and of the transition from the impression to the
idea. Perhaps it will appear in the end that the necessary
connexion depends on the inference, instead of the inference's depending on the necessary connexion.

Since it appears that the transition from an impression
present to the memory or senses to the idea of an object,
which we call cause or effect, is founded on past *experience*, and on our remembrance of their *constant conjunction*, the next question is, Whether experience produces the
idea by means of the understanding or of the imagination;
whether we are determined by reason to make the transition, or by a certain association and relation of perceptions. If reason determined us, it would proceed upon that
principle *that instances, of which we have had no experience must resemble those of which we have had experience, and that the course of nature continues always uni-
formly the same.* In order, therefore, to clear up this
matter, let us consider all the arguments upon which such
a proposition may be supposed to be founded; and as
these must be derived either from *knowledge* or *probability*, let us cast our eye on each of these degrees of evidence,
and see whether they afford any just conclusion of this
nature.

Our foregoing method of reasoning will easily convince
us that there can be no *demonstrative* arguments to prove
*that those instances of which we have had no experience
resemble those of which we have had experience.* We can
at least conceive a change in the course of nature; which
sufficiently proves that such a change is not absolutely im-

possible. To form a clear idea of anything is an undeniable argument for its possibility, and is alone a refutation of any pretended demonstration against it.

Probability, as it discovers not the relations of ideas, considered as such, but only those of objects, must, in some respects, be founded on the impressions of our memory and senses, and in some respects on our ideas. Were there no mixture of any impression in our probable reasonings, the concluson would be entirely chimerical: And were there no mixture of ideas, the action of the mind, in observing the relation, would, properly speaking, be sensation, not reasoning. It is, therefore, necessary that in all probable reasonings there be something present to the mind, either seen or remembered; and that from this we infer something connected with it, which is not seen nor remembered.

The only connexion or relation of objects which can lead us beyond the immediate impressions of our memory and senses, is that of cause and effect; and that because it is the only one on which we can found a just inference from one object to another. The idea of cause and effect is derived from *experience,* which informs us that such particular objects, in all past instances, have been constantly conjoined with each other: And as an object similar to one of these is supposed to be immediately present in its impression, we thence presume on the existence of one similar to its usual attendant. According to this account of things, which is, I think, in every point unquestionable, probability is founded on the presumption of a resemblance betwixt those objects of which we have had experience, and those of which we have had none; and, therefore, it is impossible this presumption can arise from probability. The same principle cannot be both the cause and effect of another; and this is, perhaps, the only proposition concerning that relation which is either intuitively or demonstratively certain.

Should any one think to elude this argument; and, without determining whether our reasoning on this subject be derived from demonstration or probability, pretend that all conclusions from causes and effects are built on solid reasoning: I can only desire that this reasoning may be produced, in order to be exposed to our examination. It may perhaps be said that after experience of the constant conjunction of certain objects, we reason in the following manner. Such an object is always found to produce another. It is impossible it could have this effect, if it was not endowed with a power of production. The power necessarily implies the effect; and therefore there is a just foundation for drawing a conclusion from the existence of one object to that of its usual attendant. The past production implies a power: The power implies a new production: And the new production is what we infer from the power and the past production.

It were easy for me to show the weakness of this reasoning, were I willing to make use of those observations I have already made, that the idea of *production* is the same with that of *causation,* and that no existence certainly and demonstratively implies a power in any other object; or were it proper to anticipate what I shall have occasion to remark afterwards concerning the idea we form of *power* and *efficacy*. But as such a method of proceeding may seem either to weaken my system, by resting one part of it on another, or to breed a confusion in my reasoning, I shall endeavour to maintain my present assertion without any such assistance.

It shall therefore be allowed for a moment, that the production of one object by another in any one instance implies a power; and that this power is connected with its effect. But it having been already proved, that the power lies not in the sensible qualities of the cause; and there being nothing but the sensible qualities present to us; I ask why in other instances you presume that the same power still exists, merely upon the appearance of these qualities? Your appeal to past experience decides nothing in the present case; and at the utmost can only prove that that very object which produced any other was, at that very instant, endowed with such a power; but can never prove that the same power must continue in the same object or collection of sensible qualities; much less that a like power is always conjoined with like sensible qualities.

Should it be said that we have experience that the same power continues united with the same object, and that like objects are endowed with like powers, I would renew my question, *why from this experience we form any conclusion beyond those past instances of which we have had experience?* If you answer this question in the same manner as the preceding, your answer gives still occasion to a new question of the same kind, even *in infinitum;* which clearly proves that the foregoing reasoning had no just foundation.

Thus, not only our reason fails us in the discovery of the *ultimate connexion* of causes and effects, but, even after experience has informed us of their *constant conjunction,* it is impossible for us to satisfy ourselves by our reason why we should extend that experience beyond those particular instances which have fallen under our observation. We suppose, but are never able to prove, that there must be a resemblance betwixt those objects of which we have had experience, and those which lie beyond the reach of our discovery. . . .

There is indeed a principle of union among ideas, which at first sight may be esteemed different from any of these, but will be found at the bottom to depend on the same origin. When every individual of any species of objects is found by experience to be constantly united with an individual of another species, the appearance of any new individual of either species naturally conveys the thought to its usual attendant. Thus, because such a particular idea is commonly annexed to such a particular word, nothing is required but the hearing of that word to produce the correspondent idea; and it will scarce be possible for the mind, by its utmost efforts, to prevent that transition. In this case it is not absolutely necessary that upon hearing such a particular sound we should reflect on any past experience, and consider what idea has been usually connected with the sound. The imagination of itself supplies the place of this reflection, and is so accustomed to pass from the word to the idea, that it interposes not a moment's delay betwixt the hearing of the one, and the conception of the other.

But though I acknowledge this to be a true principle of

association among ideas, I assert it to be the very same
with that betwixt the ideas of cause and effect, and to be an
essential part in all our reasonings from that relation. We
have no other notion of cause and effect but that of certain
objects which have been *always conjoined* together, and
which in all past instances have been found inseparable.
We cannot penetrate into the reason of the conjunction.
We only observe the thing itself, and always find that,
from the constant conjunction, the objects require an union
in the imagination. When the impression of one becomes
present to us, we immediately form an idea of its usual
attendant; and consequently we may establish this as
one part of the definition of an opinion or belief, *that it is
an idea related to or associated with a present impression.* . . .

SECTION VII. *Of the Nature of the Idea or Belief*

The idea of an object is an essential part of the belief
of it, but not the whole. We conceive many things which
we do not believe. In order, then, to discover more fully
the nature of belief, or the qualities of those ideas we assent
to, let us weigh the following considerations.

It is evident that all reasonings from causes or effects
terminate in conclusions concerning matter of fact; that
is, concerning the existence of objects or of their qualities.
It is also evident that the idea of existence is nothing different from the idea of any object, and that when after the
simple conception of anything we would conceive it as
existent, we in reality make no addition to or alteration
on our first idea. Thus, when we affirm that God is existent, we simply form the idea of such a being as he is represented to us; nor is the existence which we attribute to him
conceived by a particular idea which we join to the idea of
his other qualities, and can again separate and distinguish
from them. But I go farther; and, not content with asserting that the conception of the existence of any object is no
addition to the simple conception of it, I likewise maintain
that the belief of the existence joins no new ideas to those
which compose the idea of the object. When I think of

God, when I think of him as existent, and when I believe him to be existent, my idea of him neither encreases nor diminishes. But as it is certain there is a great difference betwixt the simple conception of the existence of an object and the belief of it, and as this difference lies not in the parts or composition of the idea which we conceive; it follows that it must lie in the *manner* in which we conceive it.

Suppose a person present with me, who advances propositions to which I do not assent, *that Caesar died in his bed, that silver is more fusible than lead, or mercury heavier than gold*; it is evident that, notwithstanding my incredulity, I clearly understand his meaning, and form all the same ideas which he forms. My imagination is endowed with the same powers as his; nor is it possible for him to conceive any idea which I cannot conceive; or conjoin any which I cannot conjoin. I therefore ask, Wherein consists the difference betwixt believing and disbelieving any proposition? The answer is easy with regard to propositions that are proved by intuition or demonstration. In that case, the person who assents not only conceives the ideas according to the proposition, but is necessarily determined to conceive them in that particular manner, either immediately, or by the interposition of other ideas. Whatever is absurd is unintelligible; nor is it possible for the imagination to conceive anything contrary to a demonstration. But as, in reasonings from causation, and concerning matters of fact, this absolute necessity cannot take place, and the imagination is free to conceive both sides of the question, I still ask, *Wherein consists the difference betwixt incredulity and belief?* since, in both cases the conception of the idea is equally possible and requisite.

It will not be a satisfactory answer to say that a person who does not assent to a proposition you advance, after having conceived the object in the same manner with you, immediately conceives it in a different manner, and has different ideas about it. This answer is unsatisfactory; not because it contains any falsehood, but because it discovers not all the truth. It is confessed that, in all cases wherein we dissent from any person, we conceive both sides of the question; but as we can believe only one, it evidently follows that the belief must make some difference betwixt that conception to which we assent, and that from which we dissent. We may mingle, and unite, and separate, and confound, and vary our ideas in a hundred different ways; but until there appears some principle which fixes one of these different situations, we have in reality no opinion: And this principle, as it plainly makes no addition to our precedent ideas, can only change the *manner* of our conceiving them.

All the perceptions of the mind are of two kinds, viz., impressions and ideas, which differ from each other only in their different degrees of force and vivacity. Our ideas are copied from our impressions, and represent them in all their parts. When you would any way vary the idea of a particular object, you can only increase or diminish its force and vivacity. If you make any other change on it, it represents a different object or impression. The case is the same as in colours. A particular shade of any colour may acquire a new degree of liveliness or brightness without any other variation. But when you produce any other variation, it is no longer the same shade or colour; so that as belief does nothing but vary the manner in which we conceive any object, it can only bestow on our ideas an additional force and vivacity. An opinion, therefore, or belief, may be most accurately defined, *A lively idea related to or associated with a present impression*

Here are the heads of those arguments which lead us to this conclusion. When we infer the existence of an object from that of others, some object must always be present either to the memory or senses, in order to be the foundation of our reasoning; since the mind cannot run up with its inferences *in infinitum*. Reason can never satisfy us that the existence of any one object does ever imply that of another; so that when we pass from the impression of one to the idea or belief of another, we are not determined by reason, but by custom, or a principle of association. But belief is somewhat more than a simple idea. It is a particular manner of forming an idea: And as the same idea can only be varied by a variation of its degree of force and vivacity; it follows upon the whole that belief is a lively idea produced by a relation to a present impression, according to the foregoing definition.

This operation of the mind, which forms the belief of any matter of fact, seems hitherto to have been one of the greatest mysteries of philosophy: though no one has so much as suspected that there was any difficulty in explaining it. For my part, I must own that I find a considerable difficulty in the case; and that even when I think I understand the subject perfectly, I am at a loss for terms to express my meaning. I conclude, by an induction which seems to me very evident, that an opinion or belief is nothing but an idea, that is different from a fiction, not in the nature, or the order of its parts, but in the *manner* of its being conceived. But when I would explain this *manner,* I scarce find any word that fully answers the case, but am obliged to have recourse to every one's feeling, in order to give him a perfect notion of this operation of the mind. An idea assented to *feels* different from a fictitious idea, that the fancy alone presents to us. And this different feeling I endeavour to explain by calling it a superior *force,* or *vivacity,* or *solidity,* or *firmness,* or *steadiness.* This variety of terms, which may seem so unphilosophical, is intended only to express that act of the mind which renders realities more present to us than fictions, causes them to weigh more in the thought, and gives them a superior influence on the passions and imagination. Provided we agree about the thing, it is needless to dispute about the terms. The imagination has the command over all its ideas, and can join, and mix, and vary them in all the ways possible. It may conceive objects with all the circumstances of place and time. It may set them, in a manner, before our eyes in their true colours, just as they might have existed. But as it is impossible that that faculty can ever of itself reach belief, it is evident that belief consists not in the nature and order of our ideas, but in the manner of their conception, and in their feeling to the mind. I confess that it is impossible to explain perfectly this feeling or manner of conception. We may make use of words that express something near it. But its true and proper name is *belief,* which is a term that every one sufficiently understands in common life. And in philosophy, we can go no farther than assert that it is something *felt* by the mind, which distinguishes the ideas of the judgment from the fictions of the imagination. It gives them more force and influence; makes them appear of greater importance; infixes them in the mind; and renders them the governing principles of all our actions.

This definition will also be found to be entirely conformable to every one's feeling and experience. Nothing is more evident than that those ideas to which we assent, are more strong, firm, and vivid than the loose reveries of a castle-builder. If one person sits down to read a book as a romance, and another as a true history, they plainly receive the same ideas, and in the same order; nor does the incredulity of the one, and the belief of the other, hinder them from putting the very same sense upon their author. His words produce the same ideas in both; though his testimony has not the same influence on them. The latter has a more lively conception of all the incidents. He enters deeper into the concerns of the persons: represents to himself their actions, and characters, and friendships, and enmities: He even goes so far as to form a notion of their features, and air, and person. While the former, who gives no credit to the testimony of the author, has a more faint and languid conception of all these particulars; and, except on account of the style and ingenuity of the composition, can receive little entertainment from it. . . .

SECTION XIV. *Of the Idea of Necessary Connexion*

Having thus explained the manner *in which we reason beyond our immediate impressions, and conclude that such particular causes must have such particular effects;* we must now return upon our footsteps to examine that question which first occurred to us, and which we dropped in our way, viz., *What is our idea of necessity, when we say that two objects are necessarily connected together?* Upon this head I repeat, what I have often had occasion to observe, that as we have no idea that is not derived from an impression, we must find some impression that gives rise to this idea of necessity, if we assert we have really such an idea. In order to this, I consider in what objects necessity is commonly supposed to lie; and, finding that it is always ascribed to causes and effects, I turn my eye to two objects supposed to be placed in that relation; and examine them in all the situations of which they are susceptible. I immediately perceive that they are *contiguous* in time and place, and that the object we call cause *precedes* the other we call effect. In no one instance can I go any farther, nor is it possible for me to discover any third relation betwixt these objects. I therefore enlarge my view to comprehend several instances; where I find like objects always existing in like relations of contiguity and succession. At first sight this seems to serve but little to my purpose. The reflection on several instances only repeats the same objects; and therefore can never give rise to a new idea. But upon further enquiry I find that the repetition is not in every particular the same, but produces a new impression, and by that means the idea which I at present examine. For, after a frequent repetition, I find that upon the appearance of one of the objects the mind is *determined* by custom to consider its usual attendant, and to consider it in a stronger light upon account of its relation to the first object. It is this impression, then, or *determination,* which affords me the idea of necessity.

I doubt not but these consequences will at first sight be received without difficulty, as being evident deductions from principles which we have already established, and which we have often employed in our reasonings. This evidence, both in the first principles and in the deductions, may seduce us unwarily into the conclusion, and make us imagine it contains nothing extraordinary, nor worthy of our curiosity. But though such an inadvertence may facilitate the reception of this reasoning, it will make it be the more easily forgot; for which reason I think it proper to give warning that I have just now examined one of the most sublime questions in philosophy, viz., *that concerning the power and efficacy of causes;* where all the sciences seem so much interested. Such a warning will naturally rouse up the attention of the reader, and make him desire a more full account of my doctrine, as well as of the arguments on which it is founded. This request is so reasonable that I cannot refuse complying with it; especially as I am hopeful that these principles, the more they are examined, will acquire the more force and evidence.

There is no question which, on account of its importance, as well as difficulty, has caused more disputes both among ancient and modern philosophers, than this concerning the efficacy of causes, or that quality which makes them be followed by their effects. But before they entered upon these disputes, methinks it would not have been improper to have examined what idea we have of that efficacy, which is the subject of the controversy. This is what I find principally wanting in their reasonings, and what I shall here endeavour to supply.

I begin with observing that the terms of *efficacy, agency, power, force, energy, necessity, connexion,* and *productive quality,* are all nearly synonymous; and therefore it is an absurdity to employ any of them in defining the rest. By this observation we reject at once all the vulgar definitions which philosophers have given of power and efficacy; and instead of searching for the idea in these definitions, must look for it in the impressions from which it is originally derived. If it be a compound idea, it must arise from compound impressions. If simple, from simple impressions.

I believe the most general and most popular explication of this matter is to say that, finding from experience that there are several new productions in matter, such as the motions and variations of body, and concluding that there must somewhere be a power capable of producing them, we arrive at last by this reasoning at the idea of power and efficacy. But, to be convinced that this explication is more popular than philosophical, we need but reflect on two very obvious principles. *First,* That reason alone can never give rise to any original idea; and, *secondly,* that reason, as distinguished from experience, can never make us conclude that a cause or productive quality is absolutely requisite to every beginning of existence. Both these considerations have been sufficiently explained; and therefore shall not at present be any farther insisted on.

I shall only infer from them that since reason can never give rise to the idea of efficacy, that idea must be derived from experience, and from some particular instances of this efficacy which make their passage into the mind by the common channels of sensation or reflexion. Ideas always represent their objects or impressions; and vice versa, there are some objects necessary to give rise to every idea. If we pretend, therefore, to have any just idea of this efficacy, we must produce some instance wherein the efficacy is plainly discoverable to the mind, and its operations obvious to our consciousness or sensation. By the refusal of this, we acknowledge that the idea is impossible and imaginary; since the principle of innate ideas, which alone can save us from this dilemma, has been already refuted, and is now almost universally rejected in the learned world. Our present business, then, must be to find some natural production, where the operation and efficacy of a cause can be clearly conceived and comprehended by the mind, without any danger of obscurity or mistake.

In this research we meet with very little encouragement from that prodigious diversity which is found in the opinions of those philosophers who have pretended to explain the secret force and energy of causes. There are some who maintain that bodies operate by their substantial form; others, by their accidents or qualities; several, by their matter and form; some, by their form and accidents; others, by certain virtues and faculties distinct from all this. All these sentiments, again, are mixed and varied in a thousand different ways; and form a strong presumption that none of them have any solidity or evidence, and that the supposition of an efficacy in any of the known qualities of matter is entirely without foundation. This presumption must increase upon us when we consider that these principles of substantial forms, and accidents, and faculties are not in reality any of the known properties of bodies, but are perfectly unintelligible and inexplicable. For it is evident philosophers would never have recourse to such obscure and uncertain principles, had they met with any satisfaction in such as are clear and intelligible; especially in such an affair as this, which must be an object of the simplest understanding, if not of the senses. Upon the whole, we may conclude that it is impossible, in any one instance, to show the principle in which the force and agency of a cause is placed; and that the most refined and most vulgar understandings are equally at a loss in this particular. If any one think proper to refute this assertion, he need not put himself to the trouble of inventing any long reasonings; but may at once show us an instance of a cause where we discover the power or operating principle. This defiance we are obliged frequently to make use of, as being almost the only means of proving a negative in philosophy. . . .

Some have asserted that we feel an energy or power in our own mind; and that, having in this manner acquired the idea of power, we transfer that quality to matter, where we are not able immediately to discover it. The motions of our body, and the thoughts and sentiments of our mind (say they) obey the will; nor do we seek any farther to acquire a just notion of force or power. But to convince us how fallacious this reasoning is, we need only consider that the will being here considered as a cause has no more a discoverable connexion with its effects than any material cause has with its proper effect. So far from perceiving the connexion betwixt an act of volition and a motion of the body; it is allowed that no effect is more inexplicable from the powers and essence of thought and matter. Nor is the empire of the will over our mind more intelligible. The effect is there distinguishable and separable from the cause, and could not be foreseen without the experience of their constant conjunction. We have command over our mind to a certain degree, but beyond *that* lose all empire over it: And it is evidently impossible to fix any precise bounds to our authority, where we consult not experience. In short, the actions of the mind are, in this respect, the same with those of matter. We perceive only their constant conjunction; nor can we ever reason beyond it. No internal impression has an apparent energy, more than external

objects have. Since, therefore, matter is confessed by philosophers to operate by an unknown force, we should in
vain hope to attain an idea of force by consulting our own
minds. . . .

The idea of necessity arises from some impression.
There is no impression conveyed by our senses which can
give rise to that idea. It must, therefore, be derived from
some internal impression or impression of reflection.
There is no internal impression which has any relation
to the present business but that propensity, which custom
produces, to pass from an object to the idea of its usual
attendant. This, therefore, is the essence of necessity.
Upon the whole, necessity is something that exists in the
mind, not in objects; nor is it possible for us ever to form
the most distant idea of it, considered as a quality in bodies. Either we have no idea of necessity, or necessity is
nothing but that determination of the thought to pass from
causes to effects, and from effects to causes, according to
their experienced union.

Thus, as the necessity, which makes two times two equal
to four, or three angles of a triangle equal to two right
ones, lies only in the act of the understanding, by which
we consider and compare these ideas; in like manner the
necessity or power which unites causes and effects, lies in
the determination of the mind to pass from the one to the
other. The efficacy or energy of causes is neither placed
in the causes themselves, nor in the deity, nor in the concurrence of these two principles; but belongs entirely to
the soul, which considers the union of two or more objects
in all past instances. It is here that the real power of causes
is placed, along with their connexion and necessity.

I am sensible that of all the paradoxes which I have
had, or shall hereafter have, occasion to advance in the
course of this treatise, the present one is the most violent,
and that it is merely by dint of solid proof and reasoning
I can ever hope it will have admission, and overcome the
inveterate prejudices of mankind. . . .

There may two definitions be given of this relation,
which are only different by their presenting a different

view of the same object, and making us consider it either as a *philosophical* or as a *natural* relation; either as a comparison of two ideas, or as an association betwixt them. We may define a *cause* to be "An object precedent and contiguous to another, and where all the objects resembling the former are placed in like relations of precedency and contiguity to those objects that resemble the latter." If this definition be esteeemed defective, because drawn from objects foreign to the cause, we may substitute this other definition in its place, viz., "A *cause* is an object precedent and contiguous to another, and so united with it that the idea of the one determines the mind to form the idea of the other, and the impression of the one to form a more lively idea of the other." Should this definition also be rejected for the same reason, I know no other remedy than that the persons who express this delicacy should substitute a juster definition in its place. But, for my part, I must own my incapacity for such an undertaking. When I examine, with the utmost accuracy, those objects which are commonly denominated causes and effects, I find, in considering a single instance, that the one object is precedent and contiguous to the other; and in enlarging my view to consider several instances, I find only that like objects are constantly placed in like relations of succession and contiguity. Again, when I consider the influence of this constant conjunction, I perceive that such a relation can never be an object of reasoning, and can never operate upon the mind but by means of custom, which determines the imagination to make a transition from the idea of one object to that of its usual attendant, and from the impression of one to a more lively idea of the other. However extraordinary these sentiments may appear, I think it fruitless to trouble myself with any farther enquiry or reasoning upon the subject, but shall repose myself on them as on established maxims.]

SO MUCH FOR THE INSOLUBLE PROBLEM—A LOGICAL squaring of the circle—of how to "justify" induction, without introducing illegitimate a priori laws of nature, by means of some principle or truth compatible with empiri-

cism, itself neither merely probable nor yet accepted un-
critically—"on instinct." The passages which follow contain Hume's treatment of a closely related and equally
central topic: what we mean by material objects, and in
particular by their continuous identity in time and space.
And once the identity of things is considered, the identity
of persons turns out to be a notion equally obscure. The
nature of selves as opposed to things is something left un-
discussed, save in very glancing terms, by Locke and
Berkeley, though the latter throws out some obscure sug-
gestions about the connection of spirits with action or volition rather than perception which were later echoed by
German and French anti-sensationalist metaphysicians.
But the honor of exploding the dogmatic assumptions
about substantive selves, timeless and unchanging, which
were common to the theories of knowledge of rationalists
and theists, belongs to Hume alone. His analysis of the self
is perhaps the most characteristically devastating application of his empirical method, and has, in its own way,
caused as much scandal during the two hundred years that
followed as his undermining of the a priori basis of induction. Material objects are to Hume a harmless illusion,
but an illusion nevertheless.

Once again we find Hume claiming to give a psychological explanation—the imagination is as usual the culprit—
of why we hold a certain false belief ("a very little reflection and philosophy is sufficient to make us see the fallacy
of this opinion") where we should today be inclined to say
that what he was doing was to elucidate the nature of certain of our criteria, in this case, the criteria for physical
objects. If we hold, as Hume held, somewhat inconsist-
ently with his empirical premises, a metaphysical theory
about the external world according to which all that exists
are collections of swiftly flowing, exceedingly short-lived,
"impressions," then how are material objects—or what
goes under that notion—compounded out of them? What
are the characteristics of a particular set of sense data in
virtue of which they are thought of as uniquely belonging
to, or being "of," one object?

This question as it stands comprises two distinct, though

overlapping, problems: that of belonging to the same object; and that of continuity in time. An example of the first
question is this. As I sit writing, what are the characteristics of the sensations that I am now experiencing, in
virtue of which the shape, colour, smell, etc., "of the
paper" present themselves to me as *properties of the same
object*—the piece of paper—as distinct from the shape of
the hand, the smell of the paper, and the colour of my pen,
which are not, though equally coexistent, properties of the
same single object? This question is answered by empiricists mainly in terms of the "spatial cohesion" of the properties of the paper: when one of the properties of the
paper moves, the others (and only they) always move
with it, and so on. And if we ask, in a different sense, the
Humean question, why we collect properties together in
bundles in this, rather than any other, way, the reasons are
pragmatic (and partly biological); they have to do with
our basic needs, as well as ease and convenience in our
transactions with the outside world.

This, however, is not the question which Hume dis-
cusses. He is concerned rather with continuity. Given
Berkeley's (and usually Locke's) position that all that we
are acquainted with are "ideas," or, in Hume's terminology, "impressions" (what English philosophers in our own
time have called "sense data"), on what principles do we
"collect" together certain (interrupted) temporal se-
quences of these sense data, and take them to be part of
the unbroken history of one object, and regard this object
as having a *distinct* and *continued* existence, *external* to
and causally *independent* of our minds.[6]

Hume answers this question in terms of what he calls
"constancy" and "coherence." Provided that the data remain relatively stable—or change in such a way that the
assumption that the change is continuous, even if unperceived, is not inconsistent with our other data—we speak
of an object as identical through change. His answer may
be criticized in detail and it is certainly carelessly formu-

[6] The four words in italics denote the properties of objects discussed by Hume, although Hume of course regards them as fictitiously ascribed to mythical substrata.

lated at some points. Nevertheless, his contribution is of the highest importance. Any philosopher who accepts a sense-datum theory of the external world must sooner or later come to terms with the problem Hume is considering. However much subsequent solutions may differ in detail or in the accuracy of their formulation, they inevitably resemble Hume's in major points of principle. In asking the question, and providing the definite ground plan for an answer, Hume made an important advance in the theory of perception which stems from Berkeley.

Hume, of course, does not think that he is simply giving a theory of perception or even of the criteria for the application of the concept of material identity, or of a material object. He thinks that he is giving a psychological explanation of our false beliefs in certain "fictions." Among these is our fictitious ascription of *identity* to objects. Hume himself is very much perplexed by the notion of identity (as was F. H. Bradley a century and a half later). He cannot see how we could truly utter a proposition of the form "A is identical with B," or, in more ordinary language, "A is the same (person, tree, ship, etc.) as B." For if "A" and "B" really do denote the *same* entity, then the form of words does not, so Hume thinks, state a significant proposition at all; ("nor would the proposition contain a predicate and a subject, which, however, are implied in this affirmation"). It is in effect saying "A is A," which seems a tedious tautology. But if they do not denote literally the same entity, then the proposition—by identifying entities which are *ex hypothesi* not identical—is clearly false.

Hume, in fact, adopts a concept of identity which has no application, except perhaps in mathematics and logic: that of literal identity, identity in all respects whatever. Such a concept can have no application to the real world. When we affirm truly that this is the same tree as the one we saw ten years ago in the same garden, we do not mean that it (or the garden) is the same in absolutely all respects; we do not, for example, wish to deny that the tree has acquired new cells and lost old ones. Even with such a stable object as a stone, we should still call it the same even if a bit had been chipped off; and we certainly do not wish to deny that there have been changes in the distribution of electrons. And in the case of, let us say, houses or towns or flowers, we allow a very great deal of change before we become dubious about whether they are the same. Now one consequence of Hume's "ideal limit" concept of identity is this. Wherever we should say that he was describing the criteria (different in each case) for the truth of such propositions as "He is the same person I met a year ago in London," "That is the same ship that I saw in the Mediterranean in 1946," he regards himself as giving a psychological explanation of our invariably false ascriptions of identity. These ascriptions are false, but we cannot, apparently, avoid making them: they are a kind of necessary illusion. This paradoxical theory dominates Hume even more obsessively in his celebrated discussion of personal identity which follows upon that of material objects.

The following is from Part IV, *Of the Sceptical and other Systems of Philosophy.*

[SECTION II. *Of Scepticism with Regard to the Senses*

Thus the sceptic still continues to reason and believe, even though he asserts that he cannot defend his reason by reason; and by the same rule he must assent to the principle concerning the existence of body, though he cannot pretend, by any arguments of philosophy, to maintain its veracity. Nature has not left this to his choice, and has doubtless esteemed it an affair of too great importance to be trusted to our uncertain reasonings and speculations. We may well ask, *What causes induce us to believe in the existence of body?* but it is in vain to ask, *Whether there be body or not?* That is a point which we must take for granted in all our reasonings.

The subject, then, of our present enquiry, is concerning the *causes* which induce us to believe in the existence of body: And my reasonings on this head I shall begin with a distinction which at first sight may seem superfluous, but which will contribute very much to the perfect understanding of what follows. We ought to examine apart those two questions which are commonly confounded together, viz., Why we attribute a *continued* existence to objects, even when they are not present to the senses; and why we suppose them to have an existence *distinct* from the mind and perception. Under this last head I comprehend their situation as well as relations, their *external* position as well as the *independence* of their existence and operation. These two questions concerning the continued and distinct existence of body are intimately connected together. For if the objects of our senses continue to exist even when they are not perceived, their existence is of course independent of and distinct from the perception; and, vice versa, if their existence be independent of the perception and distinct from it, they must continue to exist even though they be not perceived. But though the decision of the one question decides the other; yet that we may the more easily discover the principles of human nature, from whence the decision arises, we shall carry along with us this distinction, and shall consider whether it be the *senses, reason,* or the *imagination,* that produces the opinion of a *continued* or of a *distinct* existence. These are the only questions that are intelligible on the present subject. For as to the notion of external existence, when taken for something specifically different from our perceptions, we have already shown its absurdity.

To begin with the *senses,* it is evident these faculties are incapable of giving rise to the notion of the *continued* existence of their objects after they no longer appear to the senses. For that is a contradiction in terms, and supposes that the senses continue to operate even after they have ceased all manner of operation. These faculties, therefore, if they have any influence in the present case, must produce the opinion of a distinct, not of a continued, existence; and in order to that, must present their impressions either as images and representations, or as these very distinct and external existences.

That our senses offer not their impressions as the images of something *distinct,* or *independent,* and *external,* is evident; because they convey to us nothing but a single perception, and never give us the least intimation of anything beyond. A single perception can never produce the idea of a double existence, but by some inference either of the reason or imagination. When the mind looks farther than what immediately appears to it, its conclusions can never be put to the account of the senses; and it certainly looks farther, when from a single preception it infers a double existence, and supposes the relations of resemblance and causation betwixt them. . . .

To begin with the question concerning *external* existence, it may perhaps be said that, setting aside the metaphysical question of the identity of a thinking substance, our own body evidently belongs to us; and, as several impressions appear exterior to the body, we suppose them also exterior to ourselves. The paper on which I write at present is beyond my hand. The table is beyond the paper. The walls of the chamber beyond the table. And in casting my eye towards the window, I perceive a great extent of fields and buildings beyond my chamber. From all this it may be inferred that no other faculty is required beside the senses to convince us of the external existence of the body. But to prevent this inference, we need only weigh the three following considerations. *First,* That, properly speaking, it is not our body we perceive when we regard our limbs and members, but certain impressions, which enter by the senses; so that the ascribing a real and corporeal existence to these impressions, or to their objects, is an act of the mind as difficult to explain as that which we examine at present. *Secondly,* Sounds, and tastes, and smells, though commonly regarded by the mind as continued independent qualities, appear not to have any existence in extension, and consequently cannot appear to the senses as situated externally to the body. The reason why we ascribe a place to them shall be considered afterwards. *Thirdly,* Even our sight informs us not of distance or outness (so to speak), immediately and without a certain reasoning and experience, as is acknowledged by the most rational philosophers.

As to the *independency* of our perceptions on ourselves, this can never be an object of the senses; but any opinion we form concerning it must be derived from experience and observation: And we shall see afterwards that our conclusions from experience are far from being favourable to the doctrine of the independency of our perceptions. Meanwhile, we may observe that when we talk of real distinct existences, we have commonly more in our eye their independency than external situation in place, and think an object has a sufficient reality when its Being is uninterrupted, and independent of the incessant revolutions which we are conscious of in ourselves.

Thus to resume what I have said concerning the senses; they give us no notion of continued existence, because they cannot operate beyond the extent in which they really operate. They as little produce the opinion of a distinct existence, because they neither can offer it to the mind as represented, nor as original. To offer it as represented, they must present both an object and an image. To make it appear as original, they must convey a falsehood; and this falsehood must lie in the relations and situation: In order to which, they must be able to compare the object with ourselves; and even in that case they do not, nor is it possible they should, deceive us. We may therefore conclude with certainty that the opinion of a continued and of a distinct existence never arises from the senses.

To confirm this, we may observe that there are three different kinds of impressions conveyed by the senses. The first are those of the figure, bulk, motion, and solidity of bodies. The second, those of colours, tastes, smells, sounds, heat, and cold. The third are the pains and pleasures that arise from the application of objects to our bodies, as by the cutting of our flesh with steel, and such like. Both philosophers and the vulgar suppose the first of these to have a distinct continued existence. The vulgar only regard the second as on the same footing. Both philosophers and the vulgar, again, esteem the third to be merely perceptions; and, consequently, interrupted and dependent beings.

Now, it is evident that whatever may be our philosophical opinion, colours, sounds, heat, and cold, as far as appears to the senses, exist after the same manner with motion and solidity; and that the difference we make betwixt them, in this respect, arises not from the mere perception. So strong is the prejudice for the distinct continued existence of the former qualities that when the contrary opinion is advanced by modern philosophers, people imagine they can almost refute it from their feeling and experience, and that their very senses contradict this philosophy. It is also evident, that colours, sounds, &c., are originally on the same footing with the pain that arises from steel, and pleasure that proceeds from a fire; and that the difference betwixt them is founded neither on perception nor reason, but on the imagination. For as they are confessed to be, both of them, nothing but perceptions arising from the particular configurations and motions of the parts of body, wherein possibly can their difference consist? Upon the whole, then, we may conclude that, as far as the senses are judges, all perceptions are the same in the manner of their existence.

We may also observe, in this instance of sounds and colours, that we can attribute a distinct continued existence to objects without ever consulting *reason,* or weighing our opinions by any philosophical principles. And, indeed, whatever convincing arguments philosophers may fancy they can produce to establish the belief of objects independent of the mind, it is obvious these arguments are known but to very few; and it is not by them that children, peasants, and the greatest part of mankind, are induced to attribute objects to some impressions, and deny them to others. Accordingly, we find that all the conclusions which the vulgar form on this head, are directly contrary to those which are confirmed by philosophy. For philosophy informs us that everything which appears to the mind is nothing but a perception, and is interrupted and dependent on the mind; whereas the vulgar confound perceptions and objects, and attribute a distinct continued existence to the very things they feel or see. This sentiment, then, as it is entirely unreasonable, most proceed from some other faculty than the understanding. To which we may add that, as long as we take our perceptions and objects to be the same, we can never infer the existence of

the one from that of the other, nor form any argument
from the relation of cause and effect; which is the only one
that can assure us of matter of fact. Even after we distinguish our perceptions from our objects, it will appear presently that we are still incapable of reasoning from the
existence of one to that of the other: So that, upon the
whole, our reason neither does, nor is it possible it ever
should, upon any supposition give us an assurance of the
continued and distinct existence of body. That opinion
must be entirely owing to the *imagination*: which must
now be the subject of our enquiry.

Since all impressions are internal and perishing existences, and appear as such, the notion of their distinct and
continued existence must arise from a concurrence of some
of their qualities with the qualities of the imagination; and
since this notion does not extend to all of them, it must
arise from certain qualities peculiar to some impressions.
It will, therefore, be easy for us to discover these qualities
by a comparison of the impressions to which we attribute
a distinct and continued existence, with those which we
regard as internal and perishing.

We may observe, then, that it is neither upon account
of the involuntariness of certain impressions, as is commonly supposed, nor of their superior force and violence,
that we attribute to them a reality and continued existence
which we refuse to others that are voluntary or feeble.
For it is evident our pains and pleasures, our passions
and affections, which we never suppose to have any existence beyond our perception, operate with greater violence,
and are equally involuntary, as the impressions of figure
and extension, colour and sound, which we suppose to be
permanent beings. The heat of a fire, when moderate, is
supposed to exist in the fire; but the pain which it causes
upon a near approach is not taken to have any being except in the perception.

These vulgar opinions, then, being rejected, we must
search for some other hypothesis, by which we may discover those peculiar qualities in our impressions which
make us attribute to them a distinct and continued existence.

After a little examination, we shall find that all those objects to which we attribute a continued existence, have a peculiar *constancy*, which distinguishes them from the impressions whose existence depends upon our perception. Those mountains, and houses, and trees which lie at present under my eye, have always appeared to me in the same order; and when I lose sight of them by shutting my eyes or turning my head, I soon after find them return upon me without the least alteration. My bed and table, my books and papers, present themselves in the same uniform manner, and change not upon account of any interruption in my seeing or perceiving them. This is the case with all the impressions whose objects are supposed to have an external existence; and is the case with no other impressions, whether gentle or violent, voluntary or involuntary.

This constancy, however, is not so perfect as not to admit of very considerable exceptions. Bodies often change their position and qualities, and, after a little absence or interruption, may become hardly knowable. But here it is observable that even in these changes they preserve a *coherence,* and have a regular dependence on each other; which is the foundation of a kind of reasoning from causation, and produces the opinion of their continued existence. When I return to my chamber after an hour's absence, I find not my fire in the same situation in which I left it: But then I am accustomed, in other instances, to see a like alteration produced in a like time, whether I am present or absent, near or remote. This coherence, therefore, in their changes, is one of the characteristics of external objects, as well as their constancy.

Having found that the opinion of the continued existence of body depends on the *coherence* and *constancy* of certain impressions, I now proceed to examine after what manner these qualities give rise to so extraordinary an opinion. To begin with the coherence; we may observe that though those internal impressions which we regard as fleeting and perishing, have also a certain coherence or regularity in their appearances, yet it is of somewhat a different nature from that which we discover in bodies.

Our passions are found by experience to have a mutual connexion with and dependence on each other; but on no occasion is it necessary to suppose that they have existed and operated when they were not perceived, in order to preserve the same dependence and connexion of which we have had experience. The case is not the same with relation to external objects. Those require a continued existence, or otherwise lose, in a great measure, the regularity of their operation. I am here seated in my chamber, with my face to the fire; and all the objects that strike my senses are contained in a few yards around me. My memory, indeed, informs me of the existence of many objects; but, then, this information extends not beyond their past existence, nor do either my senses or memory give any testimony to the continuance of their being. When, therefore, I am thus seated, and revolve over these thoughts, I hear on a sudden a noise as of a door turning upon its hinges; and a little after see a porter who advances towards me. This gives occasion to many new reflexions and reasonings. First, I never have observed that this noise could proceed from anything but the motion of a door; and therefore conclude that the present phaenomenon is a contradiction to all past experience, unless the door, which I remember on the other side the chamber, be still in being. Again, I have always found that a human body was possessed of a quality which I call gravity, and which hinders it from mounting in the air, as this porter must have done to arrive at my chamber, unless the stairs I remember be not annihilated by my absence. But this is not all. I receive a letter, which, upon opening it, I perceive by the handwriting and subscription to have come from a friend, who says he is two hundred leagues distant. It is evident I can never account for this phaenomenon, conformable to my experience in other instances, without spreading out in my mind the whole sea and continent between us, and supposing the effects and continued existence of posts and ferries, according to my memory and observation. To consider these phaenomena of the porter and letter in a certain light, they are contradictions to common experience, and may be regarded as objections

to those maxims which we form concerning the connexions
of causes and effects. I am accustomed to hear such a
sound, and see such an object in motion, at the same time.
I have not received, in this particular instance, both these
perceptions. These observations are contrary, unless I
suppose that the door still remains, and that it was opened
without my perceiving it: And this supposition, which was
at first entirely arbitrary and hypothetical, acquires a force
and evidence by its being the only one upon which I can
reconcile these contradictions. There is scarce a moment
of my life wherein there is not a similar instance presented
to me, and I have not occasion to suppose the continued
existence of objects, in order to connect their past and
present appearances, and give them such a union with
each other as I have found, by experience, to be suitable
to their particular natures and circumstances. Here, then,
I am naturally led to regard the world as something real
and durable, and as preserving its existence, even when it
is no longer present to my perception. . . .

When we have been accustomed to observe a constancy
in certain impressions, and have found that the perception
of the sun or ocean, for instance, returns upon us, after
an absence or annihilation, with like parts and in a like
order as at its first appearance, we are not apt to regard
these interrupted perceptions as different (which they
really are), but on the contrary consider them as individually the same, upon account of their resemblance. But
as this interruption of their existence is contrary to their
perfect identity, and makes us regard the first impression
as annihilated, and the second as newly created, we find
ourselves somewhat at a loss, and are involved in a kind
of contradiction. In order to free ourselves from this difficulty, we disguise, as much as possible, the interruption,
or rather remove it entirely, by supposing that these interrupted perceptions are connected by a real existence of
which we are insensible. This supposition, or idea of continued existence, acquires a force and vivacity from the
memory of these broken impressions, and from that propensity which they give us to suppose them the same; and

according to the precedent reasoning, the very essence of belief consists in the force and vivacity of the conception. . . .

We shall afterwards see many instances of this tendency of relation to make us ascribe an *identity* to *different* objects; but shall here confine ourselves to the present subject. We find by experience that there is such a *constancy* in almost all the impressions of the senses that their interruption produces no alteration on them, and hinders them not from returning the same in appearance and in situation as at their first existence. I survey the furniture of my chamber; I shut my eyes, and afterwards open them; and find the new perceptions to resemble perfectly those which formerly struck my senses. This resemblance is observed in a thousand instances, and naturally connects together our ideas of these interrupted perceptions by the strongest relation, and conveys the mind with an easy transition from one to another. An easy transition or passage of the imagination, along the ideas of these different and interrupted perceptions, is almost the same disposition of mind with that in which we consider one constant and uninterrupted perception. It is therefore very natural for us to mistake the one for the other.

The persons who entertain this opinion concerning the identity of our resembling perceptions, are in general all the unthinking and unphilosophical part of mankind (that is, all of us at one time or another), and, consequently, such as suppose their perceptions to be their only objects, and never think of a double existence internal and external, representing and represented. The very image which is present to the senses is with us the real body; and it is to these interrupted images we ascribe a perfect identity. But as the interruption of the appearance seems contrary to the identity, and naturally leads us to regard these resembling perceptions as different from each other, we here find ourselves at a loss how to reconcile such opposite opinions. The smooth passage of the imagination along the ideas of the resembling perceptions makes us ascribe to them a perfect identity. The interrupted manner of their appearance makes us consider them as so many resembling, but still distinct, beings, which appear after certain intervals. The perplexity arising from this contradiction produces a propension to unite these broken appearances by the fiction of a continued existence, which is the *third* part of that hypothesis I proposed to explain. . . .

This sceptical doubt, both with respect to reason and the senses, is a malady which can never be radically cured, but must return upon us every moment, however we may chase it away, and sometimes may seem entirely free from it. It is impossible, upon any system, to defend either our understanding or senses; and we but expose them farther when we endeavour to justify them in that manner. As the sceptical doubt arises naturally from a profound and intense reflection on those subjects, it always encreases the farther we carry our reflections, whether in opposition or conformity to it. Carelessness and inattention alone can afford us any remedy. For this reason I rely entirely upon them; and take it for granted, whatever may be the reader's opinion at this present moment, that an hour hence he will be persuaded there is both an external and internal world; and, going upon that supposition, I intend to examine some general systems, both ancient and modern, which have been proposed of both, before I proceed to a more particular enquiry concerning our impressions. This will not, perhaps, in the end, be found foreign to our present purpose.

SECTION V. *On the Immateriality of the Soul*

Having found such contradictions and difficulties in every system concerning external objects, and in the idea of matter, which we fancy so clear and determinate, we shall naturally expect still greater difficulties and contradictions in every hypothesis concerning our internal perceptions, and the nature of the mind, which we are apt to imagine so much more obscure and uncertain. But in this we should deceive ourselves. The intellectual world, though involved in infinite obscurities, is not perplexed with any such contradictions as those we have discovered in the natural. What is known concerning it agrees with itself; and what is unknown we must be contented to leave so.

It is true, would we hearken to certain philosophers, they promise to diminish our ignorance; but I am afraid it is at the hazard of running us into contradictions from which the subject is of itself exempted. These philosophers are the curious reasoners concerning the material or immaterial substances in which they suppose our perceptions to inhere. In order to put a stop to these endless cavils on both sides, I know no better method than to ask these philosophers in a few words, *What they mean by substance and inhesion?* And after they have answered this question, it will then be reasonable, and not till then, to enter seriously into the dispute.

This question we have found impossible to be answered with regard to matter and body: But besides that in the case of the mind it labours under all the same difficulties, it is burdened with some additional ones which are peculiar to that subject. As every idea is derived from a precedent impression, had we any idea of the substance of our minds, we must also have an impression of it; which is very difficult, if not impossible, to be conceived. For how can an impression represent a substance otherwise than by resembling it? And how can an impression resemble a substance, since, according to this philosophy, it is not a substance, and has none of the peculiar qualities or characteristics of a substance?

But leaving the question of *what may or may not be,* for that other *what actually is,* I desire those philosophers who pretend that we have an idea of the substance of our minds, to point out the impression that produces it, and tell distinctly after what manner that impression operates, and from what object it is derived. Is it an impression of sensation or of reflection? Is it pleasant, or painful, or indifferent? Does it attend us at all times, or does it only return at intervals? If at intervals, at what times principally does it return, and by what causes is it produced?

If, instead of answering these questions, any one should

evade the difficulty by saying that the definition of a substance is *something which may exist by itself;* and that this
definition ought to satisfy us: Should this be said, I should
observe that this definition agrees to everything that can
possibly be conceived; and never will serve to distinguish
substance from accident, or the soul from its perceptions.
For thus I reason. Whatever is clearly conceived may
exist; and whatever is clearly conceived, after any manner, may exist after the same manner. This is one principle which has been already acknowledged. Again, everything which is different is distinguishable, and everything
which is distinguishable is separable by the imagination.
This is another principle. My conclusion from both is that
since all our perceptions are different from each other, and
from everything else in the universe, they are also distinct
and separable, and may be considered as separately existent, and may exist separately, and have no need of anything else to support their existence. They are therefore
substances, as far as this definition explains a substance.

Thus, neither by considering the first origin of ideas,
nor by means of a definition, are we able to arrive at any
satisfactory notion of substance; which seems to me a
sufficient reason for abandoning utterly that dispute concerning the materiality and immateriality of the soul, and
makes me absolutely condemn even the question itself.
We have no perfect idea of anything but of a perception.
A substance is entirely different from a perception. We
have therefore no idea of a substance. Inhesion in something is supposed to be requisite to support the existence
of our perceptions. Nothing appears requisite to support
the existence of a perception. We have therefore no idea
of inhesion. What possibility then of answering that question, *Whether perceptions inhere in a material or immaterial substance,* when we do not so much as understand
the meaning of the question? . . .

This argument affects not the question concerning the
substance of the soul, but only that concerning its *local
conjunction* with matter; and therefore it may not be improper to consider in general what objects are, or are not,

susceptible of a local conjunction. This is a curious question, and may lead us to some discoveries of considerable moment. . . .

It will not be surprising, after this, if I deliver a maxim which is condemned by several metaphysicians, and is esteemed contrary to the most certain principles of human reason. This maxim is, *that an object may exist, and yet be nowhere*: and I assert that this is not only possible, but that the greatest part of beings do and must exist after this manner. An object may be said to be nowhere, when its parts are not so situated with respect to each other as to form any figure or quantity; nor the whole with respect to other bodies so as to answer to our notions of contiguity or distance. Now this is evidently the case with all our perceptions and objects except those of the sight and feeling. A moral reflection cannot be placed on the right or on the left hand of a passion, nor can a smell or sound be either of a circular or a square figure. These objects and perceptions, so far from requiring any particular place, are absolutely incompatible with it, and even the imagination cannot attribute it to them. And as to the absurdity of supposing them to be nowhere, we may consider that if the passions and sentiments appear to the perception to have any particular place, the idea of extension might be derived from them as well as from the sight and touch; contrary to what we have already established. If they *appear* not to have any particular place, they may possibly *exist* in the same manner; since whatever we conceive is possible.

It will not now be necessary to prove that those perceptions which are simple and exist nowhere, are incapable of any conjunction in place with matter or body, which is extended and divisible; since it is impossible to found a relation but on some common quality. It may be better worth our while to remark that this question of the local conjunction of objects does not only occur in metaphysical disputes concerning the nature of the soul, but that even in common life we have every moment occasion to examine it. Thus, supposing we consider a fig at one end of the

table, and an olive at the other, it is evident that, in forming the complex idea of these substances, one of the most
obvious is that of their different relishes; and it is as evident that we incorporate and conjoin these qualities with
such as are coloured and tangible. The bitter taste of the
one, and sweet of the other, are supposed to lie in the very
visible body, and to be separated from each other by the
whole length of the table. This is so notable and so natural
an illusion that it may be proper to consider the principles
from which it is derived.

Though an extended object be incapable of a conjunction in place with another that exists without any place or
extension, yet are they susceptible of many other relations.
Thus the taste and smell of any fruit are inseparable from
its other qualities of colour and tangibility; and whichever
of them be the cause or effect, it is certain they are always
coexistent. Nor are they only coexistent in general, but
also contemporary in their appearance in the mind; and
it is upon the application of the extended body to our
senses we perceive its particular taste and smell. These
relations, then, of *causation, and contiguity in the time of
their appearance,* betwixt the extended object and the
quality, which exists without any particular place, must
have such an effect on the mind that, upon the appearance of one, it will immediately turn its thought to the
conception of the other. Nor is this all. We not only turn
our thought from one to the other upon account of their
relation, but likewise endeavour to give them a new relation, viz., that of *a conjunction in place,* that we may render the transition more easy and natural. For it is a quality
which I shall often have occasion to remark in human nature, and shall explain more fully in its proper place, that,
when objects are united by any relation, we have a strong
propensity to add some new relation to them, in order to
complete the union. In our arrangement of bodies, we
never fail to place such as are resembling in contiguity to
each other, or, at least, in correspondent points of view:
Why? but because we feel a satisfaction in joining the relation of contiguity to that of resemblance, or the resemblance of situation to that of qualities. The effects of this

propensity have been already observed in that resemblance which we so readily suppose betwixt particular impression and their external causes. But we shall not find a more evident effect of it than in the present instance, where, from the relations of causation and contiguity in time betwixt two objects, we feign likewise that of a conjunction in place, in order to strengthen the connexion.

But whatever confused notions we may form of a union in place betwixt an extended body, as a fig, and its particular taste, it is certain that, upon reflexion, we must observe in this union something altogether unintelligible and contradictory. For, should we ask ourselves one obvious question, viz., if the taste, which we conceive to be contained in the circumference of the body, is in every part of it, or in one only, we must quickly find ourselves at a loss, and perceive the impossibility of ever giving a satisfactory answer. We cannot reply that it is only in one part: For experience convinces us that every part has the same relish. We can as little reply that it exists in every part: For then we must suppose it figured and extended; which is absurd and incomprehensible. Here, then, we are influenced by two principles, directly contrary to each other, viz., that *inclination* of our fancy by which we are determined to incorporate the taste with the extended object, and our *reason,* which shows us the impossibility of such a union. Being divided betwixt these opposite principles, we renounce neither one nor the other, but involve the subject in such confusion and obscurity that we no longer perceive the opposition. We suppose that the taste exists within the circumference of the body, but in such a manner that it fills the whole without extension, and exists entire in every part without separation. In short, we use in our most familiar way of thinking that scholastic principle which, when crudely proposed, appears so shocking, of *totum in toto, et totum in qualibet parte:* Which is much the same as if we should say that a thing is in a certain place and yet is not there.

All this absurdity proceeds from our endeavouring to bestow a place on what is utterly incapable of it; and that endeavour again arises from our inclination to complete a union which is founded on causation and a contiguity of time, by attributing to the objects a conjunction in place. But if ever reason be of sufficient force to overcome prejudice, it is certain that, in the present case, it must prevail. For we have only this choice left, either to suppose that some beings exist without any place; or that they are figured and extended; or that when they are incorporated with extended objects, the whole is the whole, and the whole in every part. The absurdity of the two last suppositions proves sufficiently the veracity of the first. Nor is there any fourth opinion. For as to the supposition of their existence in the manner of mathematical points, it resolves itself into the second opinion, and supposes that several passions may be placed in a circular figure, and that a certain number of smells, conjoined with a certain number of sounds, may make a body of twelve cubic inches; which appears ridiculous upon the bare mentioning of it. . . .

From these hypotheses concerning the *substance* and *local conjunction* of our preceptions, we may pass to another, which is more intelligible than the former, and more important than the latter, viz., concerning the *cause* of our perceptions. Matter and motion, it is commonly said in the schools, however varied, are still matter and motion, and produce only a difference in the position and situation of objects. Divide a body as often as you please, it is still body. Place it in any figure, nothing ever results but figure, or the relation of parts. Move it in any manner, you still find motion or a change of relation. It is absurd to imagine that motion in a circle, for instance, should be nothing but merely motion in a circle; while motion in another direction, as in an ellipse, should also be a passion or moral reflexion: That the shocking of two globular particles should become a sensation of pain, and that the meeting of two triangular ones should afford a pleasure. Now as these different shocks and variations and mixtures are the only changes of which matter is susceptible, and as these never afford us any idea of thought or perception, it is concluded to be impossible that thought can ever be caused by matter.

Few have been able to withstand the seeming evidence of this argument; and yet nothing in the world is more easy than to refute it. We need only reflect on what has been proved at large, that we are never sensible of any connexion betwixt causes and effects, and that it is only by our experience of their constant conjunction we can arrive at any knowledge of this relation. Now as all objects which are not contrary are susceptible of a constant conjunction, and as no real objects are contrary; I have inferred from these principles that, to consider the matter a priori, any thing may produce any thing, and that we shall never discover a reason why any object may or may not be the cause of any other, however great or however little the resemblance may be betwixt them. This evidently destroys the precedent reasoning concerning the cause of thought or perception. For though there appear no manner of connexion betwixt motion and thought, the case is the same with all other causes and effects. Place one body of a pound weight on one end of a lever, and another body of the same weight on another end; you will never find in these bodies any principle of motion dependent on their distances from the centre, more than of thought and perception. If you pretend, therefore, to prove a priori, that such a position of bodies can never cause thought; because, turn it which way you will, it is nothing but a position of bodies; you must, by the same course of reasoning, conclude that it can never produce motion; since there is no more apparent connexion in the one case than in the other. But as this latter conclusion is contrary to evident experience, and as it is possible we may have a like experience in the operations of the mind, and may perceive a constant conjunction of thought and motion; you reason too hastily when, from the mere consideration of the ideas, you conclude that it is impossible motion can ever produce thought, or a difference position of parts give rise to a different passion or reflexion. Nay, it is not only possible we may have such an experience, but it is certain we have it, since every one may perceive that the different dispositions of his body change his thoughts and sentiments. And should it be said that this depends on the union of soul and body, I would answer that we must separate the question concerning the substance of the mind from that concerning the cause of its thought; and that, confining ourselves to the latter question, we find, by the comparing their ideas, that thought and motion are different from each other, and by experience, that they are constantly united; which being all the circumstances that enter into the idea of cause and effect, when applied to the operations of matter, we may certainly conclude that motion may be, and actually is, the cause of thought and perception. . . .

To pronounce, then, the final decision upon the whole; the question concerning the substance of the soul is absolutely unintelligible: All our perceptions are not susceptible of a local union, either with what is extended or unextended; there being some of them of the one kind, and some of the other: And as the constant conjunction of objects constitutes the very essence of cause and effect, matter and motion may often be regarded as the causes of thought, as far as we have any notion of that relation. . . .

There is no foundation for any conclusion a priori, either concerning the operations or duration of any object of which it is possible for the human mind to form a conception. Any object may be imagined to become entirely inactive, or to be annihilated in a moment; and it is an evident principle *that whatever we can imagine is possible*. Now this is no more true of matter than of spirit; of an extended compounded substance, than of a simple and unextended. In both cases the metaphysical arguments for the immortality of the soul are equally inconclusive; and in both cases the moral arguments and those derived from the analogy of nature are equally strong and convincing. If my philosophy therefore makes no addition to the arguments for religion, I have at least the satisfaction to think it takes nothing from them, but that everything remains precisely as before.]

HUME BEGINS HIS CONTRIBUTION TO THE PHILOSOPHICAL question of the self with an attack on the notion of self as substance, the doctrine, held for example by Descartes and Leibniz and their followers, that there exists a single unitary soul-substance persisting always the same through time, underlying all our "impressions and ideas" and in which these latter "inhere"—bearing, in fact, the same sort of relation to our impressions and ideas as does Locke's material substratum to the qualities of bodies. Against this time-honored view Hume argues as follows:

(1) What is *meant* by the expressions "substance" and "inhesion"? These expressions have never been satisfactorily explained.

(2) How can we find out anything about this substance? We cannot have an impression of it. For an impression could only be an impression of the substance by resembling it. But the very starting point of those who believe that the soul is a substance is that impressions are utterly unlike substances, and it is for this reason that impressions require a substance in which to "inhere." (It will be remembered that Berkeley, who believed in a substantive soul, declared that we have no *"idea"* of it, but only a "relative notion.")

(3) Argument (2) is logical, being designed to show the logical impossibility of our having an impression of a substance called soul. Hume reinforces this with an empirical argument, an appeal to experience. In Chapter V he taunts the substance theorists: "Is it [the impression of the soul-substance] pleasant or painful or indifferent? Does it attend us at all times or only at intervals?" and so on. In Chapter VI he makes a more formidable point: he says that when we look within we never in fact come upon any such idea as that of a single unitary self, continuing the same throughout our lives. On the contrary, we only meet, as always, with some *particular* perception or other or a cluster of them; and these numerous particular per-

ceptions "succeed each other with an inconceivable rapidity."

(4) It was argued by the old metaphysicians that only substances are (logically) capable of "existing by them-selves" and therefore there must be a soul-substance in which impressions inhere. To this Hume replies that, since he can conceive of impressions "existing by themselves," it must be logically possible that they should so exist; so that on this definition of substance, impressions them-selves turn out to be substances, and certainly have no need of a further substance to prop them up.

He concludes that "the question concerning the sub-stance of the soul is wholly unintelligible." He can find no such entity: only collections of data, a stream—or several parallel streams—of thoughts, images, feelings, percep-tions, loosely connected. The mind is nothing but "a bun-dle or collection of different perceptions." And so he is left with the problem of explaining what it is that makes us "collect together" certain perceptions and not others as the history of any one single mind. Following his treat-ment of the notion of material things, he similarly dis-perses minds or selves. And where we should today be inclined to say that Hume was trying to establish the cri-terion for correctly describing certain ideas as belonging to the mental history of a particular person, he regards himself as providing a psychological explanation for our tendency fictitiously to ascribe identity to a set of wholly discrete impressions and ideas, since we have a "natural propension . . . to imagine that simplicity and identity" which in reality does not exist.

We have seen that absolute identity, in the logical or mathematical sense, has no relevance to the identification of things or persons. It cannot have, for the good empirical reason that we do often utter such statements as: "The Mr. Jones I saw yesterday is the same (person) as the Mr. Jones I knew in London five years ago," or "The table on which I am now writing is the same (table) as the one that has been in my study for fifteen years," or "The chest-nut tree in the square is the same (tree) as has been there for two hundred years." And we call some of these statements *true* and others *false*. It follows that we have criteria for the correct use of such statements. In no empirical case will these criteria amount to the absolute identity of Hume; and in different empirical cases (different sorts of objects) the criteria are, as a matter of fact, of different kinds and of different degrees of elasticity and vagueness. Thus where Hume supposes that he is overthrowing the metaphysics of substance in favor of the (equally indemonstrable) metaphysics of sense data, and is, in addition, giving a psychological explanation of our fictitious ascription of (metaphysical) identity to non-identical (empirical) objects of various sorts, he is in fact performing the more useful, in appearance less exciting, task of giving the criteria for the correct use of the expression "the same as," applied to different classes of objects.

Hume explains the "fictitious ascription of identity" as being due to the imagination, which passes so smoothly over the ideas of the separate perceptions that it comes to think of them as not a rain of discrete data, but rather a single "uninterrupted and invariable" object. Finally to justify itself, as it were, it "feigns" some soul or self or substance, which really would, if it existed, be a single unchanging object. As usual, the principles of association by which the imagination is led to this deceptively smooth transition are resemblance, contiguity, and causation, though, in this case, Hume says, contiguity plays little part.

Hume's own constructive "theory of the self" is not satisfactory, as he himself realizes (see the memorable passage in the Appendix). In particular, he is in some confusion as to whether memory *produces* or *discovers* personal identity, i.e., whether or not some memory relation between the discrete impressions and ideas constitutes the meaning or part of the meaning of the expression "the same as" as applied to persons, or whether, rather, it is by means of memory that we find out that several discrete impressions and ideas "belong" to the history of the "same" person. It is not clear that these two questions are as distinct as Hume thought them. Be that as it may, he has failed to give us a satisfactory account of what it is in a set of impressions and ideas that makes it the sort of "bundle" that we call the history of a single person and not of several persons at once, or of none. What is the unifying tie of such a bundle?

One of the difficulties here is that we do not feel quite sure what we want a "theory of the self" to do. If all that is being asked for is an account of the criteria by which in fact we judge of the truth or falsehood of statements of the form "A (at time t_2) is the same person as B (at time t_1)," the answer is comparatively clear. As usual in questions of this sort, there are several criteria which normally —but not always—accompany each other:

(1) We go by a certain continuity (allowing, of course, for changes due to age and physical state, etc.) of bodily appearance. This is the first criterion we apply on meeting someone we know.

(2) We pay attention to a certain continuity of behavior pattern, both physical and "psychical." It is worth noticing in this context the semimetaphysical idioms, "He is not himself today" and "He is beside himself with rage," as denoting discontinuous data, not persistent or violent enough to destroy identity.

(3) We rely mainly on memory. Of course, we can directly appeal only to our own memory; but we do also appeal to the memories of others. For example if a man whom I meet today claims to be the Mr. Smith that I met in Paris in 1947, and if, despite a resemblance of appearance, he gives an entirely false account of what I remember myself and Smith to have been doing in Paris in 1947, this, in the absence of information, e.g., that he has lost his memory, constitutes prima facie evidence for the hypothesis that he is an impostor, i.e., not the Mr. Smith he claims to be.

These are only examples of the kind of criteria we use. That there are yet further criteria is proved by the fact that we are very inclined to say that Dr. Jekyll and Mr. Hyde were the same person, although the composite Jekyll-Hyde fails to satisfy any of the above three criteria. I think our inclination arises from the fact that anyone who had been in the room when Jekyll drank the potion and turned into Hyde would have seen a physical human body occupying a volume of space continuously. We are less inclined to assert identity if sudden violent physical change occurs, even though mental continuity persists: e.g., if, as in Kafka's story, a man turns into a cockroach while preserving his human memories. In such cases we feel rather more nervous about saying that the cockroach *is* the commercial traveler who occupied the bed a moment before. From which it seems to follow that we attend more to physical than to mental characteristics. This criterion (4) consists in continuous occupation of a space-time track, and seems more fundamental than other criteria, just as it alone is fundamental in the case of physical objects.

Puzzles arise when these criteria, which in the vast majority of cases go together and are useful precisely for this reason, fail to occur. For example, schizophrenics (the most notorious case is Sally Beauchamp, who, as reported by Dr. Morton Prince, had no fewer than five personalities) fulfill (1) and (4), fail in (2) and fulfill (3) with varying degrees of imperfection. Amnesiacs fulfill (1) and (4), fail in (3), and may fail in varying degrees in (2), and so on. The puzzle here is less about what is the case, than of what to say. The relevant facts are before us; what we feel uncertain about is whether we should or should not use the expression "the same person" with all that this implies. And we are puzzled as to what to say precisely because criteria which normally agree here conflict; there is no philosophical crux here, for the criteria are, of course, logically independent of each other. We are not confronted with conflicting evidence as to the presence of a unitary substance called "the self," but rather with having to decide what to say if we are not to mislead ourselves or others. Sometimes we escape this by explaining that from some points of view the entity before us is the same person; from other points of view, two (or more) different people. For example an official issuing a railroad ticket to a schizophrene regards him as one person; a psychiatrist may be inclined to think of him as two; a judge called on to determine the validity of his will, is involved in a borderline case of the identity of his legal personality.

Yet this account, plausible so far as it goes, leaves us dissatisfied. For it seems to leave out of account the central fact of self-consciousness, the " 'I think' which accompanies all our representations," as Kant expresses it, that which makes my experience *mine,* especially in action and volition. We are not content to dismiss this as merely an extra introspectible feeling or "feeling-tone," on a level with other elements of some "neutral stuff" waiting to be sorted out into separate bundles called persons, in terms of practical criteria, none of them very definite. This may do for identifying "one" cloud or "one" wave, which may melt into each other (as my headache cannot, in some sense of "cannot," melt into yours) but seems to omit the seemingly impenetrable barrier which divides one person from another, and makes their individual experiences—their vantage points—unique to them, and opaque, impenetrable, to one another, as clouds and waves are not. Quasi-mechanical models, such as Hume attempts to construct, of the relations between perceptions, which make them the perceptions of *one* person, seem not only unplausible but irrelevant to the question of what we mean by personal identity. Much remains to be done in clarifying what questions we are asking, and why we reject some answers as shallow or paradoxical when we demand a philosophical analysis of the self.

Two other important and neglected doctrines of Hume's should be noticed in the passage above.

(1) That an object may exist, and yet be nowhere. Hume himself makes but a poor use of this dictum. He tries to show by means of it that our idea that, e.g., the taste of an olive is spatially conjoined with the actual extended body, the olive, must be an illusion, since the taste, being a perception, cannot properly be said to be anywhere in space. But he is forgetting, that on his view, the extension, bulk, etc., of the olive are no more and no less our perceptions than is the taste, and that he has not explained what he means by "somewhere in space." However, despite the fact that Hume makes use of the dictum only to

land himself in inconsistency, it is, as so often with his *aperçus,* of first-rate importance. It is logically absurd to talk of a mind (and a fortiori an idea "in" a mind) being *somewhere.* Spatial predicates do not apply to minds or ideas. And, with this discovery, Hume liberates us from the Cartesian picture, shared to some extent by Locke, of the mind literally situated within the brain, a picture according to which, just as light rays in a mechanical way produce physical changes in the eyes, the optic nerves and finally the brain, so—the last link in the causal chain —the brain in a quasi-mechanical way produces ideas in the mind.

(2) It had been held by, e.g., certain Cartesians, that matter and motion on the one hand and ideas on the other are so different in kind that it is impossible that either should leap over the gulf to "cause" the other. Hume points out that once we realize that cause is nothing but regularity, "constant conjunction," there can be no a priori reason why anything should not cause anything else. The importance of his principle that there are no impassable "natural" barriers between kinds of things or events, and that no causal connections between any sorts of events can ever be ruled out a priori, remains worthy of notice even in the twentieth century.

[SECTION VI. *Of Personal Identity*

There are some philosophers who imagine we are every moment intimately conscious of what we call our *self;* that we feel its existence and its continuance in existence; and are certain, beyond the evidence of a demonstration, both of its perfect identity and simplicity. The strongest sensation, the most violent passion, say they, instead of distracting us from this view, only fix it the more intensely, and make us consider their influence on *self* either by their pain or pleasure. To attempt a farther proof of this were to weaken its evidence; since no proof can be derived from any fact of which we are so intimately conscious; nor is there any thing of which we can be certain if we doubt of this.

Unluckily, all these positive assertions are contrary to that very experience which is pleaded for them, nor have we any idea of *self* after the manner it is here explained. For, from what impression could this idea be derived? This question it is impossible to answer without a manifest contradiction and absurdity; and yet it is a question which must necessarily be answered, if we would have the idea of self pass for clear and intelligible. It must be some one impression that gives rise to every real idea. But self or person is not any one impression, but that to which our several impressions and ideas are supposed to have a reference. If any impression gives rise to the idea of self, that impression must continue invariably the same, through the whole course of our lives; since self is supposed to exist after that manner. But there is no impression constant and invariable. Pain and pleasure, grief and joy, passions and sensations, succeed each other, and never all exist at the same time. It cannot, therefore, be from any of these impressions, or from any other, that the idea of self is derived; and consequently there is no such idea.

But, farther, what must become of all our particular perceptions upon this hypothesis? All these are different, and distinguishable, and separable from each other, and may be separately considered, and may exist separately, and have no need of anything to support their existence. After what manner therefore do they belong to self; and how are they connected with it? For my part, when I enter most intimately into what I call *myself,* I always stumble on some particular perception or other, of heat or cold, light or shade, love or hatred, pain or pleasure. I never can catch *myself* at any time without a perception, and never can observe any thing but the perception. When my perceptions are removed for any time, as by sound sleep; so long am I insensible of *myself,* and may truly be said not to exist. And were all my perceptions removed by death, and could I neither think, nor feel, nor see, nor love, nor hate, after the dissolution of my body, I should be entirely annihilated, nor do I conceive what is farther requisite to make me a perfect nonentity. If any one, upon serious and unprejudiced reflection, thinks he has a different notion of *himself,* I must confess I can reason no longer with him. All I can allow him is, that he may be in the right as well as I, and that we are essentially different in this particular. He may, perhaps, perceive something simple and continued, which he calls *himself;* though I am certain there is no such principle in me.

But setting aside some metaphysicians of this kind, I may venture to affirm of the rest of mankind that they are nothing but a bundle or collection of different perceptions, which succeed each other with an inconceivable rapidity, and are in a perpetual flux and movement. Our eyes cannot turn in their sockets without varying our perceptions. Our thought is still more variable than our sight; and all our other senses and faculties contribute to this change; nor is there any single power of the soul which remains unalterably the same, perhaps for one moment. The mind is a kind of theatre, where several perceptions successively make their appearance; pass, repass, glide away, and mingle in an infinite variety of postures and situations. There is properly no *simplicity* in it at one time, nor *identity* in different; whatever natural propension we may have to imagine that simplicity and identity. The comparison of the theatre must not mislead us. They are the successive perceptions only, that constitute the mind; nor have we the most distant notion of the place where these scenes are represented, or of the materials of which it is composed.

What, then, gives us so great a propension to ascribe an identity to these successive perceptions, and to suppose ourselves possessed of an invariable and uninterrupted existence through the whole course of our lives? In order to answer this question we must distinguish betwixt personal identity, as it regards our thought or imagination, and as it regards our passions or the concern we take in ourselves. The first is our present subject; and to explain it perfectly we must take the matter pretty deep, and account for that identity which we attribute to plants and animals; there being a great analogy betwixt it and the identity of a self or person.

We have a distinct idea of an object that remains invariable and uninterrupted through a supposed variation of time; and this idea we call that of *identity* or *sameness*. We have also a distinct idea of several different objects existing in succession, and connected together by a close relation; and this to an accurate view affords as perfect a notion of *diversity* as if there was no manner of relation among the objects. But though these two ideas of identity, and a succession of related objects, be in themselves perfectly distinct, and even contrary, yet it is certain that, in our common way of thinking, they are generally confounded with each other. That action of the imagination, by which we consider the uninterrupted and invariable object, and that by which we reflect on the succession of related objects, are almost the same to the feelings; nor is there much more effort of thought required in the latter case than in the former. The relation facilitates the transition of the mind from one object to another, and renders its passage as smooth as if it contemplated one continued object. This resemblance is the cause of the confusion and mistake, and makes us substitute the notion of identity, instead of that of related objects. However at one instant we may consider the related succession as variable and interrupted, we are sure the next to ascribe to it a perfect identity, and regard it as invariable and uninterrupted. Our propensity to this mistake is so great from the resemblance above-mentioned that we fall into it before we are aware; and though we incessantly correct ourselves by reflexion, and return to a more accurate method of thinking, yet we cannot long sustain our philosophy, or take off this bias from the imagination. Our last resource is to yield to it, and boldly assert that these different related objects are in effect the same, however interrupted and variable. In order to justify to ourselves this absurdity, we often feign some new and unintelligible principle that connects the objects together, and prevents their interruption or variation. Thus we feign the continued existence of the perceptions of our senses, to remove the interruption; and run into the notion of a *soul,* and *self*, and *substance,* to disguise the variation. But, we may farther observe that where we do not give rise to such a fiction, our propension to confound identity with relation is so great that we are apt to imagine something unknown and mysterious, connecting the parts, beside their relation; and this I take to be the case with regard to the identity we ascribe to plants and vegetables. And even when this does not take place, we still feel a propensity to confound these ideas, though we are not able fully to satisfy ourselves in that particular, nor find anything invariable and uninterrupted to justify our notion of identity.

Thus the controversy concerning identity is not merely a dispute of words. For when we attribute identity, in an improper sense, to variable or interrupted objects, our mistake is not confined to the expression, but is commonly attended with a fiction, either of something invariable and uninterrupted, or of something mysterious and inexplicable, or at least with a propensity to such fictions. What will suffice to prove this hypothesis to the satisfaction of every fair enquirer, is to show, from daily experience and observation, that the objects which are variable or interrupted, and yet are supposed to continue the same, are such only as consist of a succession of parts, connected together by resemblance, contiguity, or causation. For as such a succession answers evidently to our notion of diversity, it can only be by mistake we ascribe to it an identity; and as the relation of parts which leads us into this mistake is really nothing but a quality which produces an association of ideas, and an easy transition of the imagination from one to another, it can only be from the resemblance which this act of the mind bears to that by which we contemplate one continued object, that the error arises. Our chief business, then, must be to prove that all objects to which we ascribe identity, without observing their invariableness and uninterruptedness, are such as consist of a succession of related objects.

In order to this, suppose any mass of matter, of which the parts are contiguous and connected, to be placed before us; it is plain we must attribute a perfect identity to this mass, provided all the parts continue uninterruptedly and invariably the same, whatever motion or change of place we may observe either in the whole or in any of the parts. But supposing some very *small* or *inconsiderable* part to be added to the mass, or subtracted from it; though this absolutely destroys the identity of the whole, strictly speaking; yet as we seldom think so accurately, we scruple not to pronounce a mass of matter the same, where we find so trivial an alteration. The passage of the thought from the object before the change to the object after it, is so smooth and easy, that we scarce perceive the transition, and are apt to imagine that it is nothing but a continued survey of the same object.

There is a very remarkable circumstance that attends this experiment; which is, that though the change of any considerable part in a mass of matter destroys the identity of the whole, yet we must measure the greatness of the part, not absolutely, but by its *proportion* to the whole. The addition or diminution of a mountain would not be sufficient to produce a diversity in a planet; though the change of a very few inches would be able to destroy the identity of some bodies. It will be impossible to account for this, but by reflecting that objects operate upon the mind, and break or interrupt the continuity of its actions, not according to their real greatness, but according to their proportion to each other: And, therefore, since this interruption makes an object cease to appear the same, it must be the uninterrupted progress of the thought which constitutes the imperfect identity.

This may be confirmed by another phaenomenon. A change in any considerable part of a body destroys its identity; but it is remarkable that, where the change is produced *gradually* and *insensibly,* we are less apt to ascribe it to the same effect. The reason can plainly be no other than that the mind, in following the successive changes of the body, feels an easy passage from the surveying its condition in one moment, to the viewing of it in another, and at no particular time perceives any interruption in its actions. From which continued perception, it ascribes a continued existence and identity to the object.

But whatever precaution we may use in introducing the changes gradually, and making them proportionable to the whole, it is certain that where the changes are at last observed to become considerable, we make a scruple of ascribing identity to such different objects. There is, however, another artifice by which we may induce the imagination to advance a step farther; and that is, by producing a reference of the parts to each other, and a combination to some *common end* or purpose. A ship of which a considerable part has been changed by frequent reparations, is still considered as the same; nor does the difference of the materials hinder us from ascribing an identity to it. The common end in which the parts conspire, is the same under all their variations, and affords an easy transition of the imagination from one situation of the body to another. . . .

We now proceed to explain the nature of *personal identity,* which has become so great a question in philosophy, especially of late years in England, where all the abstruser sciences are studied with a peculiar ardour and application. And here it is evident the same method of reasoning must be continued which has so successfully explained the identity of plants, and animals, and ships, and houses, and of all the compounded and changeable productions either of art or nature. The identity which we ascribe to the mind of man is only a fictitious one, and of a like kind with that which we ascribe to vegetables and animal bodies. It cannot therefore have a different origin, but must proceed from a like operation of the imagination upon like objects.

But lest this argument should not convince the reader, though in my opinion perfectly decisive, let him weigh the following reasoning, which is still closer and more immediate. It is evident that the identity which we attribute to the human mind, however perfect we may imagine it to be, is not able to run the several different perceptions into one, and make them lose their characters of distinction and difference, which are essential to them. It is still true that every distinct perception which enters into the composition of the mind is a distinct existence, and is different, and distinguishable, and separable from every other perception, either contemporary or successive. But as, notwithstanding this distinction and separability, we suppose the whole train of perceptions to be united by identity, a question naturally arises concerning this relation of identity; whether it be something that really binds our several perceptions together, or only associates their ideas in the imagination; that is, in other words, whether, in pronouncing concerning the identity of a person, we observe some real bond among his perceptions, or only feel one among the ideas we form of them. This question we might easily decide, if we would recollect what has already been proved at large, that the understanding never observes any real connexion among objects, and that even the union of cause and effect, when strictly examined, resolves itself into a customary association of ideas. For from thence it evidently follows that identity is nothing really belonging to these different perceptions, and uniting them together; but is merely a quality which we attribute to them, because of the union of their ideas in the imagination when we reflect upon them. Now, the only qualities which can give ideas a union in the imagination are these three relations above-mentioned. These are the uniting principles in the ideal world, and without them every distinct object is separable by the mind, and may be separately considered, and appears not to have any more connexion with any other object than if disjoined by the greatest difference and remoteness. It is therefore on some of these three relations of resemblance, contiguity and causation, that identity depends; and as the very essence of these relations consists in their producing an easy transition of ideas; it follows that our notions of personal identity proceed entirely from the smooth and uninterrupted progress of the thought along a train of connected ideas, according to the principles above-explained.

The only question, therefore, which remains is, by what relations this uninterrupted progress of our thought is produced, when we consider the successive existence of a mind or thinking person. And here it is evident we must confine ourselves to resemblance and causation, and must drop contiguity, which has little or no influence in the present case.

To begin with *resemblance;* suppose we could see clearly into the breast of another, and observe that succession of perceptions which constitutes his mind or thinking principle, and suppose that he always preserves the memory of a considerable part of past perceptions; it is evident that nothing could more contribute to the bestowing a relation on this succession amidst all its variations. For what is the memory but a faculty by which we raise up the images of past perceptions? And as an image necessarily resembles its object, must not the frequent placing of these resembling perceptions in the chain of thought convey the imagination more easily from one link to another, and make the whole seem like the continuance of one object? In this particular, then, the memory not only discovers the identity, but also contributes to its production, by producing the relation of resemblance among the perceptions. The case is the same, whether we consider ourselves or others.

As to *causation;* we may observe that the true idea of the human mind is to consider it as a system of different perceptions or different existences, which are linked together by the relation of cause and effect, and mutually produce, destroy, influence, and modify each other. Our impressions give rise to their correspondent ideas; and these ideas, in their turn, produce other impressions. One thought chases another, and draws after it a third, by which it is expelled in its turn. In this respect, I cannot compare the soul more properly to anything than to a republic or commonwealth, in which the several members are united by the reciprocal ties of government and subordination, and give rise to other persons who propagate the same republic in the incessant changes of its parts. And as the same individual republic may not only change its members, but also its laws and constitutions; in like manner, the same person may vary his character and disposition, as well as his impressions and ideas without losing his identity. Whatever changes he endures, his several parts are still connected by the relation of causation. And in this view our identity with regard to the passions serves to corroborate that with regard to the imagination, by the making our distant perceptions influence each other and by giving us a present concern for our past or future pains or pleasures.

As memory alone acquaints us with the continuance and extent of this succession of perceptions, it is to be considered, upon that account chiefly, as the source of personal identity. Had we no memory, we never should have any notion of causation, nor consequently of that chain of causes and effects which constitute our self or person. But having once acquired this notion of causation from the memory, we can extend the same chain of causes, and consequently the identity of our persons, beyond our memory, and can comprehend times, and circumstances, and actions, which we have entirely forgot, but suppose in general to have existed. For how few of our past actions are there of which we have any memory? Who can tell me, for instance, what were his thoughts and actions on the first of January 1715, the eleventh of March 1719, and the third of August 1733? Or will he affirm, because he has entirely forgot the incidents of these days, that the present self is not the same person with the self of that time; and by that means overturn all the most established notions of personal identity? In this view, therefore, memory does not so much *produce* as *discover* personal identity, by showing us the relation of cause and effect among our different perceptions. It will be incumbent on those who affirm that memory produces entirely our personal identity, to give a reason why we can thus extend our identity beyond our memory.

The whole of this doctrine leads us to a conclusion, which is of great importance in the present affair, viz., that all the nice and subtile questions concerning personal identity can never possibly be decided, and are to be regarded rather as grammatical than as philosophical difficulties. Identity depends on the relations of ideas; and these relations produce identity by means of that easy transition they occasion. But as the relations, and the easiness of the transition may diminish by insensible degrees, we have no just standard by which we can decide any dispute concerning the time when they acquire or lose a title to the name of identity. All the disputes concerning the identity of connected objects are merely verbal, except so far as the relation of parts gives rise to some fiction or imaginary principle of union, as we have already observed.

What I have said concerning the first origin and uncertainty of our notion of identity, as applied to the human mind, may be extended with little or no variation to that of *simplicity*. An object whose different coexistent parts are bound together by a close relation operates upon the imagination after much the same manner as one perfectly simple and indivisible, and requires not a much greater stretch of thought in order to its conception. From this similarity of operation we attribute a simplicity to it, and feign a principle of union as the support of this simplicity, and the centre of all the different parts and qualities of the object.

Thus we have finished our examination of the several systems of philosophy, both of the intellectual and moral world; and in our miscellaneous way of reasoning, have been led into several topics, which will either illustrate and confirm some preceding part of this discourse, or prepare the way for our following opinions. It is now time to return to a more close examination of our subject, and to proceed in the accurate anatomy of human nature, having fully explained the nature of our judgment and understanding.]

SO MUCH FOR HUME'S EPOCH-MAKING ANALYSES OF THE notion of natural necessity, cause, substance, identity, personality, and the relation of words, concepts and things. At the end of it he felt acute intellectual discomfort, which, with characteristic candor and charm, he sets forth, in the famous statement that follows, of the skepticism to which his philosophy has led him. So long as he reasons, as opposed to "playing a game of backgammon," he is "environed with the deepest darkness" and can give no good reason for believing anything. From this "philosophical melancholy and delirium" only nature—upon whom he looks with trust and affection—can cure him. Philosophy pulls him one way: but "the current of nature" draws him toward "indolent belief in the general maxims" accepted by ordinary men, even though they are demonstrably fallacious. But at least his "follies," if they cannot be avoided, shall be "natural and agreeable." Yet we have seen that

Hume's results are not really as paradoxical or wildly at odds with common sense as he himself thinks. What he has done is to expose the arguments of those who demanded "real" necessary connections in nature, or an unbreakable guarantee that her unobserved parts resemble the observed, or looked for an *ex hypothesi* unobservable material substratum underlying each physical identity, or a simple, continuous, timeless, unobservable self "beneath" or "within" each person's mind. Hume showed that to ask for this was either not to understand what one was asking, or to ask for the logically impossible. In the course of this he threw original light on the way in which the notion of cause in fact functions, and on the related concepts of material and personal identity, and the relations of empirical and a priori propositions, and so inaugurated a great debate on these topics of which the end is not in sight.

[SECTION VII. *Conclusion of this Book*

. . . For I have already shown that the understanding, when it acts alone, and according to its most general principles, entirely subverts itself, and leaves not the lowest degree of evidence in any proposition, either in philosophy or common life. We save ourselves from this total scepticism only by means of that singular and seemingly trivial property of the fancy, by which we enter with difficulty into remote views of things, and are not able to accompany them with so sensible an impression as we do those which are more easy and natural. Shall we, then, establish it for a general maxim, that no refined or elaborate reasoning is ever to be received? Consider well the consequences of such a principle. By this means you cut off entirely all science and philosophy: You proceed upon one singular quality of the imagination, and by a parity of reason must embrace all of them: And you expressly contradict yourself; since this maxim must be built on the preceding reasoning. . . . What party, then, shall we choose among these difficulties? If we embrace this principle, and condemn all refined reasoning, we run into the most manifest absurdities. If we reject it in favour of these reasonings, we subvert entirely the human understanding. We have therefore no choice left but betwixt a false reason and none at all. For my part, I know not what ought to be done in the present case. I can only observe what is commonly done; which is, that this difficulty is seldom or never thought of; and even where it has once been present to the mind is quickly forgot, and leaves but a small impression behind it. Very refined reflexions have little or no influence upon us; and yet we do not, and cannot, establish it for a rule that they ought not to have any influence; which implies a manifest contradiction.

But what have I here said, that reflexions very refined and metaphysical have little or no influence upon us? This opinion I can scarce forbear retracting and condemning from my present feeling and experience. The *intense* view of these manifold contradictions and imperfections in human reason has so wrought upon me, and heated my brain, that I am ready to reject all belief and reasoning, and can look upon no opinion even as more probable or likely than another. Where am I, or what? From what causes do I derive my existence, and to what condition shall I return? Whose favour shall I court, and whose anger must I dread? What beings surround me? and on whom have I any influence, or who have any influence on me? I am confounded with all these questions, and begin to fancy myself in the most deplorable condition imaginable, environed with the deepest darkness, and utterly deprived of the use of every member and faculty.

Most fortunately it happens that, since reason is incapable of dispelling these clouds, nature herself suffices to that purpose, and cures me of this philosophical melancholy and delirium, either by relaxing this bent of mind, or by some avocation, and lively impression of my senses, which obliterate all these chimeras. I dine, I play a game of backgammon, I converse, and am merry with my friends; and when, after three or four hours' amusement, I would return to these speculations, they appear so cold, and strained, and ridiculous, that I cannot find in my heart to enter into them any farther.

Here, then, I find myself absolutely and necessarily de-

termined to live, and talk, and act, like other people in
the common affairs of life. But notwithstanding that my
natural propensity, and the course of my animal spirits
and passions, reduce me to this indolent belief in the general maxims of the world, I still feel such remains of my
former disposition that I am ready to throw all my books
and papers into the fire, and resolve never more to renounce the pleasures of life for the sake of reasoning and
philosophy. For those are my sentiments in that splenetic
humour which governs me at present. I may, nay I must,
yield to the current of nature, in submitting to my senses
and understanding; and in this blind submission I show
most perfectly my sceptical disposition and principles. But
does it follow that I must strive against the current of
nature, which leads me to indolence and pleasure; that I
must seclude myself, in some measure, from the commerce
and society of men, which is so agreeable; and that I must
torture my brain with subtilities and sophistries, at the very
time that I cannot satisfy myself concerning the reason-
ableness of so painful an application, nor have any tolerable prospect of arriving by its means at truth and certainty? Under what obligation do I lie of making such an
abuse of time? And to what end can it serve, either for the
service of mankind, or for my own private interest? No: If
I must be a fool, as all those who reason or believe any
thing *certainly* are, my foilies shall at least be natural and
agreeable. Where I strive against my inclination I shall
have a good reason for my resistance; and will no more
be led a wandering into such dreary solitudes, and rough
passages, as I have hitherto met with. . . .

An Appendix on the Treatise

I had entertained some hopes that, however deficient our
theory of the intellectual world might be, it would be free
from those contradictions and absurdities which seem to
attend every explication that human reason can give of the
material world. But upon a more strict review of the section concerning *personal identity,* I find myself involved in
such a labyrinth that, I must confess, I neither know how

to correct my former opinions, nor how to render them consistent. If this be not a good *general* reason for scepticism it is at least a sufficient one (if I were not already abundantly supplied) for me to entertain a diffidence and modesty in all my decisions. I shall propose the arguments on both sides, beginning with those that induced me to deny the strict and proper identity and simplicity of a self or thinking being.

When we talk of *self* or *substance,* we must have an idea annexed to these terms, otherwise they are altogether unintelligible. Every idea is derived from preceding impressions; and we have no impression of self or substance as something simple and individual. We have, therefore, no idea of them in that sense.

Whatever is distinct, is distinguishable; and whatever is distinguishable, is separable by the thought or imagination. All perceptions are distinct. They are, therefore, distinguishable and separable, and may be conceived as separately existent, and may exist separately, without any contradiction or absurdity.

When I view this table and that chimney, nothing is present to me but particular perceptions, which are of a like nature with all the other perceptions. This is the doctrine of philosophers. But this table, which is present to me, and that chimney, may and do exist separately. This is the doctrine of the vulgar, and implies no contradiction. There is no contradiction, therefore, in extending the same doctrine to all the perceptions.

In general, the following reasoning seems satisfactory. All ideas are borrowed from preceding perceptions. Our ideas of objects, therefore, are derived from that source. Consequently no proposition can be intelligible or consistent with regard to objects, which is not so with regard to perceptions. But it is intelligible and consistent to say that objects exist distinct and independent, without any common *simple* substance or subject of inhesion. This proposition, therefore, can never be absurd with regard to perceptions.

When I turn my reflection on *myself,* I never can perceive this *self* without some one or more perceptions; nor can I ever perceive any thing but the perceptions. It is the composition of these, therefore, which forms the self.

We can conceive a thinking being to have either many or few perceptions. Suppose the mind to be reduced even below the life of an oyster. Suppose it to have only one perception, as of thirst or hunger. Consider it in that situation. Do you conceive any thing but merely that perception? Have you any notion of *self* or *substance?* If not, the addition of other perceptions can never give you that notion.

The annihilation, which some people suppose to follow upon death, and which entirely destroys this self, is nothing but an extinction of all particular perceptions; love and hatred, pain and pleasure, thought and sensation. These therefore must be the same with self; since the one cannot survive the other.

Is *self* the same with *substance?* If it be, how can that question have place, concerning the subsistence of self under a change of substance? If they be distinct, what is the difference betwixt them? For my part, I have a notion of neither, when conceived distinct from particular perceptions.

Philosophers begin to be reconciled to the principle, *that we have no idea of external substance, distinct from the ideas of particular qualities.* This must pave the way for a like principle with regard to the mind, *that we have no notion of it, distinct from the particular perceptions.*

So far I seem to be attended with sufficient evidence. But having thus loosened all our particular perceptions, when I proceed to explain the principle of connexion which binds them together, and makes us attribute to them a real simplicity and identity; I am sensible that my account is very defective, and that nothing but the seeming evidence of the precedent reasonings could have induced me to receive it. If perceptions are distinct existences, they form a whole only by being connected together. But no connexions among distinct existences are ever discoverable by human understanding. We only *feel* a connexion or determination of the thought to pass from one object to another. It follows, therefore, that the thought alone finds

personal identity, when reflecting on the train of past perceptions that compose a mind; the ideas of them are felt to
be connected together, and naturally introduce each other.
However extraordinary this conclusion may seem, it need
not surprise us. Most philosophers seem inclined to think
that personal identity *arises* from consciousness; and consciousness is nothing but a reflected thought or perception.
The present philosophy, therefore, has so far a promising
aspect. But all my hopes vanish when I come to explain the
principles that unite our successive perceptions in our
thought or consciousness. I cannot discover any theory
which gives me satisfaction on this head.

In short, there are two principles, which I cannot render
consistent; nor is it in my power to renounce either of
them; viz., *that all our distinct perceptions are distinct
existences,* and *that the mind never perceives any real connexion among distinct existences.* Did our perceptions
either inhere in something simple and individual, or did
the mind perceive some real connexion among them, there
would be no difficulty in the case. For my part, I must
plead the privilege of a sceptic, and confess that this difficulty is too hard for my understanding. I pretend not, however, to pronounce it absolutely insuperable. Others
perhaps, or myself upon more mature reflexions, may
discover some hypothesis, that will reconcile those contradictions.]

CHAPTER V

Thomas Reid

THE LIFE OF THOMAS REID WAS WHOLLY UNEVENTFUL. His career is characteristic of his time and country and milieu: he was born in 1710, became a minister of the Scottish Church at the age of twenty-seven, taught philosophy at Aberdeen, and succeeded Adam Smith as Professor of Moral Philosophy at Glasgow in 1764. His most famous work, *The Essays on the Intellectual Powers of Man,* was published when he was seventy-five years of age. He died in 1796.

The principal importance of Reid's philosophical views lies in his bold attempt to rehabilitate the "common sense" view of the external world against the disturbing paradoxes of Berkeley and Hume. Despite all Locke's efforts to break out of the charmed circle of his own "ideas," within which each individual observer is confined; despite Berkeley's reiterated plea that his views are identical with those of ordinary men, that his "ideas" are what are normally called "things," that it is not he, but the physicists with their invisible particles and mysterious activities of nonsensible properties, who are responsible for inventing a strange and unintelligible universe, remote from the familiar human world; despite Hume's half-hearted assertion that to look for a solid reality "behind" or "beyond" sense "impressions," and the "ideas" that are but decayed "impressions" is meaningless; despite all this, there is, of course, an undeniable tendency towards a solipsist metaphysics in this out-and-out phenomenalism. It does suggest that there is no existence but in the observer's awareness, and the solid "objective" world is made to melt into the "subjective" experience of particular streams of consciousness, which between them comprise all there is. Reid attempts to cut this knot by arguing that Berkeley was right in maintaining that sensations, indeed, were purely subjective, that sounds, scents, tastes, color sensations, existed only in being heard or smelled or seen, as pains only existed in sensations of pain; that physical things which could not smell or look, did not, of course, possess such sensations any more than they were able to feel aches. But from this it does not follow at all that there are no material objects, possessing, for the most part, just such qualities as we take them to have, when we are not suffering from hallucinations. We do not, indeed, *sense* these qualities (sensations *are* private and subjective) but *perceive* them, the *sensing* being the *occasion* of the *perceiving,* which occurs concomitantly with it, and which we do not, in ordinary speech, trouble to distinguish from the sensing: for the distinction is of interest solely to "philosophers." With this theory Reid may claim to be the father of British (and indeed Anglo-American) "realism." The "Scottish" or "Common Sense" school descended from him adumbrated the approach which, principally in the works of G. E. Moore and his followers, took the form of insisting that words like "knowledge" and "acquaintance" meant nothing if they could not be properly applied to the most familiar objective facts of our lives: that we lived in a space containing three-dimensional chairs which we *knew* that we occasionally sat in, that we *knew* that our bodies had never risen many thousands of miles above the surface of the earth, and so on. For to deny this in favor of some theoretical consideration is to deny the premises on which all our thought about the external world must rest, the common foundations of scientific or common-sense beliefs— the notion that there exists an external world of public objects which can be discussed, to which our symbols, whether words or images, are intended to refer, and which alone make communication possible. To deny or doubt this is, it is maintained, to pretend to disbelieve the axioms from which we must inevitably all begin, and with which we must, if we are not to stultify our arguments, all end.

For critical thought can elucidate ideas, rearrange and systematize them, classify their types and uses, and remove confusions and fallacies, but it cannot by itself provide information about the universe, which cancels or alters the basic data of direct human experience. For this central doctrine in modern philosophy Reid struck the first effective blow.

The following extracts are from *Essay on the Intellectual Powers of Man* (*Essay II*).

[CHAPTER XIV. *Reflections on the Common Theory of Ideas*

. . . When we see the sun or moon, we have no doubt that the very objects which we immediately see are very far distant from us, and from one another. We have not the least doubt that this is the sun and moon which God created some thousands of years ago, and which have continued to perform their revolutions in the heavens ever since. But how are we astonished when the philosopher informs us that we are mistaken in all this; that the sun and moon which we see are not, as we imagine, many miles distant from us, and from each other, but that they are in our own mind; that they had no existence before we saw them, and will have none when we cease to perceive and to think of them; because the objects we perceive are only ideas in our own minds, which can have no existence a moment longer than we think of them!

If a plain man, uninstructed in philosophy, has faith to receive these mysteries, how great must be his astonishment! He is brought into a new world, where everything he sees, tastes, or touches, is an idea—a fleeting kind of being which he can conjure into existence, or can anni- hilate in the twinkling of an eye.

After his mind is somewhat composed, it will be natural for him to ask his philosophical instructor: Pray, Sir, are there then no substantial and permanent beings called the sun and moon, which continue to exist whether we think of them or not? . . .

CHAPTER XVI. *Of Sensation*

. . . Almost all our perceptions have corresponding sensations which constantly accompany them, and, on that account, are very apt to be confounded with them. Neither ought we to expect that the sensation, and its corresponding perception, should be distinguished in common language, because the purposes of common life do not require it. Language is made to serve the purposes of ordinary conversation, and we have no reason to expect that it should make distinctions that are not of common use. Hence it happens that a quality perceived, and the sensation corresponding to that perception, often go under the same name.

This makes the names of most of our sensations ambiguous, and this ambiguity hath very much perplexed philosophers. It will be necessary to give some instances to illustrate the distinction between our sensations and the objects of perception.

When I smell a rose, there is in this operation both sensation and perception. The agreeable odour I feel, considered by itself without relation to any external object, is merely a sensation. It affects the mind in a certain way; and this affection of the mind may be conceived without a thought of the rose, or any other object. This sensation can be nothing else than it is felt to be. Its very essence consists in being felt, and, when it is not felt, it is not. There is no difference between the sensation and the feeling of it— they are one and the same thing. It is for this reason that we before observed that, in sensation, there is no object distinct from that act of the mind by which it is felt—and this holds true with regard to all sensations.

Let us next attend to the perception which we have in smelling a rose. Perception has always an external object; and the object of my perception, in this case, is that quality in the rose which I discern by the sense of smell. Observing that the agreeable sensation is raised when the rose is near, and ceases when it is removed, I am led, by my nature, to conclude some quality to be in the rose which is the cause of this sensation. This quality in the rose is the object perceived; and that act of my mind by which I have the conviction and belief of this quality is what in this case I call perception.

But it is here to be observed that the sensation I feel, and the quality in the rose which I perceive, are both called by the same name. The smell of a rose is the name given to both: so that this name hath two meanings; and the distinguishing its different meanings removes all perplexity and enables us to give clear and distinct answers to questions about which philosophers have held much dispute.

Thus, if it is asked whether the smell be in the rose, or in the mind that feels it, the answer is obvious: That there are two different things signified by the smell of a rose; one of which is in the mind, and can be in nothing but in a sentient being; the other is truly and properly in the rose. The sensation which I feel is in my mind. The mind is the sentient being; and, as the rose is insentient, there can be no sensation, nor anything resembling sensation, in it. But this sensation in my mind is occasioned by a certain quality in the rose, which is called by the same name with the sensation, not on account of any similitude, but because of their constant concomitancy.

All the names we have for smells, tastes, sounds, and for the various degrees of heat and cold, have a like ambiguity; and what has been said of the smell of a rose may be applied to them. They signify both a sensation and a quality perceived by means of that sensation. The first is the sign, the last the thing signified. As both are conjoined by nature, and as the purposes of common life do not require them to be disjoined in our thoughts, they are both expressed by the same name: and this ambiguity is to be found in all languages, because the reason of it extends to all.}

CHAPTER VI

Condillac

ÉTIENNE BONNOT DE CONDILLAC WAS A TYPICAL ATHEISTI-cal abbé of the eighteenth century. Born in 1715, he entered the priesthood with no apparent discomfort to his materialistic beliefs. He lived the life of a French savant of the enlightenment, and died in 1780. His works had a far greater, often indirect, influence on French—and European—naturalism in the nineteenth century, more particularly in literature and popular science, than is commonly supposed.

Condillac is perhaps the most representative of the French "sensationalist" *philosophes*. A devoted follower of Locke, he was convinced that all mental processes could be analyzed into atomic constituents consisting of basic, irreducible, units of sensation. To demonstrate this he used the famous image of a statue which was endowed with new "senses"—smell, taste, etc.—gradually, one by one; and in this way attempts to "construct" the world of normal human beings, bit by bit, and to show that everything in it is wholly analyzable into the results of the physical functioning of the senses in their normal interplay with each other. One of the difficulties of Locke's original theory was to account for judgment—that is the capacity to affirm and deny, believe and disbelieve, and in general reflect *about* data, rather than merely register them as they showered in upon the passive *tabula rasa* which the mind is conceived as being. Such experiences as reflection and judgment, which seem to require activities such as comparing, distinguishing, classifying, etc., do not prima facie seem compatible with the purely passive photographic film that the *tabula rasa* resembles. Condillac attempts to im-

266

prove on Locke's inadequate account of "ideas of reflection" by explaining them as the results of "attention," which is, for him, merely another sensation. His theory cannot be regarded as successful, as anyone who troubles to read relevant discussions in the works of Kant or of Maine de Biran can see for himself. Attention, comparison, belief, knowledge, cannot be identified with "pure sensation" which is, presumably, pure receptivity, incapable of rounding on itself and choosing, weighing, rejecting, and building theories out of the undifferentiated "raw material" which, *ex hypothesi,* is all that it itself is. A succession of sensations cannot be turned into a sensation of succession. Similar difficulties have been encountered by all those who identify knowledge with sensation, or belief with the succession of atomic data, from Condillac to Carnap. But Condillac's careful analysis of actual sensations, which constitute more of our experience than had hitherto been allowed, and his emphasis on the central importance of attention, are still interesting.

The following is from the *Treatise on Sensations* (1784).

[As soon as there is twofold attention, there is comparison, because to attend to two ideas or to compare them is the same. However, one cannot compare them without seeing some difference or some resemblance between them; to see such relations is to judge. The acts of comparing and of judging are, thus, nothing but attention itself: it is in this way that sensation becomes successively attention, comparison, judgment.

The objects which we compare possess numerous relations, whether because the impressions they make upon us are themselves wholly different, or because these impressions differ solely in degree, or because the impressions, though similar themselves, yet combine differently in each object. In such cases, the attention that we give the objects starts by enveloping all the sensations which they occasion. But this attention being so much divided, our comparisons are vague, the relations that alone we grasp are confused, our judgments are imperfect or unsure. Hence we are compelled to shift our attention from one object to another, regarding their qualities separately. After, for example, judging their color, we judge their shape, and after that their size; and by running through in this way all the sensations that the objects make upon us, we discover, by means of a succession of comparisons and judgments, the relations that obtain between the objects, and the result of these judgments is the idea which we form of each object. The attention thus directed is like a beam of light which is reflected from one body to another to illuminate them both, and this I call reflection. Thus sensation, after becoming attention, comparison, judgment, ends by becoming reflection too.]

CHAPTER VII

La Mettrie

JULIEN OFFRAY DE LA METTRIE WAS BORN IN 1709. BY profession a physician, he enjoyed the patronage of Frederick the Great of Prussia and achieved a *succès de scandale* with his books *L'Homme Machine* and *L'Homme Plante*. He died at the relatively early age of forty-one. His books are the first full-blown essays in behaviorism, according to which every human characteristic and activity can be completely accounted for by a purely mechanistic explanation; "secondary" causes are those which are patent for us all to study; "primary" causes are the occult ultimate causes whereby God or Nature operates—figments to La Mettrie, like those metaphysical "wings" with which man has vainly tried to soar above the painfully slow road of patient empirical research. When his disciple the physician Cabanis later declared that the brain secretes thought as the liver bile, and, like Dr. Watson in our own day, believed that one could provide an exhaustive explanation of mental and moral life in physio-chemical terms, his approach represented the culmination of La Mettrie's method.

〖 THE MAN-MACHINE (1748)

Man is a machine so compounded that it is at first impossible to form a clear idea of it, and consequently to define it. That is why all the investigations which the greatest philosophers have conducted a priori, that is to say by trying to lift themselves somehow on the wings of their intellect, have proved vain. Thus, it is only a posteriori or by seeking to unravel the soul, as it were, via the organs of the body, that one can, I do not say lay bare human nature itself in a demonstrative fashion, but attain to the highest degree of probability possible on this topic.

Let us then lean on the staff of experience, and eschew the history of all the unprofitable opinions of the philosophers. To be blind and to believe that one can dispense with the aid of this staff is the very height of blindness. How right is modern man to say that it is but vanity alone which fails to draw from secondary causes those very consequences that it draws from the primary ones! One can, and indeed one should, admire all those fine geniuses even in their most useless labors, the Descartes, the Malebranches, the Leibnizes, the Wolffs, etc.; but where is the fruit, I ask you, of all their profound meditations and all their works? Let us therefore begin and let us look, not at what men have thought, but at what one needs to think, if one is to attain a life of peace. . . .

The soul is, then, an empty symbol of which one has no conception, and which a sound mind could employ only in order to denote that which thinks in us. Given the least principle of movement, animate bodies will possess all they need in order to move, sense, think, repeat, and behave, in a word, all they want of the physical; and of the mental, too, which depends thereon.]

CHAPTER VIII

Johann Georg Hamann

BY THE MID-CENTURY THE TRIUMPH OF THE BRITISH EM-
piricist philosophy seemed assured; in particular that of
the systematic materialism which the French *philosophes*
had derived from it, and by means of which the most eminent among them, and in particular the contributors to the
great Encyclopaedia edited by Diderot and d'Alembert,
were successfully undermining the theological, political
and moral foundations of the established order. It is interesting to observe that it is about this time that the reaction
against this mood begins in Germany. The main current
of philosophical thought in that country—derived from
Leibniz and fed by French positivism—was no less enlightened, humane, rational and optimistic than elsewhere
in the West. But, little by little, discordant voices began to
be heard: humiliated German feeling began to assert itself
against the cosmopolitan, egalitarian, scientific, materialistic deism or atheism of the French, and advanced against
it the notion of importance of imponderable, unanalyzable, qualitative differences, of the uniqueness of individuals
and traditions and customs—and later of race, language,
churches, nations. They proclaimed the supreme value
of intuition, imagination, historical sense, of the vision
of the prophet or of the inspired historian or poet or
artist, of the sudden illumination of genius, of the im-
memorial wisdom of tradition or of the common people—
beings untouched by sophistication or too much logic—
simple rustic sages or the inspired bards of a nation. These
ideas, some of which found moral and political expression in the writings of Rousseau and Burke, found their
metaphysical formulation in the works of the German ro-

mantic thinkers—Herder, Fichte, the Schlegels, Schelling, and, to some degree, Hegel.

Among their predecessors the most arresting is J. G. Hamann, the "magician of the North," a solitary, isolated thinker inclined to mysticism, the friend and one of the sharpest opponents of Kant, whose writings were deeply admired by Herder and Goethe, but who is today a half-forgotten figure. He was born in 1730 and died in 1788, having lived all his life in poverty and neglect. Yet this neglect is undeserved, for he was a man of original opinions, the importance of which has become apparent only in our own time. His views are a queer mixture of visionary pietism and skeptical empiricism: deeply influenced by Hume's attacks on rationalism, Hamann believed that there was no bridge between the a priori propositions of logic and mathematics and factual statements asserting truths about the world. All the efforts to *prove* truths of fact—whether about the existence of God, or the immortality of the soul, or the origins and structure of the universe, whether undertaken by Thomists or Cartesians or the followers of Leibniz and Wolff, he regarded as idle fantasy. But whereas Hume at this point rests content with the probabilities towards which "nature" conducts all sound and balanced intelligences, Hamann invokes faith:*

[Our own existence, and the existence of all things outside us, must be *believed* and cannot be determined in any other way.] [Author's italics. II., p. 35]

In Hamann's case, belief took the form of absolute faith in Holy Writ, mystical interpretation of revealed truth, and an acute distrust of the rationalizing intellect which drew artificial distinctions in the seamless whole of nature and

---

* The passages given below are quoted from the translations made by Mr. James C. O'Flaherty in his *Unity and Language, A study in the philosophy of Johann Georg Hamann* (Chapel Hill, North Carolina: The University of North Carolina Press, 1952). Copyright, 1952, by the University of North Carolina. The references are to the volumes of *Johann Georg Hamann; Schriften*, ed. F. Roth und G. I. Wiener (Berlin, 1824), or, if preceded by the letter "G," to C. H. Gildemeister's *J. G. Hamanns, des Magus im Norden, Leben und Schriften* (Gotha, 1868).

experience as given to the intuitive imagination, and in particular an antipathy to the great metaphysical and scientific systems which created neat but fictitious frameworks which they passed off as reality and thereby bred spurious problems, insoluble because founded on fallacies. He is a solitary figure in his century, hostile to its spirit, contemptuous of its triumphs, and forms a link between German mystical visionaries like Eckhart and Boehme on the one hand, and anti-rationalist romantic thinkers like Herder, Schelling, Kierkegaard and Bergson and their existentialist followers in the two hundred years that followed. As with Giambattista Vico half a century before, whom (as Goethe noted) he much resembles, Hamann's darkly oracular writings are often penetrated by flashes of insight of a very arresting order. His greatest discovery is that language and thought are not two processes but one: that language (or other forms of expressive symbolism—religious worship, social habits and so on) conveys directly the innermost soul of individuals and societies; that we do not first form (or receive) "ideas" and then clothe them in words, but that to think *is* to use symbols—images or language—and that, therefore, philosophers who think that they are studying concepts or ideas or categories of reality are in fact studying means of human expression—language —which is at once the vehicle of men's views of the universe and of themselves, and part and parcel of that world itself, which is not something separable from the ways in which it is experienced or thought about. Our troubles come from the fact that "The philosophers have always given truth a bill of divorcement, in that they have separated what nature has joined together, and vice versa." [IV, p. 45] And again:

[Metaphysics misuses the word-signs and figures of speech of our empirical knowledge as pure hieroglyphs and types of ideal relations, and works over by means of this learned mischief the *straightforwardness* of language into such a hot, unstable, indefinite something = x, that nothing remains but the soughing of the wind, a magic phantasmagoria at the most, as the wise Helvétius says, the talisman and rosary of a transcendental, superstitious belief in *entia rationis,* its empty bags, and slogans.} [Author's italics. VII, p. 8]

Ideas and things can and must be studied only in their concrete contexts, i.e., as they occur in the thought, that is, language, used by human beings, otherwise they will be misunderstood and perverted:

{ O for a muse like the fire of a goldsmith and like the soap of the fullers!—She will dare to cleanse the *natural use of the senses from* the *unnatural use of abstractions,* by which our *concepts* of things are just as mutilated as the name of the creator is *suppressed* and blasphemed.} [Author's italics. II., pp. 283-84]

There is no instrument of discovery called reason, whatever Aristotle or Leibniz may say:

{ All idle talk about reason is mere wind; language is its organon and criterion. [VI., p. 365]
With me the question is not so much: What is reason? but rather: What is language? and here I presume to be the basis of all paralogisms and antinomies which one blames on the former; therefore it happens that one takes words for concepts and concepts for the things themselves. [G., V., p. 15]
My reason is invisible without language . . . [G., V., p. 508] Togetherness [*Geselligkeit*] is the true principle of reason and language, by means of which our sensations and representations [*Vorstellungen*] are modified.} [G., V., p. 515]

The critique of systems of concepts is a critique, above all, of language. To understand the ideas of others, or our own, about anything whatever, is to understand how language enters into the non-linguistic elements of our total experience, and how it modifies our language. This is the task of philosophy.

〔 If I were as eloquent as Demosthenes, I would do no more than repeat one sentence three times: Reason is language, Logos. On this marrow-bone I gnaw, and I shall gnaw myself to death on it. There still remains darkness upon the face of this deep for me; I still wait for an apocalyptic angel with a key to this abyss. [Letter to Herder, 1784. VII., pp. 151-52]

If it therefore still remains a principal question, as to *how the capacity to think is possible*—the capacity to think, *to the right of* and *to the left of, before* and *without, with* and *beyond* experience, no deduction is necessary to establish the genealogical priority of *language* and its heraldry over the seven sacred functions of logical propositions and conclusions. Not only the entire capacity to think rests on language . . . but language is also the *center of the misunderstanding of reason with itself* . . .〕 [Author's italics. VII., p. 9]

ONE NEED NOT ACCEPT HAMANN'S THEOLOGICAL BELIEFS or his anti-scientific bias to realize the depth and originality of his ideas about the relations of thought, reason, semi-inarticulate emotional (and spiritual) life, the cultural institutions in which this last is embodied, and the languages and symbolisms of mankind. There is something of this view in the French ultramontane Catholic writers Bonald and de Maistre; but it is not till our own day, and especially as a result of the ideas of Wittgenstein and his disciples, that the cardinal importance of such an approach to the problems of philosophy was realized. A uniquely independent thinker who resisted (sometimes blindly and perversely) the very powerful stream of eighteenth-century scientific enlightenment (and was duly punished by neglect or relegation to learned footnotes, usually in company with the even more gifted Vico, as an author of darkly mystical writings who dared to criticize the greatest thinkers of his age) Hamann deserves an act of belated homage in the twentieth century whose most revolutionary philosophical innovations he did something to anticipate.

CHAPTER IX

Georg Christoph Lichtenberg

BORN IN DARMSTADT IN 1742, LICHTENBERG STUDIED AT the University of Göttingen, where he remained to become professor of physics. Astronomer, art critic, geometer, satirist, a man of wide and varied attainments, Lichtenberg's life was spent in academic pursuits, outwardly peaceful enough. He died in 1799. He composed aphorisms, some of which possess a degree of startling originality and set up trains of thought very unlike the normal sensible sentiments of the eighteenth century, whether they originate among the French *lumières* or in the German *Aufklärung* (Enlightenment). Even the few *obiter dicta* here quoted suffice to show the quality of mind possessed by this remarkable and unclassifiable man.

This is his description of "my body," and its connection with "my mind" and it alone. It cuts a great deal deeper than the account of the "psychosomatic" relationship in the average textbook of psychology or physiology. [From *Aphorismen.**]

〔 My body is that part of the world which can be altered by my thoughts. Even imaginary illnesses can become real. In the rest of the world my hypotheses cannot disturb the order of things.〕

And this is his definition of man:

〔 Man is a cause-seeking creature; in the spiritual order he could be called the cause-seeker. Other minds perhaps think things in other—to us inconceivable—categories.〕

* The best known editions of his works are those of Grisebach (1871) and Wilbrandt (1893). The *Aphorismen* were first published in 1902.

These words have a Kantian flavor, especially the implication that the category of causality is so deeply rooted in us as to act as a defining characteristic of mankind; but that nevertheless it is only a "brute" fact (and not an a priori "necessity") that we think of things in exclusively causal terms; for other beings might think and sense within other frames of reference, but what these experiences could be is beyond our ken, because we are as we are, and cannot see beyond our own—evidently unalterable—horizon.

Finally the definition of philosophy itself:

[Philosophy is ever the art of drawing distinctions, look at the matter how you will. The peasant uses all the propositions of the most abstract philosophy, but wrapped up, embedded, tangled, *latent,* as physicists and chemists say; the philosopher gives us the propositions in their pure state.]

In this aphorism Lichtenberg expresses very succinctly the notion that philosophy is what in our own time came to be called "analysis"—not an instrument of discovery of new truths about the world, so much as of eliciting, with the greatest possible exactness and rigor, that which is already contained in common speech, in order to discriminate, isolate, study, classify, examine the interrelations and the functions of, types of expression and ways of speech (or thought), the peculiarities of which cannot be observed so well (or at all) in the rich amalgam—vague, blurred, ambiguous and "impure"—in which ordinary language must of necessity always remain if it is to be useful in the practical conduct of life. The task of the philosopher is to "unpack" sentences which give rise to philosophical problems into their ingredients, and so disentangle the thick rope of daily talk into its constituent strands, without which the problems cannot be solved or "dissolved." This is certainly one of the most original remarks ever made about philosophy.

Recommended Further Reading

JOHN LOCKE

An Essay Concerning Human Understanding, abridged and edited by A. Seth Pringle-Pattison. London: Oxford University Press, 1924.

An Essay Concerning Human Understanding, edited by Alexander Campbell Fraser. Oxford: The Clarendon Press, 1894 (2 v.).

Of Civil Government: Two Treatises. London: J. M. Dent & Sons, Ltd., 1924. (Everyman's Library.)

The Philosophical Works of John Locke, edited by J. A. St. John. London: G. Bell & Sons, 1902-03. (Bohn's Standard Library, 2 v.)

The Second Treatise of Civil Government and a Letter Concerning Toleration, edited by J. W. Gough. Oxford: B. Blackwell, 1946.

Two Treatises of Government, edited by Thomas I. Cook. New York: Hafner Publishing Company, 1947.

The Works of John Locke. London: W. Otridge & Son, 1812 (11th edition; 10 v.).

VOLTAIRE

Extraits en Prose de Voltaire, edited by Lucien Brunel. Paris: Hachette et Cie., 1914.

Oeuvres Complètes, edited by Louis Moland. Paris: Garnier, 1877-85 (52 v.).

Philosophical Dictionary, selected and translated by H. I. Woolf. New York: Alfred A. Knopf, Inc., 1938.

Selections from Voltaire, edited by George R. Havens. New York and London: The Century Company, 1925.

GEORGE BERKELEY

A New Theory of Vision and Other Select Philosophical Writings, edited by Ernest Rhys. London: J. M. Dent & Sons,

Ltd. New York: E. P. Dutton & Company, Inc., 1910. (Everyman's Library.)

Three Dialogues between Hylas and Philonous. La Salle, Illinois: Open Court Publishing Company, 1920. (Religion of Science Library, No. 49.)

A Treatise Concerning the Principles of Human Knowledge. La Salle, Illinois: Open Court Publishing Company, 1915. (Religion of Science Library, No. 48.)

The Works of George Berkeley, edited by Alexander Campbell Fraser. Oxford: The Clarendon. Press, 1901 (4 v.).

The Works of George Berkeley, edited by A. A. Luce and T. E. Jessop. London: T. Nelson, 1948— (7 volumes to date).

DAVID HUME

An Enquiry Concerning the Human Understanding and an Enquiry Concerning the Principles of Morals, edited by L. A. Selby-Bigge. Oxford: The Clarendon Press, 1894; 2nd edition, 1936.

Essays, Moral, Political, and Literary, edited by T. H. Green and T. H. Grose. London: Longmans, Green and Company, 1875.

Hume's Dialogues Concerning Natural Religion, edited by Norman Kemp Smith. Oxford: The Clarendon Press, 1935; 2nd edition, 1947.

Moral and Political Philosophy, edited by Henry D. Aiken. New York: Hafner Publishing Company, 1948.

Selections, edited by Charles W. Hendel, Jr. New York: Charles Scribner's Sons, 1927.

A Treatise of Human Nature, edited by L. A. Selby-Bigge. Oxford: The Clarendon Press, 1896.

A Treatise of Human Nature and Dialogues Concerning Natural Religion, edited by T. H. Green and T. H. Grose. London: Longmans, Green and Company, 1878 (2 v.).

THOMAS REID

Essays on the Intellectual Powers of Man, edited and abridged by A. D. Woozley. New York: The Macmillan Company, 1941.

The Works of Thomas Reid, edited by Sir William Hamilton. Edinburgh: Machlachlan and Stewart, 1872 (7th edition).

CONDILLAC

Oeuvres Philosophiques de Condillac, edited by Georges Le Roy. Paris: Presses Universitaires de France, 1947— (3 volumes to date).

Condillac's Treatise on the Sensations, translated by Geraldine Carr. Los Angeles: University of Southern California, School of Philosophy, 1930.

LA METTRIE

L'Homme Machine, edited by F. Assérat. Paris, 1865.

Man a Machine, translated by Gertrude Carman Bussey. La Salle, Illinois: Open Court Publishing Company, 1912.

JOHANN GEORG HAMANN

Sämmtliche Werke, edited by A. von Josef Nadler. Vienna: Thomas-Morus-Presse im Verlag Herder, 1949-53 (5 v.).

GEORG CHRISTOPH LICHTENBERG

Gesammelte Werke, edited by Wilhelm Grenzmann. Frankfurt: Halle Verlag, 1949.

ANTHOLOGIES

The Age of Enlightenment, an Anthology of 18th Century French Literature, edited by Otis E. Fellows and Norman L. Torrey. New York: Crofts, 1942.

British Empirical Philosophers, edited by A. J. Ayer and Raymond Winch. London: Routledge and Kegan Paul, 1952.

The English Philosophers from Bacon to Mill, edited by E. A. Burtt. New York: Random House, 1939. (Modern Library.)

Index of Names